THE "OTHER" PSYCHOLOGY OF JULIAN JAYNES

ANCIENT LANGUAGES, SACRED VISIONS, AND FORGOTTEN MENTALITIES

Brian J. McVeigh

imprint-academic.com

Copyright © Brian J. McVeigh, 2018

The moral rights of the authors have been asserted.
No part of this publication may be reproduced in any form
without permission, except for the quotation of brief passages
in criticism and discussion.

Published in the UK by
Imprint Academic, PO Box 200, Exeter EX5 5YX, UK

Distributed in the USA by
Ingram Book Company,
One Ingram Blvd., La Vergne, TN 37086, USA

ISBN 9781845409517

A CIP catalogue record for this book is available from the
British Library and US Library of Congress

Contents

Acknowledgments	v
Notes to the Reader and Abbreviations	vi
Introduction: The Need for a Cultural-Historical Psychology	1
Chapter 1: Julian Jaynes and the Promise of the "Other" Psychology	6
Chapter 2: The Neurocultural Malleability of Psyche	31
Chapter 3: Bronze Age Super-Religiosity: Linguistic Evidence for Pre-conscious Mentalities	45
Chapter 4: Ancient China: Social Complexity, Cognitive Adaptation, and Linguistic Change	67
Chapter 5: The Metaphors of Mind-Words in Modern Mandarin	84
Chapter 6: Hallucinations as Superceptions: Hearing Voices as Adaptive Behavior	96
Conclusion: Final Thoughts — Psychohistorical Ruptures and Stratigraphic Psychology	124
Appendices	
A Types of Ceptions	129
B Types of Adaptive Mentalities	130
C Statistical Analyses for Chapter 3	132
D Datasets for Chapter 3	138
E Statistical Analyses for Chapters 4 and 5	172
F Datasets for Chapters 4 and 5	176
G Abnormal Hallucinations	229
Bibliography	236
Index	257
About the Author	265

Acknowledgments

I would like to thank Rabbi James Cohn, Marcel Kuijsten, Michael Carr, Yu-Hui Chen, Bill Rowe, Scott Greer, Carole Brooks Platt, John Hainly, William Woodward, Yeufen Hsieh, Todd Gibson, and Barbara Greene for their advice and helpful comments. As always, my wife and family have been a source of support, comfort, and inspiration.

The germ for Chapter 6 was a graduate school paper entitled "Auditory Verbal Hallucinations and Right Hemispheric Activity: Evidence and Implications." I am grateful to Prof. Donald Graves (Sage Graduate School) for offering invaluable advice.

Notes to the Reader and Abbreviations

Though Jaynes used "consciousness" in his writings, this term is vague, multi-referential, and misleading; in English "consciousness" has at least four very different meanings: (1) the physiological state of not sleeping; (2) the physiological state of not being in a coma; (3) a vague usage to describe some form of cognition, thinking, perception, or awareness; and (4) what one's inner self introspects upon. For the sake of clarity I prefer "conscious interiority," though throughout this book I will use consciousness and conscious interiority interchangeably; both refer to Jaynes's particular understanding of consciousness (note that the Psychologist John Limber coined "J-con" — i.e. Jaynesian consciousness — to avoid confusion [2006]).

As much as possible I have attempted to present my arguments without cluttering the text with tables and charts, though to some degree this is unavoidable. Statistical analyses are placed in appendices, as are the corresponding datasets upon which the analyses are based. In order to make the hypotheses understandable while at the same time referencing relevant data and statistical evidence, I use six types of figures: (1) *Charts* offering basic facts; (2) *Tables* presenting numerical data; (3) *App Calculations* in appendices displaying statistical analyses and are referred to in chapters; (4) *Hypothesis Logs* summarizing research findings; (5) *Datasets* in appendices providing raw numbers; and (6) *Graphs* that visually quantify numerical values.

One final note: I distinguish between the academic discipline of Psychology (with a capitalized "P") and the psychological (with a small "p") or what since the late nineteenth century has been called mind or emotional, perceptive, and cognitive processes.

Abbreviations

ADC: Auxiliary Divine Communication
AIMP: "As If" Mortuary Practices
ARCC: Authority-Radiating Ceremonial Complexes
AVH: Auditory Verbal Hallucination
BA: Bronze Age
BCI Hypothesis: Bicameral Civilization Inventory Hypothesis
CAW: Centrality of Ancestor Worship
CG: Complex Graph
Chi-Sq G of F: Chi-Square Goodness of Fit
df: Degrees of Freedom
EmPL: Embryonic Psycholexicon
ePSD: Electronic Pennsylvania Sumerian Dictionary
ES: Effect Size
ETCSL: Electronic Text Corpus of Sumerian Literature
EV: Emotional Valence
HG: Hittite Grammar
IB: Intermediary Beings
IMRHA: Induction Methods for Right-Hemisphere Activation
LRC – UTA: Linguistics Research Center – University of Texas
MW: Mind–Word
NE: Negative Emotion
OHF: Objects of Hallucinatory Focus
PBCI Hypothesis: Postbicameral Civilization Inventory Hypothesis
PE: Positive Emotion
PL: Psycholexicon (Psychological Lexicon)
PS: Pictophonetic; Signific
RHD: Right-Hemisphere Dominance
RL: Religious Lexicon
SV: Supernatural Visitations
The Origin: *The Origin of Consciousness in the Breakdown of the Bicameral Mind* (book by Julian Jaynes published in 1976)
TSO: Theocentric Social Order
VB: Vestigial Bicameralism (after ca. 1000 BCE)
VV: Voice–Volition

Introduction

The Need for a Cultural-Historical Psychology

"Could it be that ... silent 'speech' areas on the right hemisphere had some function at an earlier stage in man's history that now they do not have?" — Julian Jaynes

When I was a high school student my mother, always interested in anything off the beaten track, gave me a copy of *The Origin of Consciousness in the Breakdown of the Bicameral Mind* (1976) (henceforth *The Origin*) in which Julian Jaynes (1920–1997) argued that before approximately 1200 BCE people possessed a different mentality. Boldly interdisciplinary and iconoclastic, Jaynes marshaled evidence from neuroscience, Psychology, archeology, history, linguistics, and the analysis of ancient texts. What Jaynes had to say about the duplex nature of the psyche resonated with something my mother used to say to me when as a young boy I would grumble about not being able to accomplish some difficult task: "Stop your complaining. If your brain hears you saying you can't do something, it will believe you." The mind, I concluded, is not unitary despite the strange illusion that it is. This piqued my interest in how the mind is put together. However, it was my older brother, Billy, who also has something to do with how my interests in the human mind developed. Diagnosed with autism from a very early age, Billy had an angelic countenance, was ordinarily shy, and hardly spoke. When he did, what he had to say was done in a telegraphic, soft-spoken, and gentle manner. But occasionally Billy would erupt, volcano-like, in extremely violent psychomotor seizures. These were ferocious but fortunately brief. Accompanying these attacks were guttural shouts, fearsome grunts, murderous threats, and language so foul and vile we could only wonder from where he had acquired such a formidable linguistic arsenal. It was as if an angry demon resided somewhere in his person. Surely, I thought, the individual psyche must be composed of different parts that, while perhaps ordinarily integrated, manifest themselves under the right conditions as independent entities.

Critically acclaimed but controversial, *The Origin* was far ahead of its time. Now Jaynes's theories are increasingly gaining traction in a number of fields. With his unconventional theories that consciousness only emerged three thousand years ago and of the role of hallucinations in history, he relied heavily on extra-laboratory, non-experimental research to demonstrate how consciousness rests upon strata of accumulated ideas, i.e. consciousness is socially scaffolded through layers of time. He has been described as a "maverick" — I once asked a graduate student in Princeton University's Psychology Department what Jaynes's colleagues thought of him: a "well-regarded kook" was the answer. However, if viewed objectively against the backdrop of the history of Psychology and the original promise of this field, his approach is actually not that unusual. One may question his startling conclusions, but his premise that cultural and historical studies are indispensable for understanding psyche was not a foreign concept to the pioneers and founders of what would become modern Psychology. The likes of Wilhelm Wundt (1832–1920), William James (1842–1910), and Pierre Janet (1859–1947) all recognized the saliency and significance of long-term temporal changes, customs, religion, and anomalous behavior (e.g. hypnosis and trance). Indeed, an irony of intellectual history is how Wundt, though often regarded as the originator of experimental-laboratory Psychology, considered his ten-volume work on ethnocultural Psychology (*Völkerpsychologie*, 1900–1920) to be his more important, signature contribution.

Clarifying the Confusion around "Consciousness"

The search is on for the neural correlates of consciousness. Popular contenders include the claustra (which have extensive linkages to other parts of the brain) and the temporoparietal junction. It has been suggested that gamma waves, which are strongest when one is concentrating, may have something to do with conscious states. The problem with such theories is that they confuse perception with introspection, sensation with subjectivity, and sensory experiences with that ineffable feeling of self-reflexiveness and "me-ness." Such muddled thinking assumes consciousness to be essentially neurological, reducible to brain anatomy, and physically locatable. In fact, like cognition in general, consciousness is sociocultural and since it consists of information, ideational and relational (i.e. not existing in physical space). It is a conceptual system sustained and networked throughout society and transmitted down through time in the same way knowledge about politics, economics, and religion is. Reductionistic attempts

Introduction 3

to understand consciousness account for why some have such a difficult time at least entertaining the notion that conscious subjective mind is a cultural and historical product and process.

The Legacy of Julian Jaynes

This work offers another view, one informed by Julian Jaynes. Jaynes explained the nature and origins of consciousness; more specifically, unlike other theorists, he defines consciousness with a welcome, laser-focused clarity and, in doing so, provides a compelling and more accurate account of our history as a species. Allow me to cut to the chase and stress that Jaynes had something quite particular in mind when he theorized about consciousness (or as I prefer for the sake of clarity, "conscious interiority"), i.e. he had a narrower, well-defined and delineated understanding of this type of cognition, which is

> an analog of what is called the real world. It is built up with a vocabulary or lexical field whose terms are all metaphors or analogs of behavior in the physical world. Its reality is of the same order as mathematics. It allows us to shortcut behavioral processes and arrive at more adequate decisions. Like mathematics, it is an operator rather than a thing or repository. And it is intimately bound up with volition and decision. (Jaynes 1976: 55)

Jaynes's thinking can be broken down into four independent hypotheses: (1) consciousness—as Jaynes carefully defined it—is learned and therefore an acquired process grounded in metaphorical language. Jaynes asserted that consciousness did not arise far back in human evolution but came into existence relatively recently via enculturation; (2) before the cultural emergence of consciousness a different mentality based on hallucinations governed civilizations. In place of an internal dialogue, an earlier mentality generated "voices" (and sometimes visions) directing the actions of individuals, similar to the command hallucinations experienced by many people who hear voices today. These experiences were interpreted as the instructions of chiefs, ancestors, or deities; (3) consciousness developed around the end of the second millennium BCE (with some exceptions, this transition occurred at different times in other parts of the world); and (4) the neurological model for the bicameral ("two-chambered") mind. Prior to the development of consciousness, a dominant "god" side (now partially vestigial linguistic areas in the right hemisphere) spoke to a "mortal" side (linguistic areas in the left hemisphere). Hypnosis, spirit possession, imaginary companions, and glossolalia are vestiges of bicamerality.

The "other" Psychology of Julian Jaynes—one grounded in cultural-historical approaches—can help us better understand the origins of religion, worldwide psychohistorical patterns, cognitive adaptation, the development of mental lexicons, and the continuing evolution of consciousness. He explains a wide range of otherwise inexplicable phenomena — divination, idol worship, monumental mortuary architecture, and supernatural visitations and visions. Jaynes's theories have profound implications for human history as well as for a variety of aspects of modern society such as our susceptibility to persuasion, how technology configures mental processes, and psychological anomalies.

Jaynes's theories are increasingly receiving the attention they deserve, as recent advances in neurology and dozens of brain imaging studies support and confirm his ideas. From a practical perspective, Jaynes's work provides a historical context for hearing voices and therefore can make important contributions to mental health. His ideas give us a neurological model for hearing voices which may be comforting to those who have such experiences. Such research could help lead to future treatments for those with persistent, obtrusive voices (visit Hearing Voice Network or Intervoice: The International Hearing Voices Network to gain a sense of how common "hearing voices" still is).

Purpose of this Book

This book is neither a rehashing of what Jaynes has already written nor does it explain in detail his basic ideas. This has been done rather effectively by Jaynes himself and interested readers are directed to his *The Origin* as well as works by others listed by the Julian Jaynes Society on www.julianjaynes.org where a wealth of research, resources, and relevant materials can be found. In particular, the reader is directed to several collections edited by Marcel Kuijsten: *Reflections on the Dawn of Consciousness: Julian Jaynes's Bicameral Mind Theory Revisited* (2006a); *The Julian Jaynes Collection: Biography, Articles, Lectures, Interviews, Discussion* (2012); and *Gods, Voices, and the Bicameral Mind* (2016). A number of my own works, especially *How Religion Evolved: Explaining the Living Dead, Talking Idols, and Mesmerizing Monuments* (2016a), have applied Jaynesian concepts: *A Psychohistory of Metaphors: Envisioning, Time, Space, and Self through the Centuries* (2016b); *Discussions with Julian Jaynes: The Nature of Consciousness and the Vagaries of Psychology* (2016c); and *The History of Japanese Psychology: Global Perspectives, 1875–1950* (2106d). Also relevant is my *The Propertied Self: The Psychology of Economic History* (2015).

Chapter Outline

Chapter 1 positions Jaynes's singular contribution to intellectual history by introducing his "other" Psychology. Here "other" means not just another scholarly legacy but is intended to evoke forgotten civilizations, lost ways of understanding the world, and the spooky presence of disembodied voices, ghostly visions, and spectral sights. These otherworldly entities, that still haunt our popular imagination, demand scientific explanation. Chapter 2 lays out the intellectual framework by discussing several overarching and interrelated themes that thread their way throughout this book. Chapter 2 sets the tone for the following chapters in how it points to other paths that a productive, culturally-sensitive, and historically-informed Psychology might take. A guiding principle of this book is that certain questions and problems cannot be resolved unless we inject Psychology with a healthy dose of cultural and historical studies. Chapter 3 provides empirical support for claims about linguo-conceptual and cognitive changes and explores the notion of the super-religiosity of Bronze Age civilizations. Specifically, it marshals linguistic evidence of bicameral mentality by utilizing the Embryonic Psycholexicon Hypothesis.

In order to continue my arguments about what Jaynes's other Psychology can look like if applied to historical linguistics, Chapters 4 and 5 explore the development of the psychological lexicon in Mandarin using statistical analyses. These chapters also demonstrate how language change can be seen as an adaptive system. Thanks to the picto- and ideographic nature of Chinese we can easily discern (perhaps more readily than alphabetic languages) the traces of the trajectory of psychohistorical scaffolding. In other words, Chinese logographs (or characters or logograms) are excellent examples of linguo-conceptual remnants.

Informed by a detailed literature review on recent research on hallucinations, Chapter 6 argues that such experiences were at one time in history adaptive in function, as is interior conscious experience as presently experienced. Indeed, consciousness, understood as the ability to "see" things that do not exist and conjure up nonexistent, imaginary sceneries, is semi-hallucinatory in nature and is therefore an evolutionary descendant of hallucinations.

The agenda of this book is not to "prove" a list of theories. My investigations in Chapters 3 through 5 are limited by what remains of written and archeological records. Nevertheless, it is possible to offer persuasive explanations for an array of patterns by proposing probabilistic claims. The goal is to argue my case by providing a preponderance of the evidence.

Chapter 1

Julian Jaynes and the Promise of the "Other" Psychology

"As soon as I really understood the theory of evolution, it became obvious to me that that's the answer of everything." — Julian Jaynes

Ironies in the History of Psychology

With the publication of *The Origin* in 1976, Julian Jaynes made startling claims about language, its relation to the cultural adaptive function of conscious interiority, and the role of hallucinations in history.[1] I will intellectually contextualize his ideas by highlighting their linkages to the precursors of what has become, broadly understood, cultural (-historical) Psychology. In doing so, two notable ironies of the history of Psychology will be revealed. While explicating these ironies, I pay attention to several themes: the role of culture in relation to conscious interiority; to what degree does psyche change through history; under-theorized anomalous behavior; the importance of aesthetics for understanding different mentalities; and tensions in Psychology between *nomos* (variant human convention) and *physis* (invariant natural laws) approaches. Jaynes's contribution, whatever one may conclude about his findings, was to highlight the need for anti-reductionistic, non-experimental, and interdisciplinary approaches. I conclude with some general observations about the implications of a Jaynesian Psychology.

The first irony concerns how it took a comparative Psychologist—i.e. Jaynes—who had made a name for himself experimentally investigating animal behavior, to acknowledge the inadequacy of natural-scientific methods for understanding conscious interiority. In other words, Jaynes came to realize that conscious interiority is a cultural (learned), not biological (bioevolutionary), development. The second irony concerns Wilhelm Wundt (1832–1920), who occupies a canonical place in the history of Psychology, being credited with establishing the first laboratory, textbook, journal, and PhD program in experimental Psychology.[2] But by now all good students of the history of Psychology learn (or at least they should) about how Wundt's actual accomplishments went well beyond founding experimental Psychology (which he considered a branch of philosophy). Notably, Wundt devoted a not insubstantial amount of his efforts in attempting to establish a cultural (-historical) Psychology *(Völkspsychologie)*. This "second Psychology" would explore "higher mental processes" that went beyond the purview of laboratory Psychology and be devoted to a non-experimental, comparative, and historical investigation of the mental products of different cultural communities.

Jaynes is not a direct intellectual heir to Wundt and he never explicitly aligned his agenda with a specifically Wundtian *Völkspsychologie*. However, he certainly recognized the indispensible role of culture and history for understanding psyche. Jaynes's conclusions about neurocultural plasticity are a stimulating integration of the explanatory/natural and interpretive/social sciences. In a sense, then, Jaynes's contribution is an important step toward fulfilling the promise of a "second" or "other" Psychology that does not reduce psyche to an invariant "central processing unit" untouched by cultural content and historical change (cf. Shweder 1991).

Julian Jaynes: A "Well-regarded Kook"

The son of a Unitarian minister, Jaynes was born on February 27, 1920 in West Newton, Massachusetts. In 1937 he entered the University of Virginia, transferred to Harvard College for one year (1939), but was then offered a scholarship to attend McGill University and graduated in 1941 with a degree in Psychology. While a student he was attracted to philosophy and liked Prof. George S. Brett (1879-1944), author of *A History of Psychology* (1912-21). After a year of graduate work in neurology at the University of Toronto, Jaynes registered for the draft in the summer of 1942 and was granted conscientious objector status (he had requested in 1939 to be listed as a conscientious objector in case America went to war). He was sent to a Civilian Service work camp near Thornton, New Hampshire.

From his Unitarian upbringing Jaynes was instilled with "serious purpose," "freedom of belief," and "principled action" (Woodward and Tower 2007: 14-15). Perhaps this explains why he wrote the Attorney General of the United States stating that he would leave the work camp in violation of the Selective Training and Service Act of 1940, which Jaynes described as a "nationalistic conscription" and a "totalitarian measure." He left the work camp and was soon arrested and sentenced to four years at the U.S. Penitentiary at Lewisburg, Pennsylvania. He worked in the prison hospital and volunteered to help out in the Protestant chapel where he played the organ. In 1946 he was discharged for good behavior, one year before the end of his sentence. Now 26, he enrolled at Yale University and planned to study animal behavior to search for clues to the beginnings of conscious interiority, a life-long interest and passion. Under the guidance of the ethologist and co-author of the influential *Patterns of Sexual Behavior* Frank Beach (1911–88),[3] he finished his dissertation in 1949 on the maternal behavior of animals of different species. However, Jaynes refused to submit his dissertation, later telling his student William R. Woodward that the PhD is a "license" that produces "conformity and reduces originality" and that a "senior faculty member had disagreed with him on some point and he refused the degree rather than change something he knew to be right" (Woodward and Tower 2007: 25). Greer adds that another possible reason was that he desired to pursue research outside of experimental Psychology and somehow saw the doctorate degree as restricting his options.

Whatever his motivation, Jaynes would establish a reputation for himself as an iconoclast who had become disenchanted with the restrictive domain of establishment experimental Psychology (Greer 2006: 241). He described Psychology as "bad poetry disguised as science" (Hilts 1981: 87; Keen 1977: 66) and criticized the university apprenticeship system for how it instills students with their mentors' theoretical prejudices and churns out "unoriginal and uninspired research" (Jaynes 1966; cited in Greer 2006: 241; see also Gliedman 1982). In a swipe at the inferiority complex of mainstream Psychologists that compels them to become "guilty of aping the physical scientist in their frantic rush to construct a scientific discipline" (cited in Woodward and Tower 2007: 29), Jaynes accused Psychologists of "toad-eating with the positivists" (the attendant of a charlatan who eats, or pretends to, poisonous toads to make his master appear to have the power to expel poison).

In order to his pursue his artistic interests as a playwright and actor, in 1949 Jaynes moved to Salisbury, England, where he spent the next four years. Beginning in 1960, he spent another three-year stint in England, pursuing again his thespian endeavors.[4] He returned to Yale in 1954 where he taught as an instructor and lecturer. Between 1954 and 1960 he published portions of his dissertation, as well as co-authoring works with Frank Beach and Arthur Zitrin. In 1964 he was offered a research associate position at Princeton University's Psychology Department where he would work until 1995. A popular instructor, he was known for his undergraduate course on consciousness (that this author attended).

Jaynes would eventually become close friends with the historian of Psychology Edwin G. Boring (1886–1968) and wrote his obituary for the *Journal of the History of the Behavioral Sciences* in April 1969 (Jaynes 1969a). In September 1969 Jaynes organized a session at the American Psychological Association called "In Memory of E.G. Boring." Jaynes was one of the founders of the International Society for the History of the Behavioral Sciences (eventually called Cheiron). Meanwhile he was busy at work developing his thought-provoking theories about conscious interiority.

Jaynes passed away on Prince Edward Island on November 21, 1997.

The Origin of Consciousness in the Breakdown of the Bicameral Mind

In 1969 Jaynes was invited to lecture on his theories at the American Psychological Association (1969b). That same year he also spoke at the State University of New York in the "Frontiers of Social Science" series and the Smithsonian Institution "Symposium on Man and Beast." During the summer of that year he penned a 50-page manuscript called "A New Theory of Consciousness." After working on what would become *The Origin* in the early 1970s, he finally published his monumental and controversial work in 1976. It met with generally positive reviews and articles about Jaynes and his book began to appear. In 1977, after friends and colleagues petitioned the University to accept his original research, he finally accepted his PhD from Yale. In 1978 his book was named a runner-up for the National Book Award for nonfiction.

Much has been written about *The Origin* and here I do not intend to provide a detailed explanation or critique. However, it is important to at least offer an overview of what I take to be five key theoretical perspectives of what Jaynes had to say. These will be revisited in the next chapter and expanded upon in more detail.

(1) *Bicamerality: Hallucinations as Evolutionary Adaptation.* Challenges brought about by the agricultural revolution—e.g. increased demographic scale, economic specialization, more explicit social roles—configured a neurocultural adaptation called bicamerality. This describes how the "two-chambered" brain lateralized language so that decision-making took the form of hallucinatory divine voices (right hemisphere) that commanded the "listener"/"obeyer" (left hemisphere). Such interhemispheric communication is an example of the provisional, inefficient, and cumbersome design that characterizes brain evolution.

A perusal of a collection of sermons written by Jaynes's father, composed well before Julian was even born, reveals telling precursors of the latter's theory that individuals at one time possessed "two selves" (subserved by the left and right hemispheres). Jaynes greatly admired his father's ideas. Jaynes senior wrote that the individual is "not a single homogenous self, but is, so to speak, a group of selves," or "several fragmentary personalities" dominated by whichever one takes over (J.C. Jaynes 1922: 169). Jaynes senior asked about the "presence of the watcher," and who or what stands outside a "company of selves," "watching them, counting them, criticizing them, applauding them?" Who or what "does the *observing*?" (J.C. Jaynes 1922: 169, 171, emphasis in original). "It is ... this evolution of personality that measures the advance of man up to the stairway of the ages" (J.C. Jaynes 1922: 172).

Additional evidence exists that Jaynes senior influenced his son's provocative ideas. In 1981 Jaynes was invited to give the Sunday sermon at the First Unitarian Society in Newton, Massachusetts, where his father had been minister. His talk was called "The Magic Well of Consciousness," "Magic Wells" being borrowed from the title of a 1922 collection of his father's sermons (Woodward and Tower 2007: 52). In 1985 Jaynes was invited to speak at the 100th anniversary of his father's ordination and read the sermon that his father had given called "A Religion of Selfhood" (Woodward and Tower 2007: 52).

(2) *Bicameral Breakdown: A Major Change in Human Mentality*. Increasing social complexity eroded the efficacy of the gods' voices. Consequently, conscious interiority evolved as a cultural adaptation toward the end of second millennium BCE.

(3) *The Singularity of Conscious Interiority: A New Cognitive Ability*. A distinct form of cognition, conscious interiority is not needed for thinking, reasoning, learning, or perception. These forms of cognition existed during the bicameral period without conscious interiority; the latter is a supplemental form of cognition adapted to social complexity. Conscious interiority is a product of cultural changes, not biological evolution. It has more to do with sociopolitical arrangements than neurological structures. Conscious interiority, not being physiologically innate, is learned anew by each generation. In the same way that hallucinations were an adaptation, mental imagery was a revolutionary change in how we interacted with the world.

(4) *The Role of Linguistic Concepts*. Conscious interiority is grounded in (but not determined by) metaphoric expressions that culturally construct a subjective introcosm. Jaynes (1976) never claimed that the brains of ancient peoples were anatomically different; the hardware is the same, but new software (configured by the sociolinguistic

environment) led to the linguo-cultural invention of an introspectable mental space in which a self dwells.

(5) *Bicameral Remnants: Anomalous Behavior as Relics of Vestigial Neurostructures.* A perusal of historical and ethnographic records shows that hypnosis, spirit possession, channeling, autoscopy, and "speaking in tongues" (glossolalia) are far from rare. Indeed, they fill ancient sacred texts and contemporary anthropological accounts. And though it would be inaccurate to claim that they have not been investigated by research Psychologists, very few have bothered to integrate what we know into a comprehensive account of how and why the human psyche produces such behavior. Instead, many mainstream research Psychologists have relegated peculiar phenomena to superstitious eras, exotic locales, or unstable personalities. However, despite attempts at official banishment from mainstream Psychology, unusual behaviors loiter around our dwellings of rational thought, pressing against the doors of "normal" inquiry and eerily peering in through the windows of our commonsensical understandings. As uninvited as they may be, these uncanny phenomena remind us of our ignorance when faced with the richness and puzzles of human psychic diversity.

The Nineteenth Century: Promises and Prospects

Woodward and Tower wrote that the values of Jaynes "often seemed of the nineteenth century" but yet "his mind seemed to surge far into the 21st century" (Woodward and Tower 2007: 60). I would rewrite this by stating that, while his fundamental intellectual orientation was shaped by nineteenth-century concerns, his conclusions about conscious interiority were so revolutionary that findings of the twentieth century were mere stepping-stones to his theories. Three perspectives, rooted in the nineteenth century and explored below, are relevant for my treatment of Jaynes: (1) a focus on temporal linearity that took the specific form of evolutionary theory; (2) reliance on both natural and human sciences; and (3) the saliency of introspection or the most obvious feature of what Jaynes called consciousness.

Jaynes as the "Darwin of Psychology":
Drawing the Timelines of Nature and Humankind

Though there were eighteenth-century precursors, the nineteenth century was the heyday of the search for roots, beginnings, and starting points in the natural and social sciences. The tracing of how elementary forms unfolded into an improved complexity echoed the political and economic projects of "progress" that were sweeping the industrializing world. Of course, Darwin's *On the Origin of Species by Means of Natural*

Selection is the most representative of this great quest for first causes.[5] Note how the title of Jaynes's *The Origin* structurally resonates (whether he intended it or not) with the name of Darwin's book (Chart 1.1). Arguably, in a very general sense, Jaynes's work is a continuation of the Darwinian agenda into Psychology. Chart 1.2 list other important "origin" and "evolution" works.

Chart 1.1. Comparison of the Titles of Key Works: Darwin and Jaynes.

Author	The Beginning of Something	As Explained by
Jaynes	*Origin of Consciousness*	*Breakdown of the Bicameral Mind*
Darwin	*Origin of Species*	*Means of Natural Selection*

Chart 1.2. Other Important "Origin" and "Evolution" Works.

Author	Title
McLennan, J.F.	*Primitive Marriage: An Inquiry into the Origin of the Form of Capture in Marriage Ceremonies* (1865)
Lubbock, J.	*The Origin of Civilization and the Primitive Condition of Man: Mental and Social Condition of Savage* (1870)
LaFargue, P.	*Propriété: Origine et évolution: These communiste* (1885)
LaFargue, P.	*The Evolution of Property from Savagery to Civilization* (1890)
LeTourneau, C.	*Property: Its Origin and Development* (1892)
Guyot, Y.	*La propriété: origine et evolution* (1895)
Engels, F.	*Origin of the Family, Private Property, and the State* (1884)
Veblen, T.	*The Theory of the Leisure Class: An Economic Study in the Evolution of Institutions* (1899)
Petrucci, R.	*Les origines naturelles de la propriété: Essai de sociologie compare* (1905)
Lowie, R.	*The Origin of the State* (1927)
Lewinski, I.	*The Origin of Property and the Formation of the Village Community* (1913)
Polanyi. K.	*The Great Transformation: The Political and Economic Origins of Our Time* (1944)

Jaynes and the Journeys of Psyche

As Psychology institutionalized its agenda and ideas, it would end up conceptualizing two types of time: (1) developmental or the trajectory of the human life-span (a research concern that can be traced back to

G.S. Hall); and (2) evolutionary or the unimaginable passage of many millennia. One reason some fail to appreciate Jaynes is because his range of time does not fit with these two temporal types. What we can learn from Jaynes is that Psychology needs to acknowledge a third type of time, a mid-range temporality measured in centuries or even several millennia. Unfortunately, we ignore the "attic of history" as a treasure trove of evidence, insights, and clues for coming to terms with our psychic diversity and psychic plasticity.

For a Psychologist trained in naturalistic animal behavior, history — or time measurable in human terms, i.e. *not* the immense lengths of bioevolutionary time — played a salient role in Jaynes's thinking. This sensitive appreciation of history is crucial for two reasons. Jaynes once told me that a good Psychologist should, when investigating any mental activity (dreaming, trancing, hallucinations, an emotion, etc.), trace such phenomena back in time (when possible) (for emotions, cf. Jaynes 1982). That way the causes behind the emergence of a phenomenon — its function or purpose — becomes clear. This is the first reason for an appreciation of history. In the case of consciousness, Jaynes's rummaging through historical records revealed that attention to the interior life of the individual (i.e. consciousness) appeared roughly after 1000 BCE. This is a datum of great consequence, as it strongly suggests that conscious interiority is a cultural-historical invention, not innately neurological.

The second reason history is so important concerns intellectual trajectories. Jaynes realized that, when researching, it behooves any investigator to conduct not just the requisite literature review, but to also delve deeply into foundational assumptions and presuppositions. By being keenly aware of what had already been asked by thinkers through the centuries, Jaynes knew what questions were important, which were not, and discerned commonly repeated mistakes (see his review of previous attempts to explain conscious interiority) (Jaynes 1976: 21–47).[6]

Appreciating the Two Sciences

Another important resonance with the nineteenth century was Jaynes's intellectual promiscuity. Like his academic predecessors of a century before, who were comfortable amidst the two "sciences" — natural (*Naturwissenschaften*) and mental/human (*Geisteswissenschaften*) — Jaynes worked in the laboratory, the library, and among ancient and philological texts.[7] Consequently, Jaynes was not mired in pointless attempts to use evolution to explain away culture or reduce messy social complexity to biology or genetics. He simply embraced the fact that psyche is a nexus of neurological and cultural-historical development. The tensions between experimental Psychology and the second Psychology resonate, of course, with debates about the great intellectual divide between *nomos* (variant human convention) and *physis* (invariant natural laws). This division actually has a number of ramifications that concern objective/explanatory/nomothetic versus subjective/interpretive/idiographic approaches (cf. Cahan and White 1992: 224).[8]

A perusal of the 423 names listed in the "Index of Persons" reveals Jaynes's intellectual breadth and his ability to bridge the gap between *Naturwissenschaften* and *Geisteswissenschaften*. Expectedly, given Jaynes's original interest and training, the animal behaviorists H.S. Reimarus, G.H. Lewes, and C. Lloyd Morgan are listed. Pioneers of Psychology make an appearance: Wundt, William James, Binet, Pierre Janet, Morton Prince, Watson, R.S. Woodworth (and others who made important contributions that advanced Psychology, such as Eugen Bleuler, Hermann von Helmholtz, and Martin Jean Charcot), as well as later key figures (Clark L. Hull, Ernest Hilgard, Theodore X. Barber, and Theodore R. Sarbin). Other notables of the social sciences are also mentioned (Sir James G. Frazer, G.H. Mead, Karl Polanyi, Mary Douglas). It is also not surprising that neurologists (especially those who investigated the split brain) should appear: John Hughlings Jackson, C.S. Sherrington, Joseph E. Bogen, Michael S. Gazzaniga, Wilder Penfield, and R.W. Sperry. Given that Jaynes was posing big questions, we should expect to meet iconic intellectual giants (Galileo, Newton, Lamarck, Alfred Russell Wallace, Charles Darwin, Einstein, Thomas Henry Huxley, John Stuart Mill, Herbert Spencer), as well as the luminaries of the philosophy world (Hobbes, Leibniz, Pascal, Descartes, Locke, Rousseau, Kant, Hegel, Marx, Whitehead, Gilbert Ryle).

Though the likes of Aristotle, Socrates, and Plato (cited on 14 pages) often appear in works about consciousness, it is somewhat unusual to come across Pythagoras, Democritus, Parmenides, Archimedes, Aristophanes, Heraclitus, and Herodotus (5 pages). Even more unusual is the appearance of ancient personages, both real and fictional: Achilles (9 pages), Agamemnon (4 pages), Odysseus (4 pages), and Homer (5 pages). Biblical personages—Moses, Samuel, Saul, Jeremiah, and Paul the Apostle (5 pages)—are referenced (we should also note the mention of Augustine), as are classical writers, such as Plutarch (5 pages), Virgil, and Tacitus, as well as others known only to specialists. Rounding out his sweeping take on the ancient world are the names of important rulers: King Ashurbabipal, Tukulti-Ninurta I, Hammurabi (6 pages), Josiah (king), Constantine, and Emperor Julian. To make his arguments, Jaynes relies on prominent scholars of the ancient world:

E.R. Dodds (7 pages), Henri Frankfort, Thorkild Jacobsen, H.W.F. Saggs (10 pages), and Bruno Snell. Other historical personages (Solon, Nero, Joan of Arc, Pedro Pizarro) march across the pages. Finally, examples from Milton, Goethe, Blake, and Shelley are borrowed, demonstrating Jaynes's interest in art. It is clear Jaynes did his homework.

Jaynes as Ethologist: The Biological and Environmental Aspects of Behavior

Jaynes once advised me that no matter what psychological process one is investigating, one should search for behavioral homologies in the animal world—not to reduce human behavior to more simple forms, but to highlight similarities and differences among species. It is clear that one of the differences he was interested in was consciousness: while recounting his prison experiences, he remembered standing in the stockade and picking up a worm from the grass. He vowed that he would devote his life to "finding out the difference between the insensate earth, the sensitive worm, and my thinking self" (cited in Woodward and Tower 2007: 24).[9] While in graduate school, he diligently pursued this mission. Like all comparative Psychologists, Jaynes assumed a continuity between the natural and human worlds. So he attempted to understand consciousness by working backwards, as it were, tracing it to its most primitive elements by studying how living entities learned. He began with plants, moved on to single-celled organisms such as paramecia, protozoa, and then flat-worms, fish, reptiles, and cats (Keen 1977: 60; cited in Greer 2006: 241). But eventually he would come to admit the futility of such an approach, realizing that consciousness is a culturally-acquired human ability, completely absent among animals and not a product of natural evolution. And this is the point: *only a comparative Psychologist, pursuing strict experimental protocols, could come to acknowledge the limits of natural-scientific methods for understanding conscious interiority.*

But before Jaynes reached this insight, he researched imprinting, instinct, and the interaction of learned and innate behavior for his dissertation (published in a series of articles: 1956, 1957, 1958a,b, and 1977). With Frank Beach he co-published "Effects of Early Experience upon the Behavior of Animals" (1954; reprinted in 1960) and then three studies on maternal retrieving in rats (1956a,b,c). With Beach and Zitrin, he co-published three more articles on the neural mediation of mating in male cats (1955, 1956a,b). Much of Jaynes's work explored the differences between what is innate and what is acquired. This was the starting point for his later theory that conscious interiority cannot be equated with perception and is learned, not innate. It is also unique to humans, primates that developed adaptive skills based on exceedingly complex linguistic and sociocultural practices.

We should note that Jaynes was part of the new ethology movement that questioned the wisdom of studying learning under "artificial laboratory conditions from the perspective of inherited, unlearned instincts in natural environments." In this regard he worked at the crossroads of European field ethology ("naturalistic observation") and North American experimental learning research ("laboratory analysis") (Woodward and Tower 2007: 27).[10] For Jaynes, then, the environment—especially cultural—was key to behavior.

Incorporating Anomalous Behavior into Psychology

While science in general makes progress by specialization, increased focus, and more refined measurements, arguably this all can also lead to fragmentation and the tendency to pursue excessively narrow projects, thereby forgetting "big questions." It may be naïve to regard the aforementioned "two-sciences" approach as an antidote to research mired in details, but it does appear to inspire a more eclectic, open-minded, and unprejudiced mind-set.

With this stated, we can better appreciate Jaynes's archeo-psychological excavation of ancient civilizations and historical records. The past revealed to him a strange land. He found divine visitations accompanied by thundering voices heard by holy men, priests, and ordinary people in times past to be salient and therefore worthy of serious investigation. Some of these visitations were certainly literary inventions, especially after 1000 BCE. However, given their ubiquity in the ancient world and mountain-moving historical impact, others were undoubtedly hallucinations. From the Old Testament to the Avesta (the ancient scriptures of Zoroastrianism), ancient religious texts are replete with divine voices commanding prophets (before ca. 1000 BCE, these are, incidentally, widespread patterns, not scattered references). That our neurology would be so organized as to allow something as astonishing as "hearing voices" is a datum apparently lost on not a few researchers (or they attribute them to a few loose neurological wires within the individual's brain).

Jaynes argued that an entire family of anomalous psychological behavior—hypnotic trancing, mediums, glossolalia, hypergraphia, and spirit possession—are vestiges of bicamerality. The harassing and persecuting voices suffered by modern-day schizophrenics or the visions of more recent prophets (e.g. Joseph Smith and the Book of Mormon) are also vestiges of an earlier neurocultural arrangement. Though many have *described* these disconcerting phenomena (usually anthropologists and ethnographers), they have yet to *explain* and *incorporate* them into mainstream Psychology in a robust theoretical manner. By applying his bicameral thesis (in which the right side of the brain "spoke" through the voices of gods or deceased ancestors to the brain's left side), Jaynes attempted to explain from where this strange family of eccentric psychological behavior comes.

Lessons from Art

In the same way that serious scholars of the nineteenth century were expected to acknowledge the natural and mental/human realms, they were also expected to appreciate the arts, as being cultured allowed one to discern value in the two sciences. In Psychology attention to aesthetic principles has a long history, and can be traced back to Fechner's *Vorschule der Aesthetik* (1876). Though much has been written on the perceptual mechanics and processing of aesthetic experience (perspective, visuality, color, etc.), Jaynes saw the relation between Psychology and art in a more semiotic light, as expressions in need of interpretation that offer vital clues to cultural-historical psychological changes. Jaynes's interest in art was not just academic. As mentioned above, he spent a total of about seven years in England, writing plays and performing on stage. I myself saw some of his artistic works in his summer home in Keppoch, Prince Edward Island, Canada. We might note that William James, arguably the founder of American Psychology, desired to be a painter and for one year studied art in the studio of the painter William Morris Hunt (1824–79) (and, like James, he also suffered from depression, which apparently resulted in his suicide).

Jaynes's serious attention to aesthetic artifacts is actually an aspect of his focus on the cultural, and much of his analysis on the origins of conscious interiority relies on careful re-readings of ancient literature. Some relevant writings of Jaynes include his analysis of paleolithic cave paintings (as eidetic images) (1979a); a review of the Tutankhamun exhibition from the perspective of bicameral theory (1979b); the meaning of Shang Dynasty bronzes (2006); the visions of William Blake (1981a); as well as art and right hemispheric activity (1981b).

Introspection: The Target of Psychology?

Beginning in the eighteenth and early seventeenth centuries, what we would call "introspection" began to receive focused attention. By the late 1800s, introspection seemed to be the *raison d'être* of a supposedly "newly founded" Psychology. Indeed, according to Costall (2007), the "official" narrative of Psychology, with the main protagonist being introspection, followed a three-stage trajectory. The first stage, strongly associated with Wundt, begins with the study of mind through introspection. For Wundt, simple, elementary mental processes should be studied via "internal perception" (*innere Wahrnehmung*), but not through "self-observation" (*Selbstbeobachtung*) — advocated by J.S. Mill and eventually Edward Titchener (who had studied with Wundt). Wundt viewed *Selbstbeobachtung* as "retrospection" as informed by memory images and was therefore unreliable for experimental purposes (Diriwächter 2004). Much of Wundt's work was not experimental, as he was very interested in "higher mental processes" (thought, affect, or volition) and language and concept formation,[11] for which, at least for Wundt, experimentation were not feasible. He recognized the limitations of using "internal perception" (Diriwächter 2004: 96). In fact, he did not think that the experimental method had wide application within Psychology. Far from a "brass instruments" materialist-physicalist, we should also note that Wundt's emphasis on volition and apperception (selective and constructive attentional processes) emerges straight out of German idealist philosophy (Cahan and White 1992). He was explicitly opposed to the mechanistic Psychology of Johann Friedrich Herbart and Comtean positivism (Cahan and White 1992).

The next stage saw a rejection of introspectionism by Watson, who redefined Psychology as the science of behavior. The third stage, beginning around the 1950s, witnessed the cognitive revolution that discarded both radical behaviorism and imprecise and unquantifiable introspectionism. The mind was restored as an acceptable subject of study, but now circumscribed by rigorous experimental and statistical methods largely developed by behaviorists.

Costall judiciously contends that all three stages are largely mythical. To begin with, introspectionism was never a dominant movement. However, introspection never went away as a topic either. As Costall argues, the three-phase perspective, centered on introspectionism, is too simple. The expansion of Psychology is far more complicated, shaped by Darwinian theory, physiology, philosophy, and pedagogy, and then evolving into psychoanalysis, clinical, developmental, educational, social, and applied Psychological traditions. Moreover, the cognitive revolution of the 1950s was not so revolutionary, as indicated by those who either did not identify with behaviorism or made important non-behaviorist contributions (e.g. Gestalt Psychologists, Bartlett, Piaget, Tolman). Indeed, in some ways, cognitive Psychology has merely been an extension of the "traditional behaviorist framework" (Costall 2006: 636–37).

Complementing Costall's misgivings about Psychology's distorted history, Danziger points out that three types of introspection can be discerned: (1) classical, which characterized the era of pre-experimental

Psychology; (2) Wundtian experimental; and (3) systematic, as advocated by Titchener and the Würzburg school (Danziger 1980). Complicating matters even more, Wundt distinguished between laboratory-useful "internal perception" (*innere Wahrnehmung*) and daily "self-observation" (*Selbstbeobachtung*).

Costall writes that the final stage is not the culmination it had once seemed. Perhaps a fourth state is long overdue. However, he warns about "true cognitivism" or the "return of consciousness as a proper subject" of study through the revival of introspection (which would be the "ultimate fulfillment of the goals of the early introspectionists"") (Costall 2006: 650). With the rise of "consciousness studies" a new mistake might be made within mainstream Psychology as we still lack a "sensible, non-dualistic account of what is *really* involved in the various socially shared practices of self-observation" (Costall 2006: 651, emphasis in original).[12] After all, Watsonian behaviorists and dogmatic introspectionists (to the degree these types actually existed) argued from the same premise, i.e. "both were committed to an overly subjectivized conception of subjectivity, and an overly objectivized conception of behaviour" (also, what exactly is the meaning of "behaviorism" and "introspectionism"?) (Costall 2006: 649).

Conscious interiority (to the degree that it overlaps in meaning with introspection), then, "continues to pose a very awkward problem" for Psychology (Costall 2006: 649). Perhaps the cultural-historical approach as put forth by Jaynes can begin to remedy the situation.

Consciousness According to Jaynes

Conscious interiority is like dark matter or dark energy in physics; it occupies a huge place, but so far it is poorly understood. Perhaps this explains why so many Psychologists have simply ignored it. The problem is that currently our technical lexicon lacks the terms to adequately describe it. Part of the reason for this is that many assume that conscious interiority is perception, a mere copy of experience (this is the most common mistake). Others assume it to be a vague thought process generated by brain activity shared with animals, and because many of us take interiority for granted, we fail to appreciate its extraordinary and singular nature.

One way to conceptualize Jaynes's agenda is to postulate two modes of mentality. The first is the more basic and easy to understand, though one greatly under-appreciated because we mistakenly assume that we are always consciously "turned on": *routine-maintenance cognition*. This type of thinking is automatic and nonconscious. It describes most of our engagement with the environment (e.g. perceptual reactivity). When dealings with our surroundings are predictable, expected, ordinary, regulated, and uninterrupted, or if problems are already solved, issues decided, schedules prearranged and routine, certainty the rule, and activities continuous, habit (though of a complex sort) is usually all that is required for daily navigation. The second type of mentality, *emergency-repair cognition*, is designed to deal with unpredictable and more messy situations. In his unpublished manuscript, "A New Theory of Consciousness," Jaynes wrote that consciousness is like an "emergency repairman that goes only where he is needed" and that "the role of consciousness has been much overestimated" (cited in Woodward and Tower 2007: 36). When confronted with the unregulated, the extraordinary, or the unpredictable, or if matters uncertain, undecided, or unresolved arise, a type of meta-cognition kicks in since other neurological components are needed to communicate with each other. Episodic in nature, this type of mentality is associated with volition and intentional behavior (at least in the way we moderns understand these terms). It occurs when a chain of behaviors is interrupted or disrupted. During pre-conscious times, emergency-repair cognition took the form of commanding "voice-volitions" from the gods.

Though I have elaborated on his list (Chapter 2), Jaynes enumerated what he thought to be the most important features of conscious interiority, suggesting that there are more: (1) spatialization; (2) excerption; (3) analog "I"; (4) metaphor "me"; (5) narratization; and (6) conciliation (Jaynes 1976: 59–65).

Towards a "Second Psychology"

Cahan and White have proposed that a number of thinkers envisioned a "second Psychology" that would complement what would become, by the late nineteenth century, a laboratory, experiment-based Psychology. For example, Auguste Comte (1798–1857) wrote about *"psychics."* This denoted abstract disciplines that included the biological, sociological, and the moral/individualistic. His interest in the difficult-to-translate *"la morale positive"* was a collectivist rather than an individual-centered Psychology (cf. Cahan and White 1992: 233). John Stuart Mill (1806–73), in *On the Logic of the Moral Sciences* (1843 [1974]) (the sixth book of *A System of Logic*) argued for a "science of character formation or ethology" that would examine habits, dispositions, and conduct (Cahan and White 1992: 226). The prolific John Bascom (1827–1911) who wrote a number of books on Psychology and greatly influenced his student, G.S. Hall, argued that philosophy should take a top-down approach to humans in order to balance findings from natural-scientific research (Cahan and White 1992).

Influential thinkers such as William James (1842–1910) and George Herbert Mead (1863–1931) wrote about the possibilities of non-experimental Psychology, while James Mark Baldwin (1861–1934) and John Dewey (1859–1952) would question the unqualified importation of natural-scientific methodologies into Psychology. An important intellectual descendant of *Völkerpsychologie* took root in the Soviet Union with the work of the cultural-historical approach of Lev Vygotsky (1896–1934) (1998), Alexander Luria (1902–77) (1976), and Aleksei Leontiev (1903–79) (1978, 2005 [1940]). Vygotsky and Luria (1993 [1930]) emphasized the inherently social nature of mind, language, and thought. Higher mental processes are complex and self-regulating, social in origin, mediated, and "conscious and voluntary in their mode of functioning" (cited in Meshcheriakov 2000: 43; see Wertsch 1985, 1991). Cross-cultural, ethnopsychology, Psychological anthropology, and cultural Psychology have, in their own way, continued the hopes of a second Psychology. From an institutional perspective, interdisciplinary programs, such as the Institute of Human Relations at Yale and the Department of Social Relations at Harvard, might be viewed as attempts to establish a second Psychology outside the conventional disciplinary structure of academic Psychology (Cahan and White 1992: 231–33).

Völkerpsychologie *and the Promise of a Non-Experimental Psychology*

Völkerpsychologie predates the more familiar experimental Psychology. The first professorship in this discipline was established in 1860 at the University of Bern, Switzerland, which is concerned with the "products of collective mental processes of peoples identified as a unified body" (Diriwächter 2004: 88–89). Its underlying premise is that only through the cultural community does an individual become a "mental/spirited being" (*geistiges Wesen*) (Diriwächter 2004: 92). *Völkerpsychologie* has been rendered into English in various ways: "folk Psychology," "Psychology of peoples," "ethnic Psychology," "ethnocultural Psychology," "social Psychology," or "ethnopsychology." Wong suggests that "cultural-historical Psychology" is the most appropriate translation (2009: 230). *Völkerpsychologie* is actually one of an array of notions, such as *Volksgesit* ("spirit of the people") that indicates the collective (as opposed to "person" of "individual Psychology"). It is also related to *Volkskunde* (folklore), but pursued from a scientific perspective, not just as a "fashionable sport" (Diriwächter 2004: 93). Adolf Bastian (1826–1905), the highly influential anthropologist, searched for *Volkergedanken* (elementary "folk ideas") while Wilhelm von Humboldt looked at *Nationalcharakter*. Indeed, *Völkerpsychologie* would provide the ideological inspiration for German cultural nationalism, propounding an ethnonational "togetherness" in an area of Europe that until around 1870 was politically divided but—more or less—culturally cohesive (Diriwächter 2004: 88–89).

Völkerpsychologie harks back to an earlier nineteenth-century "nature-philosophy" that combined science, religion, philosophy, and art as evident in the thinking of luminaries such as Kant, Humboldt, Schopenhauer, Goethe, Hegel, Fechner, and Fichte (Blumenthal 1975: 1086–87). Arguably something like a *Völkerpsychologie* can be traced back even earlier, to jurist, historian, and political philosopher Giambattista Vico (1668–1744) and the philosophical anthropologist Johann Georg Hamann (1730–88). But the most important inspiration came from Johann Gottfried Herder (1744–1803) and his conceptualization of *Volker*. Herder saw psychological processes as "embedded in a trans-individual cultural medium" (Danziger 1983: 304).

By the late 1800s, attempts were made in Germany to cultivate a Psychology of culture grounded in earlier philosophies of customs, language, mythology, and history (Cahan and White 1992). In 1851, the philologists Moritz Lazarus (1824–1903) and Hajim Steinthal (1823–1899) penned "On the Concept and Possibility of a *Völkerpsychologie*." Lazarus and Steinthal pursued two goals. The first was to search out "general laws that explain humankind as a whole and the development of the human 'sprit' (*Geist*)." The second was to study the "specific characters of the various *Volker* that make up humankind and the factors that produce particular manifestations of the general laws among people in different historical circumstances" (Cahan and White 1992: 227). For Lazarus and Steinthal, individual–community relations should be a problem for Psychology, not just philosophy, legal theory, or politics, since the "inner activity of all individuals" was not metaphysical but could be a topic of investigation (Danziger 1983: 305).[13] In 1860 they established the journal *Zeitschrift für Völkerpsychologie und Sprachwissenschaft* (*Journal of Cultural Psychology and Linguistics*). This was "dedicated to the study of the mentalities of diverse human societies and the relationships of those mentalities to language" (Cahan and White 1992: 227). Indeed, language played a pivotal role. For instance, for Wilhelm von Humboldt (1767–1835), philologist, philosopher, and statesman, and founding father of the University of Berlin, language "can be seen as the creating force as well as the tools of higher mental processes" (Diriwächter 2004: 87). Like Jaynes, Humboldt believed that "social-developmental transformations of psychological phenomena are mediated by language" (Greenwood 2003: 73).

Wundt and the "Second Psychology"

The biggest objector to the limitations of laboratory-based psychology, of course, was none other than Wilhelm Wundt, the ostensible founder of experimental "physiological" Psychology. He called for a "second Psychology" to complement laboratory-based Psychology (Cahan and White 1992). Additionally, his deepest interest, to which he devoted most of his life, was in cultural-historical Psychology, as evident in his ten-volume work entitled *Völkerpsychologie: Eine Untersuchung der Entwicklungsgestze von Sprache, Mythus, und Sitte* (*Cultural Psychology: An Investigation of the Developmental Laws of Language, Myth, and Morality*, 1900–1920).

Though many have corrected the record, the Wundt portrayed in many texts and courses is "largely fictional" (Blumenthal 1975: 1082). Thanks to the biographies by G.S. Hall and Boring, Wundt's contributions and significance are greatly misunderstood. He was neither a structuralist nor introspectionist. Wundt is still mis-appreciated in some circles because graduate students are trained in the "splintered disciplinary maze" that is modern Psychology (cited in Ferrari, Robinson, and Yasnitsky 2010: 98; cf. Woodward 1982). Mainstream Psychology has taken his more limited "experimental" approach (methodologically inspired by physiology and physics) and ignored his cultural-historical Psychology. Cole makes the same point, writing about the "Two Wundt's" (1996; cited in Ferrari *et al.* 2010: 99).

According to Graumann, Wundt's concern for *Völkerpsychologie* has to do with his changing interest in unconscious processes and afterwards in consciousness activity itself. Before his Leipzig days (pre-1875), he combined introspective, experimental, historical, and statistical investigations of unconscious mental phenomena. This was his "Heidelberg Program." But his "Leipzig Program" dropped considerations of the unconscious and split into (1) simple conscious mental actions (experimental Psychology) and (2) cultural-historical *Völkerpsychologie* (1980) (cited in Ferrari *et al.* 2010: 99). In this sense he never intended to develop two types of Psychology.

There is another side to Wundt that should be interjected as it concerns the value of asking "big questions" in the human sciences (e.g. the origins of consciousness itself). According to Ferrari *et al.*, Wundt had two somewhat different careers, first as a pioneering physiologist Psychologist and then as a Psychologist-philosopher (Ferrari *et al.* 2010: 97). Indeed, he should be thought of as a "prominent German philosopher" who promoted the new Psychology as the "scientific foundation for philosophy in general" (Ferrari *et al.* 2010: 97). Wundt believed that

Psychology should not be a distinct discipline but should be part of a reformed philosophy (Ferrari et al. 2010: 99).[14]

The Völkerpsychologie of the "Other" Wundt

Wundt spent more than a third of his professional life working on *Völkerpsychologie* (Kroger and Scheibe 1990: 223). But, in the same way that Wundt's laboratory research was reduced to an "atomic mental chemistry" by his North American students, his *Völkerpsychologie* also suffered at the hands of historians (Kroger and Scheibe 1990: 221). Indeed, until not that long ago, his huge ten-volume work on the topic has been more or less ignored, at least in the Anglophone world.

Lazarus and Steinthal shared some basic understandings about *Völkerpsychologie* with Wundt: (1) individual Psychology is not sufficient to give us a comprehensive understanding of psychological processes; (2) interdependence between individuals and communities; (3) *Volksgeist* plays an important role in the development of individual psychological processes; and (4) *Volksgeist* is also a source for the interpretation of the lawfulness of psychological processes (Wong 2009: 245). Nevertheless, in 1881 Wundt wrote a critique of Lazarus and Steinthal. He argued that the less mystical sounding *Völkseele* (mind of the folk) should replace *Völkgiest* (Cahan and White 1992).

Wundt thought that while entire languages, myths, and customs cannot be investigated experimentally, "it does not obviously preclude the experimental investigation of the social [P]sychological processes of individuals that can be inferred from them (by means of the comparative-historical study of languages, myths, and customs)" (Greenwood 2003: 76). Languages, myths, and customs have properties, unlike the psychological process responsible for their production, making them analogous to "objects of nature" and therefore they may be treated as objects of pure observation (Greenwood 2003: 77). They possess a "thin-like nature" that can be investigated like "objects of nature." In fact, they provide a "more secure evidential base" for Psychological theory than the "fleeting evidential base" of experimental introspective Psychology (Greenwood 2003: 76).

Greenwood contends that Wundt *supposedly* maintained that social psychological phenomena, the topic of *Völkerpsychologie*, were not amenable to experimentation.[15] Rather, social Psychological issues should be investigated using comparative-historical methods. Greenwood doubts if Wundt actually believed this. He argues that if Wundt did take such a stance, it contradicted his own theoretical position and methodological practices. Wundt seems to have had little interest in experimental analyses of the synchronic social dynamics of psychological processes, and that most of his arguments about the inappropriateness of experimentation targeted the introspective analysis of "diachronic" historical processes (Greenwood 2003: 84).

Though Wundt saw *Völkerpsychologie* as a "socio-developmental discipline" (i.e. tracing the different steps of humankind's mental development), in principle he was opposed to integrating history (the discipline, not development *per se*) into *Völkerpsychologie* (Diriwächter 2004: 97); he did not want to psychologize history. What is "investigated is not the historicity of the psyche in and of itself, but the development of the mental objectifications of psychical activity during the course of history." In other words, the "historicity of the psyche" is not the same as "psychologizing the historical" (Diriwächter 2004: 98).

Like Darwin's "archeological method" (note how geology greatly shaped Darwin's evolutionary theory), Wundt's *Völkerpsychologie* is a science of traces, remnants, and deposits, rather than synchronic experimental intervention. While Darwin looked at the products of organic evolution, Wundt searched for the products of "cultural evolution" (Kroger and Scheibe 1990: 225). This resonates with the view of Jaynes — a psychohistory of strata with vestiges of the bicameral mind (e.g. spirit possession, hypnosis, and "hearing voices").

Despite the potential for an outside-the-laboratory cultural-historical Psychology, Wundt's own concerns in *Völkerpsychologie* "remained disappointingly individualist and universalistic" (Greenwood 1999: 511). Nevertheless, his brand of "social Psychology" was carried forward by G.H. Mead, Durkheim, Sapir, Whorf, Malinowski, Boas, W.I. Thomas, and Freud (Kroger and Scheibe 1990: 223–24).[16] More broadly, though it has not been as recognized by those writing the meta-narratives concerning what human Psychology could be about,[17] Wundt's vision lives on in the various sister fields of Psychological anthropology, cultural and cross-cultural Psychology, Vygotskian approaches, and social cognition approaches.

In certain respects *Völkerpsychologie* is a "forgotten" tradition that did not fulfill its promise. Several reasons account for this. First, "Many of our historical accounts have been heavily influenced by the partitioning of problems and approaches into the rubrics of the 'schools' of the early twentieth century" (Mueller 1979: 23–24). The study of "collective spirit expressing itself in a certain cultural products" (Wong 2009: 245) did not seem to have well-defined intellectual predecessors. In America, though social Psychology seemed to be a related discipline, this field acquired an experimental, behavioristic, and individualistic orientation that did not square easily with the group and interpretive perspective of a cultural-historical approach. The "pursuit of the social as the mere stimulus provided by the presence of others continued and continues still in the pages of major social [P]sychological journals" (Kroger and Scheibe 1990: 222). Though we now know that for Wundt *Völkerpsychologie* was never a sort of postscript to his career, it became regarded as

> vague, imprecise, unscientific, and metaphysical. At best, it was regarded as a kind of afterthought to Wundt's experimental psychology, as the indulgence of an aging academic who, in the twilight of this career, wanted to address the larger questions of human existence after having devoted a lifetime to the technicalities of elementary psychological processes in the restricted confines of the laboratory he founded in 1879. (Kroger and Scheibe 1990: 223)

Finally, *Völkerpsychologie* was tainted with the nationalist movements of the late nineteenth century (Danziger 1983: 310).

What is significant for our purposes is how two main foci of *Völkerpsychologie*, language and mythology, in many ways resonate with two crucial aspects of Jaynes's theorizing: linguistic theory (specifically, how metaphor relates to the cultural construction of mind-words) and ancient religions (in how they reveal the contours of an earlier mentality).

Cultural Psychology as a Descendant of Völkerpsychologie

The discipline that appears to be the direct descendant of *Völkerpsychologie* is cultural Psychology; Diriwächter describes *Völkerpsychologie* as cultural Psychology's "historical predecessor" or "grandfather" (Diriwächter 2004: 85). But we need to note that certain disciplines, closely related to cultural Psychology, do not in fact view culture as the medium in which "psychological processes are enacted, via practical everyday activities situated in historically conditioned contexts" (Cole 1996: 504). Perhaps this is because, "Like fish in water, we fail to 'see' culture because it is the medium within which we exist" (Cole 1996: 8). Indeed, through its history, Psychology has had the "collective habit of repressing psychological complexities (including culture) as often as has been possible" (Valsiner 2001: 6).

Shweder, a proponent of cultural Psychology, views the psyche as "content-driven, domain-specific, and constructively stimulus bound"; it "cannot be extricated from the historically variable and cross-culturally diverse intentional worlds in which it plays a coconstituting part" (Shweder 1990: 13). He explains why allied fields, while incorporating culture into their analyses, do not in fact regard psyche as inherently cultural. First, cultural Psychology differs fundamentally from mainstream Psychology because the latter de-emphasizes emotions, historical factors, and the sociocultural context in which actions or thoughts transpire (Gardner 1985: 6). Thus, "stimuli, contexts, resources, values, meanings, knowledge, religion, rituals, language, technologies, [and] institutions" are all regarded as external to mind (Shweder 1990: 5). Conventional Psychology's primary goal is to describe an abstract, fixed, and universal "central processing mechanism" (CPM) whose "invariant laws of operation" are supposedly "untainted by content and context" (Shweder 1990: 5-7).[18] The approaches of mainstream Psychology, artificially-bounded in its endeavors, can be limiting. Psychologists have little concern for the concrete, particulars, substance, or variable content that "is operated upon by the processor or may interfere with its operations" (Shweder 1990: 4). Contemporary Psychology has "developed a theoretical myopia towards seeing universality in variability." However, variability is "the *basis* for making sense of the universalist lawfulness of human psychology—rather than a technically uncomfortable aberration (or error)" (Valsiner 2001: 18, emphasis in original). And despite its focus on culture, cross-cultural Psychology merely attempts to "itemize the features of the CPM" (Shweder 1990: 9). General research Psychology has more faith in psychic unity than cultural Psychology, which has a "fundamental skepticism concerning all those fateful and presupposed distinctions" (Shweder 1990: 13).

Mainstream research Psychology has much to learn from culture-based approach. Culture should not be regarded as merely another variable (whether dependent or independent), and anti-reductionistic, non-experimental methods have an indispensable role to play. The "imposition of hypothetico-deductivism from an imaginary version of physics" (Potter 2000: 35) stifles an open-minded, creative understanding of the psyche. As Danziger puts it, "analysis in terms of variables has become a way of eliminating questions of meaning from the explanation of human conduct" (1997: 171). "Cognitivists are used to pre-defining the world—in stimulus materials, in vignettes, in fixed-choice questionnaires—that they never have to address the flexibility and rhetorically contested nature of everyday life where the world is not given in a single particular way, in particular fixed categories, but is reaccomplished and transformed" (Potter 2000: 35). Cognitivism, fixed on that which can be measured, is overly focused on an underlying competence (form, structures) that is deemed the proper topic for investigation, not the messy "surface" (content, practices) (Potter 2000: 33). But we should not forget that much of earlier Psychology, as I have tried to show, was greatly concerned with these issues.

Psychological Anthropology suffers from reductionism because it assumes that society is configured by the projection of processes "operated upon by, or expressive of, deep and invariant psychological laws or processes or motivation, affect and intellect" (Shweder 1990: 14). It does not concern itself with how the mind is "fundamentally altered by the content, stuff, material, or sociocultural environment on which it operates" (Shweder 1990: 15–16). Finally, ethnopsychology investigates mind, self, and emotions in the same way it approaches folk beliefs about botany or kinship, i.e. it is not person-centered enough. Cultural Psychology gives more attention to the experiences of actual persons (Shweder 1990: 16). Catherine Lutz, in her investigations of emotions, writes that they "can more profitably be viewed as serving complex communicative, moral, and cultural purposes rather than as labels for internal states whose nature or essence is presumed to be universal" (Lutz 1988: 5).

As powerful as it is, the assumption that beliefs (culture) are something layered over deeper, pre-cultural mental processes (psychological structures) is misleading. No fundamental division between the CPM and an individual's historical context, institutional setting, beliefs, values, and knowledge exists (Shweder 1990: 4–5). The disciplinary delineations between Psychology, sociology, anthropology, etc. do not reflect pre-given natural cleavages between person and society; drawing demarcations between individual psychological processes and sociocultural content is much more of a challenge than the landscape of departmental divisions would have us believe.

Corroboration and Applications of Jaynes's Theories

As controversial as they are, support for Jaynes's ideas have come from various quarters (see Introduction). Here I can only provide a sampling of examples. These include investigations into neurology (Sher 2000; Olin 1999; Cavanna et al. 2007; Kuijsten 2006b, 2009); hallucinations (Hamilton 2006); linguistics (Carr 1983, 1985a,b, 1989, 1996, 2006; Limber 2006; McVeigh 1996); literature (Weissman 1993); religion (McVeigh 2016a); and questions about personal agency and volition (McVeigh 2006a). Other relevant works include Rowe (2012); Sleutels (2006); and Stove (2006). From a more practical point of view, some have noted that, while hearing voices often occurs in pathological contexts, this phenomenon in and of itself, given that it occurs among the normal population more frequently than acknowledged, is not abnormal. The idea is that hearing voices is a bicameral vestige. This finding has been integrated into therapeutic settings for those suffering from unwelcome voice-hearing (Moskowitz and Corstens 2008).

Endnotes

[1] See also McVeigh (2005, 2008, 2012a,b, 2013).
[2] Of course, this canonization is somewhat misleading and depends on one's definition of "Psychology."

3   With the anthropologist Clellan S. Ford (1951).
4   It is worth pointing out that Vygotsky, another Psychologist concerned with cultural-historical developments, wrote his 1916 master's thesis on the "Tragedy of Hamlet, the Prince of Denmark, by W. Shakespeare" (1916), and his 1925 doctoral dissertation was entitled "Psychology of Art." He also became a well-known literary critic (Ferrari et al. 2010: 104).
5   The rest of the title reads: *or the Preservation of Favored Races in the Struggle for Life*.
6   In 1963 Jaynes received a letter from then seventy-seven year-old Edwin G. Boring at Harvard University. Boring asked Jaynes to write 120 pages on the history of comparative Psychology for a Basic Book series. This would never materialize. Instead, he did end up writing 500 manuscript pages which was developed into a week of lectures at the National Science Foundation "Summer Institute in the History of Psychology" at the University of New Hampshire. These were organized into twenty-one chapters (14 to 21 have not been found and were probably never written). The project begins with the "Ionian Revolution" (Chapter 2) and ends in the twentieth century with "psychoneurology." If one theme stands out, it is "evolution," as this word appears four times in the 21 chapters (Woodward and Tower 2006: 30-32). Another example of Jaynes's interest in intellectual development is his work on the history of ethology and comparative Psychology (1969c).
7   Of course, for those who were attracted to materialism, the happy marriage of the two sciences was not as appreciated.
8   Hugo Münsterberg, in his *Psychology: General and Applied* (1915), distinguished between a complementary "casual" and "purposive" Psychology that resonates with these characteristics (cited in Cahan and White 1992: 224).
9   From a recorded interview, 1984.
10 See Jaynes (1969a: 605).
11 Among his many other accomplishments, Wundt is recognized by Blumenthal (1975) and Leahey (1979) as a founder of psycholinguistics (cited in Greenwood 2003: 84).
12 Julian Jaynes once said something in a course I took with him that surprised me: he did believe in dualism, but not the kind that had plagued Psychology. He explained that it were as if human primates were, in ethological terms, following a typical trajectory but then their cognition took a sudden, sharp turn, exploding into a new complexity. What he meant was that this deviation, being part of the evolutionary story, required a scientific approach, not a postulation of a mysterious mental substance (or its denial by behaviorists). Perhaps this resonates with the physician Johann Gottlob Krüger's notion (1715-59); he argued for what would be called "empirical dualism" (1756) (in Schmidt 1796: 189), or the "position that the phenomena of mind and body form distinct subject matters, whatever the underlying ontology might be" (Hatfield 2002: 212).
13 Johann Friedrich Herbart (1776-1841), with his idea that intra-individual and inter-individual levels were somehow analogous (and famous for conceiving of Psychology as a discipline that could be mathemtaticalized), influenced Lazarus and Steinthal (Danziger 1983: 305).

14. See also Lamiell, "On Psychology's Struggle for Existence: Some Reflections on Wundt's 1913 Essay a Century On" (2013).
15. Note that Wundt did not that believe "social Psychology" was a suitable translation as it was associated with contemporary cultural phenomena (cf. Greenwood 2003: 72–73). In renderings of *Völkerpsychologie* Wundt preferred "folk" as it indicated not just entire peoples but also more limited groupings, such as families, classes, and clans.
16. Mead attended Wundt's lectures in Leipzig in 1889–90. His symbolic interactionism can be traced to Wundt (Danziger 1983: 308; Kroger and Scheibe 1990).
17. But also see works such as Werner's *Comparative Psychology of Mental Development* (1948).
18. Greenwood examines how Cole advocated a cultural Psychology sensitive to the promise of Wundt's *Völkerpsychologie* and the historical-cultural Psychology of Vygotsky and Luria. But he contends that Cole failed to "take seriously the theoretical possibility of historically and culturally local forms of cognitive processing" (Cole 1996): "None of Cole's illustrative samples of cultural [P]sychological theory and practice constitute illustrations of historically or culturally local forms of psychological functioning: they are all readily interpretable as different cultural or historical manifestations of putatively universal forms of psychological functioning" (Greenwood 1999: 511).

Chapter 2

The Neurocultural Malleability of Psyche

"The individual human organism, having two brains, is the biological substrate of *two persons*, each of which has *one mind*." —Roland Puccetti (emphasis in original)

A Primer on Jaynesian Psychology

Using evidence from Psychology, neurology, archeology, history, linguistics, and the analysis of religious texts, the late Julian Jaynes argued in *The Origin* that the neurocultural[1] organization of the human psyche is remarkably plastic. He contended that before the twelfth century BCE individuals lacked "consciousness" as we know it and possessed a different mentality. Though people could perceive their surroundings, they were not subjectively self-aware. Instead, they were governed by hallucinatory voices and visions attributed to chiefs, rulers, ancestors, and gods. Jaynes's thinking is premised on the notion that social transformations—expanding demographics, more complex political economic systems, mass migration, and technological innovations such as writing and bronze- and ironworking—led to changes in cognition.

The purpose of this book is not to explicate in detail the basic theories of Jaynes or to offer a comprehensive treatment of his contributions. But in order to appreciate how his thinking on language fits into his other theories, the reader should be oriented to the fundamentals of his ideas. Below five key theoretical perspectives postulated by Jaynes are introduced to afford some theoretical perspective.

(1) Bicamerality:
Hallucinations as Evolutionary Adaptation

The pivotal concept in Jaynes's thinking is "bicameral" ("two-chambered") psychology. This describes a pre-conscious mentality of the Mesolithic period in which the language areas of the right hemisphere organized advice and admonishments and coded them into hallucinatory experiences that were conveyed over the anterior commissure to the left hemisphere's corresponding language regions. As societies adapted to the agricultural revolution, the hallucinated voices and visions produced by bicameral mentality reflected emerging spiritual hierarchies of divinized ancestors and deities, so that the ruler or "god" side (the right side) ordered about the follower or "person" (the left side).

That hallucinations were once a useful evolutionary adaptation may at first blush sound preposterous until one puts together the pieces of neurological and historical evidence that, taken together, forms a picture that answers why divine voices, visions, and visitations were so ubiquitous in the ancient world. In the context of what we now know about cerebral lateralization from comparative Psychology, neurological plasticity, and "self talk," this theory is not as far-fetched as it might at first sound.

(2) Bicameral Breakdown:
Recognizing Major Changes in Human Mentality

Overcoming Our "Too Familiar" Sense of History

Before the first millennium BCE all known ancient civilizations exhibit some strikingly similar features which point to a "super-religious" mentality. This term is intended to highlight just how supercharged religion was in societies characterized by divine visions and visitations, monumental mortuary architecture, and the absence of skepticism vis-à-vis the gods. The super-religiosity that characterized earlier societies may not in and of itself be surprising, as it is overwhelmingly evident in archeological and historical records. But this is exactly the point: we have become so accustomed to regarding ancient civilizations as religious that we have forgotten how strange it is that before roughly 1000 BCE skepticism vis-à-vis the supernatural realm was nonexistent. Unfortunately, we have become so overly-familiarized with these worldwide patterns that we fail to see their alienness. Does an explanation exist that accounts for these unusual civilizational patterns? And how do we explain the birth of religion as we know it that, with some geographical variation, accompanied a major shift in mentality after the first millennium BCE?

Despite its original adaptive value as a psychosocial communications system, bicamerality was no match for rapidly ballooning populations, expanding sociopolitical arrangements, and technological changes of the Bronze Age. The transition to an upgraded *mentalité* took a number of centuries, but some time around the twelfth century BCE a pre-conscious cognition of hallucinated divine volitional voices and visions was replaced by a psychology of conscious interiority. The passing of bicameral civilizations, rather than something neuroanatomical, was a cultural development, i.e. psychological processes are as much sociohistorical as they are neurological.

The Bicameral Civilization Inventory Hypothesis

The Bicameral Civilization Inventory (BCI) Hypothesis was inspired by the thinking of Jaynes. It postulates that from around 3500 to 1000 BCE[2] a list of certain features characterized all civilizational cores without exception. The emphases, combinations, and permutations of the BCI traits vary by place and period, but generally the following list of ingredients are to be found in all cultures. The reader is requested to drop his or her assumptions and ask why these are universal. The challenge is to find one demographically-large society that does not fit the pattern of bicamerality (or a culture that lacks bicameral vestiges) rather than one that does.

Elements of the BCI have built upon each other through the centuries, forming worldwide stratigraphic psychological patterns as revealed in the archeological and historical record. Such evidence shows how human psychology has adapted over time. The most robust evidence for this change appears in Mesopotamia beginning around 3500 BCE, though prototypical traits date back to 10,000 BCE. Compared to Eurasian societies, bicameral features emerged later in North, South, and Central America. The Post-Bicameral Civilization Inventory (PBCI) lists vestiges of bicameral societies. The development of post-bicamerality indicates a major rupture in human history, roughly corresponding to the Late Bronze Age Collapse in the Mediterranean and Middle East.

The BCI

- *Right-Hemisphere Dominance (RHD)*. Hallucinated "self-talk" originating in right hemisphere's linguistic regions (now vestigial).
- *Voice-Volition (VV)*. As groups grow in size, social control-at-a-distance is needed; hallucinated voice-volitions (RHD) develop. VVs, attributed to absent clan leaders, ancestors, etc., provide social control and authorization.
- *Centrality of Ancestor Worship (CAW)*. Divinized rulers and ancestors become gods issuing VVs. Household ancestor cults typically nested within larger hierarchies of overarching royal ancestor-worship.
- *Theocentric Social Order (TSO)*. Theopolitical governance by divinely-deputized rulers or incarnate gods (e.g. pharaohs). Carvings,

sculptures, texts, etc. portray rulers' claim to "hear" and obey a deity's commands (RHD and VVs).
- *Objects of Hallucinatory Focus (OHF).* Hallucinatory aids broadcast instructions, commandments, warnings. Speaking idols, living statues; effigies treated as if alive, fed, paraded, taken on journeys and into battles; these emitted holy power and authorized decision-making—in some cases portable OHF were used, e.g. the Israelites' Ark of the Covenant.
- *Induction Methods for Right-Hemisphere Activation (IMRHA).* Music, poetry, and song used in induction procedures to activate linguistic regions of right-hemisphere (e.g. large eyes on statues).
- *Authority-Radiating Ceremonial Complexes (ARCC).* Influence of gods and divine rulers emanated from sacred administrative centers; these structures formed focal points of deity–mortal communication. Evolved from simpler funerary sites, monumental mortuary architecture housed divinized rulers and OHF: images, ancestral tablets, leaders' glorified remains (e.g. pyramids, ziggurats, temples, megaliths, aggrandized tombs).
- *Human Settlements Dominated by ARCC.* Urban dwellings and agricultural hinterland encircle a "house of the god(s)" or other ARCC that exercised control (TSO) over local inhabitants.
- *"As If" Mortuary Practices (AIMP).* Belief that the deceased continue living in the afterlife; graves themselves became OHF (e.g. elaborate grave furnishings, retinues, slaves, figurines that assist in afterlife, mummification).
- *Supernatural Visitations (SV).* Messages from beyond maintain moral order as direct-god–mortal communication (VVs) erodes (e.g. revenants, ghosts, demons, vengeful spirits).
- *Intermediary Beings (IB).* As deities retreat to the heavens, their VVs cease, so intercessionary beings ensure that communication between mortals and gods still transpire via angels or guardian deities.
- *Indirect Divine Communication (IDC).* As deities retreat to the heavens and their VV cease, exopsychic practices develop to communicate with them. Divination, oracles, prophets, visions, "visitation dreams," revelations by IB.
- *Secondary Burials.* When VVs of ancestors cease, then the dead are permanently interned (AIMP).
- *Multiple Souls.* One soul is divinized, one stays behinds to communicate with mortals (AIMP).
- *Undeveloped Psychological Lexicon (UPL) before ca. 1000 BCE.* Sociopolitical systems were not complex enough to require sophisticated interiorized linguo-concepts until after ca. 1000 BCE.

- *Metaphoric Mind-Words (MMW).* In response to increased social complexity, languages replace UPL and follow the same linguo-conceptual scaffolding trajectory based on spatial and bodily metaphors.
- *No Philosophical Tradition before ca. 1000 BCE.* Existence of gods not doubted; skepticism of divine order neuroculturally impossible. Absence of sustained philosophical suspicion, skepticism, or doubt regarding the supernatural did not develop until after 1000 BCE.

Post-Bicameral Civilization Inventory

- *Vestigial Bicameralism (VB) after ca. 1000 BCE.* IMRHA is utilized to culturally activate vestigial language areas of right hemisphere. Examples include shamanism, spirit possession, glossolalia, autoscopic phenomena (doppelgängers, heautoscopy), and neo-IDC. Folktales, myths, and legends about "little people" and ghost stories develop. Another example of vestigial bicamerality includes what happens when conscious interiority is suspended, i.e. hypnosis and hyper-suggestibility.

Below, building upon the BCI, I provide a sketch of how human mentality underwent neurocultural adaptation in the face of sociopolitical and techno-economic upheaval:

- *Neolithic Bicamerality: A Neurocultural Response to the Agricultural Revolution.* The transition from nomadic hunting and gathering to animal and plant domestication during the Neolithic era (roughly from 10,000 to 4000 BCE) transformed the lifestyle of *homo sapiens*. By 6000 to 5000 BCE, early agricultural settlements and pre-urban sites had developed.
- *Literate-Urban Bicameral Societies: A Neurocultural Response to the Urban Revolution.* The urban revolution, whose earliest evidence dates from approximately 3500 BCE in Mesopotamia, was a continuation of the agricultural revolution that saw the emergence of complex and literate bicameral societies characterized by more or less direct god–mortal communications (until approximately 2000 BCE). Urbanized societies during this period were "classic" bicameral, that is, they exhibited super-religious civilizational patterns. A common arrangement was the establishment of a temple around which revolved proto-urban centers; this was probably a tribal or ancestral-deity shrine that eventually housed a patron deity of the town. Initially a type of shaman-king, appointed by the gods, was put in charge. But eventually, this ruler assumed a heavier task, evolving into a god-king (as in Egypt) or a divinely-appointed ruler.

- *The Breakdown of Bicamerality: A Transitional Period.* A mentality rooted in the agricultural revolution and its impressive outcome—the strict theocratic hierarchies administrating urban centers overseeing crop-yielding hinterlands—was no match for a system of communication, command, and control that had become overextended, disordered, and weakened as the authorization of the gods no longer made sense. As demographic scale increased and more sociopolitical layers were added, the divine dominance hierarchies creaked under pressure and *more* adaptive hallucinatory experiences became necessary. Evidence of this transition in mentality is apparent in the late Bronze Age (BA) collapse (from around 1200 to 1000 BCE). The subsequent dark ages would last for centuries in parts of the Eastern Mediterranean and Southwest Asia. Out of this chaos a new cognition emerged—a conscious interiority in which divine authorization was replaced by self-authorization for more efficient decision-making.
- *Post-Bicamerality: A New Mentality of Conscious Interiority.* Some time after 1000 BCE conscious interiority, a new neurocultural adaptation, replaced semi-bicamerality, which was a jury-rigged psycho-machinery, with its difficult-to-discern divination, increasingly irrelevant ravings of wandering prophets, and admonishing revenants who, as time went by, seemed to fade like the mist from which they appeared. The post-bicameral period saw science and philosophy flower in the world's civilizational centers. This was the "axial age" (ca. 800–200 BCE) as described by the philosopher and psychiatrist Karl Jaspers: an incandescent rebirth after the late BA collapse when the great proselytizing religions were founded and modern spirituality—characterized by probing doubts and self-questioning that would have been psychologically impossible in bicameral times—took root.

(3) Conscious Interiority:
Mental Imagery as a Cultural Adaptation

According to Jaynes, introspectable conscious cognition did not arise far back in human evolution but first developed around the end of the second millennium BCE. It was out of the cauldron of cyclical civilizational collapse and chaos that a new mentality—conscious subjective "interiority"—grounded in a conscious "internal dialogue" better suited to the pressures of larger, more complex sociopolitical systems, gradually emerged by around the late second millennium BCE. Many of us assume that consciousness means cognition or that sensory perception is the same as what we "see" with our mind's eye. But we can be awake, alert, and attentive without experiencing the world in an interiorized self-aware manner. Self-conscious subjectivity as we experience it is a neurocultural adaptive add-on. With that stated, Charts 2.1 and 2.2 are intended to clarify for the reader what Jaynes meant—and did not mean—by "consciousness."

Chart 2.1. Different Understandings of "Consciousness."

	Conventional Understandings	Jaynes's Understanding
When It Emerged	Far back in evolutionary history	Late second millennium BCE
Why It Emerged	Response to long-term environmental changes	Response to relatively recent sociopolitical complexity
How It Emerged	Bioevolutionary development	Generated linguistically from metaphors
What It Is	Variously and confusingly understood as sensory perception, cognition, thinking, neurological processes, etc.	Culturally-configured "interiorized behavior" modeled on the external world
Where It Is	Neurological apparatus	As a relational phenomenon, it lacks location
Who Possesses It	Possibly animals	Only humans

Chart 2.2. Differences between Conscious Interiority and Other Cognitive Processes.

	Conscious Interiority	Other Cognitive Processes
Evolutionary Changes	Not a product of bioevolution	Certain mental abilities are products of bioevolution
Genetic Transmission	Not transmitted genetically; it is not innate	Certain mental abilities are transmitted genetically
Role of Culture	It is a product of socio-historical development and learning; it requires a cultural substratum; it is transmitted culturally	Certain mental abilities, though arguably inchoate without enculturation, do not necessarily require culture
Species Specificity	Only *homo sapiens* developed conscious interiority	Animals other than *homo sapiens* lack the prerequisite neurological apparatus needed for culture—complex sociopolitic patterns and language—they cannot be conscious

History	It appeared during a certain historical period due to socially pragmatic causes	Certain cognitive abilities have existed prehistorically
Universality	It is a sociohistorical development: before approximately 1000 BCE individuals lacked consciousness	Certain cognitive abilities are universal

The very ability itself to "see" mental imagery—the images, sceneries, and vistas that make up our introcosm—is thought by many to be innate. But Jaynes argued that it is culturally acquired and learned. Indeed, the historical record strongly suggests that it was not until three thousand years ago that people learned this ability. It developed to replace the earlier adaptation of hallucinations which had become weakened due to growing political economic complexity. Rather than the voice-volitions of gods or ancestors, an "I" populating the private psychoscape would now make the decisions for each of us. Mental imagery, then, is a cultural—not biological—adaptation that emerged relatively recently in human history.

In pre-conscious times, individuals lacked a sense of reflexivity. Since no introspecting "I" could scan a "me" or mental objects in a psychoscape, a sense of selfhood generated by internal "mirror imaging" would be impossible. Thus, individuals would not be wracked by existentialist sentiments or spiritual alienation. Indeed, it is surprising how the ancient Mesopotamians did not ask themselves questions about the origins of the world; the gods had created the cosmos and that was that. No existentialist "how's" or "why's" haunted the individual's heart (Bottéro 1992: 218). This would change during the second millennium: "It is as if an early period, still little gifted with speculation, was followed by a period of maturity, of urgency and of depth, in which the Mesopotamians expressed themselves easily and well." The "Poem of the Supersage" (or the Epic of Atrahasîs or Gilgamesh) illustrates this very gradual change. Composed around 1700 BCE, it is the "oldest known description of the ideas that mankind had developed with regard to its own origins and with regard to the sense of its existence" (Bottéro 1992: 221-222). One wonders why earlier epics that began to probe the meaning of the cosmos have not been discovered.

Features of Conscious Interiority[3]

Much confusion surrounds the meaning of "consciousness," so I use the term conscious interiority to distinguish it from perception, thinking, cognition, rational thought, and other concepts. The following is a list of the key features of conscious interiority:

- *Spatialization of Psyche*. This is the most elementary feature of conscious interiority. Linguistic expressions metaphorically hollow out the body and lay the groundwork for psychological interiority (internal organs, e.g. "heart"). Such interiorization generates an "introcosm" in opposition to both the immediate person (microcosm) and the external physical world (macrocosm).
- *Introception*. The ability to experience the introcosm as an inner place modeled after the perceptual, physical world. From this introscape is generated an "I," analogous to one's physical person, that can introspect upon inner quasi-sensory experiences.
- *Excerption*. The inner "I" excerpts from the "collection of possible attentions to a thing which comprises our knowledge of it... Actually we are never conscious of things in their true nature, only of the excerpts we make of them." This feature is "distinct from memory. An excerpt of a thing is in consciousness the representative of the thing or event to which memories adhere, and by which we can retrieve memories." Reminiscence is a "succession of excerptions" (Jaynes 1976: 61–62). Interiority is the "instance of selection that picks and chooses among the many options" that the psyche provides for us (Nørretranders 1998: 243).
- *Self-narratization*. Excerptions and mental sceneries, once unmoored from the limitations of physical reality, provide the "I" not just with a panorama of past and present events, but with imaginary "could be's." Now introspectable due to spatialization, such hypotheticals form a linear temporality leading to future possibilities upon which one's "I" moves as protagonist.
- *Self-autonomy*. Individual narratization leads to a sense of control over one's self and destiny. Intentionality and responsibility are attributed to the "I" ("inner person") rather than divine powers, social groupings, or natural forces.
- *Self-authorization*. One's own person ("I"), rather than external gods or ancestors, has immediate control over one's behavior ("me").
- *Concilience*. A "slightly ambiguous perceived object is made to conform to some previously learned schema." Consilience (or assimilation) is "doing in mind-space what narratization does in our mind-time or spatialized time. It brings things together conscious objects

just as narratization brings episodes together as a story" (Jaynes 1976: 64–65).
- *Individuation.* In the same way that one's "I" is differentiated and comes to appear unique when set against the backdrop of interiorized excerptions, the individual's personal traits are highlighted and privileged within larger collectivities.
- *Self-reflexivity.* This is the most difficult feature to describe. It occurs because the ability to excerpt, to "see" one's self ("I") in an interiorized place minus physical limitations, and to narratize not-yet versions of our future selves all generate an "I" that introspects upon a "me." Such self-introspection causes a recursively regressive mirroring effect (self observing self). This leads to a keenly-felt existentialist perspective of a highly individuated selfness that exists in opposition to others and the world.

Introspection as Controlled Hallucinations

It is easy to overlook the almost magical properties of mental imagery. Many mistakenly assume that the ability to call up mental sceneries—"unshared sensory experiences" (Stevenson 1983)—is a type of sensory perception, a mirroring of the surrounding environment, and then conclude that introspective experiences can be explained away or reduced to perceptual processes. Unfortunately, the role of conscious interior experience is gravely misunderstood. In fact, the mysterious nature of quasi-perception comes from some important affinities it shares with hallucinations, i.e. both types of experiences cannot be pointed to in the physical world and yet exert influence over our behavior. Indeed, conscious interiority gives us the ability to "see" things that do not exist and conjure up nonexistent, imaginary sceneries; it is semi-hallucinatory and is an evolutionary descendant of hallucinations.

The cultural invention of a privately-viewable place to "introceive" (*not* perceive) allows us to excerpt scenes and objects and weave "should've-could've-would've" narratives necessary for planning in increasingly complex societies. Introception is a type of adaptive hallucination, i.e. mental imagery is employed in the "selection, rehearsal, planning, and perfecting of adaptive activities," thereby providing the "means to guide experimentally and transform experience by running off activity cycles as mental simulations of the real thing." In short, a "primary function of consciousness is the mental rehearsal of adaptive, goal-directed action through the experimental manipulation of perceptual-motor imagery" (Marks 1999: 579, 567). Introceptions conveniently conjure up "viewable" cognitive maps of the world, but ones infused with a menu of maybe's, perhaps's, and possibilities. It is a post-bicameral, adaptive upgrading of our mental machinery suited to more complex sociopolitical circumstances, just as extraceptive as divine visions or disembodied voices were in bicameral times. In this sense, introception is the counterpart to exteriorized hallucinations (McVeigh 2012a,b, 2013). Introceptions and extraceptions (audiovisual hallucinations interpreted as divine voices and visitations in ancient times) can be called superceptions. Vestigial extraceptions are anomalous behaviors, e.g. hallucinations still experienced by schizophrenics, while coceptions describe how perceptions and introceptions coincide (such overlapping deludes us into assuming that interior experiences are sensory reflections of reality) (Appendix A).

If the hypothesis is correct that hallucinations were at one time in history adaptive in function — as are the semi-hallucinatory interior conscious experiences (what we see with our mind's eye) as presently experienced — then there should be a traces of a different mentality (Appendix B). The task of Chapters 3, 4, and 5 is to provide evidence for this. By offering a meta-analytical literature review, Chapter 6 utilizes recent research on the surprising ubiquity of "hearing voices" in modern times to argue that hallucinations are neurological vestiges and mental imagery — a controllable, semi-hallucinatory experience — is the successor to the hallucinations that once held societies together. In other words, modern hallucinations are vestigial experiences that once had sociopsychological utility.

(4) The Sociohistorical Evolution of Mind-Words: From the Senses, to the Body, to the Mind

Consciousness is learned and therefore an acquired cultural capability grounded in metaphorical language. Though others have written about the metaphoricity of mental idioms, Jaynes (1976) offered the most radical elaboration of what the tropic nature of mind-words (MWs) might mean, i.e. terms that refer to cognitive, emotional, volitional, and personality disposition.[4] He argued that the cultural invention of psychological descriptors granted the human species a new type of cognition: conscious interiority.

The Metaphoric Construction of the World's Psychological Lexicons

Because our inner lives have been linguistically assembled over time from things in the objective world, observable behaviors, bodily parts, physiological experiences, and religious concepts, all MWs in all languages are metaphoric in origin.[5] The tropic transfer from the physical to the psychological realm is not simply descriptive; indeed, it is transformative. Metaphors have led to changes in how we view the world and consciousness. The metaphoricity of MWs in the world's languages, then, is neither a poetic flourish nor an interesting but inconsequential fact. Rather, such metaphoricity and language evolution tell us a great deal about how the psyche has developed. Despite historical and cross-cultural variation, the metaphoric construction of mental lexicons is a universal, i.e. all languages employ tropes in order to construct notions of psychological events. Our subjective, felt experience of our bodies provides the fundamental grounding for language and thought. This is not an attempt to *reduce* subjective experience to linguistic building blocks but rather to illustrate how meaning is generated through embodiment. Also, since no simple causal relation between language and interiorized mentation exists, an examination of how a lexicon shapes psychology is not necessarily a Sapir-Whorfian application of linguistic theory.

If Jaynes's claims are correct, ancient languages for which we have written evidence should, at least until around the early part of the first millennium BCE, have a paucity of MWs. For example, the Shang Dynasty oracle bones dating from the late second millennium BCE display a "scarcity of psychological vocabulary." Indeed, MWs are "extraordinarily limited." Such a dearth of MWs would make sense in a pre-interiorized or recently interiorized civilization. Characters written with "heart" (a key metaphor for mental and emotional activity) are "exceedingly rare." However, by the early first millennium the "repertoire of psychological terms increases markedly" (Harbsmeier 2005: 491–92), which is what we would expect as Chinese culture entered a more interiorized age during the latter half of the first millennium BCE.

Furthermore, languages should exhibit the same basic pattern which can be described as a trajectory from objective sensations (auditory, visual, tactile, taste, olfactory) to subjective experience. In other words, modern wordstocks of interiority (terms related to thinking, feeling, emotions, and other psychological events) are borrowed from bodily parts and physical experiences. This cultural invention was a gradual development that followed a four-phase linguo-conceptual trajectory. During the first or "objective" phase, external, observable things or activities outside the person were borrowed to describe what we call mental events. For example, *psyche*, perhaps originally meaning air, is a good example. In Japanese *ki* (vital/cosmic energy) is the most salient word for psychological descriptors; perhaps it had its origins in some natural phenomenon, such as wind or rising steam. Eventually these terms came to indicate internal physiological sensations with the result that bodily organs began to represent places where cognitive, emotional, and volitional events occur. This was the second or "internal" phase. In the third or "subjective" phase certain words began to refer to experiences that we would classify as psychological: "They have moved from internal stimuli supposedly causing actions to internal spaces where metaphored actions may occur" (Jaynes 1976: 260). The last or "synthetic" phase transpires when the array of MWs "unite into one conscious self capable of introspection" (1976: 260).[6]

The subjective and synthetic phases aid us in appreciating the salient role of that cosmic split which has vexed thinkers since around the seventh or sixth century BCE: mind–body dualism (notably debates about this dualism are absent in the records before the first millennium BCE, as is to be expected if Jaynes's dating of the birth of conscious interiority is correct). Discussions of what we now call the psyche-physicality divide appear in the great classical civilizations in China, Greece, India, and the Middle East (or at least a type of mind–body dualism implicitly configured philosophical debates). The gap separating the external existence-versus-internal experience would grow over time, sanctioned by Descartes' detached ego observing the world from inside the head. Mind–body dualism would culminate in the strict dichotomization of objectivity–subjectivity that became the foundations of modern science as well as the guiding axiom of experimental Psychology.

Literal and Figurative Metaphors

Related to Jaynes's four-phase trajectory of linguo-concepts is what can be called *literalization* (Barclay 1997).[7] An example is how ancient peoples used heart-related expressions because they literally believed that physiological experiences felt in the chest or heart were what we would now label psychological events. In modern times people realize such heart-related expressions are figures of speech. However, in times past, people believed that the heart (and other organs) was the seat of psychological occurrences. This is a distinction between (1) *literal metaphors*—these describe how an individual interprets an analogical experience as literally true; and (2) *figurative metaphors*—these describe how an individual interprets analogical experiences as figures of speech, i.e. not in a literal sense (McVeigh 1996).

(5) Bicameral Vestiges: Anomalous Behavior as Relics of Vestigial Neurostructures

If Jaynes's contentions are correct about our neurocultural development as a species, then we should expect some vestiges of bicamerality. Consider the large family of scientifically unwelcome oddities such as hypnosis, mediums, automatic writing (hypergraphia), spirit possession, channeling, glossolalia, automatisms, oracles, poetic and religious frenzy, and the voice-volitions heard by schizophrenics. These phenomena are anything but rare. They are scattered through ancient sacred texts, historical accounts, and contemporary ethnographies. Rather than being atypical, these activities are unexplained but common and widespread; indeed, in some societies, they are routinely practiced and encouraged.

Endnotes

1. Neurocultural means the inter-evolution — i.e. the interactive development — of our innate neurological apparatus with what is learned.
2. Subsequent centuries should be regarded as the early classical and classical periods (about 1000 BCE to 500 CE).
3. From McVeigh (2016a). This list is an expansion and elaboration of Jaynes's list (1976).
4. Jaynes also theorized how metaphoric idioms self-generate, producing ever-increasingly complex lexical fields that are semantically woven together and thereby forming the foundations of thought (1976: 52-59).
5. The number of works on metaphors is immense, but recent examples include Barclay (1997); Kövecses (2000, 2002, 2003, 2004, 2005); McVeigh (2016b); Sharifian, Dirven, Yu and Niemeier, eds. (2008); Zouhair and Yu, eds. (2011).
6. Though Jaynes's four-phase sequence describes what transpired *generally* across time, exceptions exist, e.g. some mind-words rooted in borrowings from the objective world may very well have appeared after the historical "objective" first phase.
7. Literalization haunts modern science. Consider how, using advanced imaging technologies, we still attempt to localize mental processes "in" the head, misunderstanding the difference between "physical position" versus "generated by" (e.g. three apples generate "three-ness," but "three-ness" cannot be located in each apple).

Chapter 3

Bronze Age Super-Religiosity
Linguistic Evidence for Pre-conscious Mentalities

"Occam's razor would favor the bicameral explanation because it is the simplest hypothesis with the widest applicability." — Michael Carr

If Jaynes's theorizing is correct, then bicamerality should be reflected in the archeological, historical, and linguistic record. This chapter, written in the spirit of an exploratory prolegomenon that interrogates patterns of worldwide religiosity that we take for granted, will focus on language. This will be done by surveying and comparing the religious and psychological lexicons of the Near East Bronze Age (BA) civilizations (or at least what we moderns would refer to as religious and psychological terms). This exercise is inspired by the notion that, as religiosity declined, an interiorized psychologicality increased. Reviewing glossaries of languages from before roughly the 1000 BCE period should reveal a significantly longer list of religious than psychological terms.[1]

Below I outline the arguments of this chapter by introducing the Embryonic Psycholexicon (EmPL) hypothesis. Then I explain the sources used and present evidence for the EmPL hypothesis. Additionally, several supplementary sections round out this chapter that explore how and why negative emotions were more common than positive emotions (NE > PE hypothesis) and textual evidence for hallucinated "voices and visions" (the prevalence of "shining" and "brilliance" in particular are suggestive of visual hallucinations). The BCI and the PBCI afford historical context.

The Embryonic Psycholexicon Hypothesis

If Jaynes is correct that individuals lacked conscious interiority before about 1000 BCE, then this should be reflected in language. The Embryonic Psycholexicon (EmPL) hypothesis is intended to test his argument. "Embryonic" points to a weakly developed psychologicality whose linguistic forms were incipient and primordial, i.e. the first MWs were substratal building blocks upon which more abstract forms would be constructed to reflect ever increasing sociopsychological complexity. The time range of the EmPL hypothesis coincides with that of BA civilizations, give or take several centuries depending on the particular place (though in North, Central, and South America the timeline begins about one millennium later).

The EmPL hypothesis has a number of characteristics that can be assessed. First, BA psycholexicons appear restricted in size. Super-religiosity accounts for this, i.e. bicamerality means that supernatural entities (gods, ancestors, spirits, etc.) functioned as our inner selves. If this is the case, the need for an inventory of MWs would, arguably, be limited. A well-developed, nuanced psychological vocabulary was simply unnecessary in a world saturated with the supernatural, and therefore the further one goes back in time, the fewer MWs one should encounter in the written record.

Measuring and finding evidence for the EmPL hypothesis presents some challenges, but one way to illustrate this proposition is to compare PLs against religious words. Since MWs replaced a supernatural mind-set and spiritual entities, we should expect to see more religious lexemes (RL) relative to PL. Findings from the RL > PL proposition can be utilized to test the EmPL hypothesis (along with other auxiliary hypotheses to be discussed below). A second characteristic of archaic psycholexemes is their literal, behavioralist quality, which a perusal through the appended datasets indicates. Related to the second postulate is the third: elemental psycholexemes had a concreteness and physicality often reflected in their colorful metaphorical nature.[2] However, it is at least worth pointing out the metaphoric roots of psychological terms. This allows us to appreciate how physical behaviors were "interiorized" into a mind-space that developed into subjective "mental behaviors" (i.e. consciousness). The evolution of psychological lexemes took centuries, but resulted in a powerful cognitive adaptation that permitted individuals to "mentally travel" to the past and future, thereby greatly enhancing planning, organizing, and abstracting capabilities.

Though this chapter will not examine BA literature, it is important to point out that in Sumer the earliest writings, from around 3200 BCE, were for record keeping. That the earliest and most extensive type of works were administrative and commercial suggests that we are dealing with people who, strangely, saw no need to record their interior life. It was not until approximately 2600 BCE that "literature" first appeared. But this type of writing was not literature as we think of it. Rather, temple hymns, poems to gods, and other religious texts comprised most writings, as did "wisdom literature." The latter advocated obedience, promoted virtue, and admonished individuals to maintain community codes. Works such as the Sumerian *Instructions of Shuruppak* (2600 BCE) or the Egyptian *Maxims of Ptahhotep* (2350 BCE) are considered examples of the "teaching" (*sebayt*) genre on human relations and fit into the category of wisdom literature. Some ancient writings are notable for one reason or another, e.g. the Sumerian compositions by Enheduanna—or the "high priestess adornment of the god, An"—are the earliest writings for whom we have an author's name (2270 BCE). *The Epic of Gilgamesh* (from around 2200), which is often called the world's first great work of literature, has its shares of adventures, but the protagonist lacks complex motivations. Overall, despite its beauty and inherent worth, BA literature is didactic, moralistic, formulaic, and its MWs seem sparse. Here we might note that the modern reader must approach translations of ancient writings with a cautious eye, as some translators take liberties when interpreting texts.

Sources and Evidence

The number of written languages that record life before the BA collapse is not large but certainly substantial enough to survey in order to discern worldwide psychohistorical patterns, the development of mental lexicons, and cognitive adaptation. The primary focus in this chapter is Sumerian. The language of ancient Sumer, Sumerian was spoken in southern Mesopotamia. A language isolate, it began to be written down around 3200 BCE in ideographic form. Eventually ideograms were supplemented by syllabograms. Rebuses were employed to allow the representation of grammatical markers and non-Sumerian names. Gradually, Sumerian and Akkadian would mutually influence each other, thereby forming an area of linguistic convergence (*Sprachbund*). Sometime around 2000 BCE Akkadian replaced Sumerian as a spoken language. However, the latter, in written form, continued to be utilized as a sacred, ceremonial, and literary language until the first century BCE in parts of the Middle East. Other languages that will supplement my analysis include Hittite, Egyptian, and Mycenaean/Linear B.[3]

I will take advantage of a number of online resources. The first is the Electronic Text Corpus of Sumerian Literature (ETCSL),[4] which is composed of about 400 documents organized into seven groups. The first group is ancient lists of literary compositions; the second, narrative and mythological compositions; the third, royal praise poetry and compositions with a historical background; the fourth, literary letters and letter-prayers (addressed to gods); the fifth, hymns and cult songs (mostly addressed to deities); the sixth, "other" literature, and the seventh, proverbs. It should be stressed that, significantly, various genres of cult songs and prayers (in Emesal; a sociolect restricted to goddesses and women in certain literary texts, e.g. lamentations, divine love songs, proverbs, etc.) and magical incantations are not included in ETCSL. This means that certain genres typically regarded as super-religious are not included in the present analysis. However, as we shall see, an insistent and robust religiosity nevertheless permeates the seven groups of documents.

The second online resource is the electronic Pennsylvania Sumerian Dictionary (ePSD) which covers 2700 to 1600 BCE and links words to a corpus of about 90,000 texts.[5] Other sources include Hittite Grammar (HG),[6] Linguistics Research Center at the University of Texas at Austin (LRC-UTA),[7] Paul Dickson's *Dictionary of Middle Egyptian: In Gardiner Classification Order*,[8] and Markos Gavalas's Mycenaean (Linear B)–English Dictionary.[9]

Methodological Concerns

If modern translating presents significant challenges, interpreting long-forgotten languages raises even more difficulties. The presentist impulse to project modern understandings and sensibilities onto the language of ancient peoples needs to be avoided. This issue becomes especially problematic when dealing with abstract, difficult-to-define concepts, and in ancient languages, psychological terms that we assume carried a subjective sense actually denoted something more objective, concrete, and behavioral (see the relevant datasets).

A number of methodological issues that the thoughtful reader might raise as objections need to be addressed. First, my analysis is only partial; as many as 100,000 documents have been recovered but undoubtedly still more exist. Moreover, other text corpora include monumental inscriptions and cylinder seal inscriptions. But whatever the number of texts, as fragmentary as they may be, we still possess enough material to draw some conclusions. Moreover, note that my arguments apply to *all* BA written documents, i.e. patterns — specifically the EmPL hypothesis — can be discerned that are not limited to only one culture. This fact in and of itself is an interesting datum.

A second objection concerns spoken language. For obvious reasons, we will only be examining the written record. Some might object that such documentation is incomplete and does not reflect what was actually spoken. However, our analysis surveys some ten centuries; one would imagine that such a temporal span would include enough opportunities to register a representative number of spoken terms.

A third issue relates to interpretive context: for example, how do we know if an item of material culture belongs in the mundane/secular or religious/sacred realm? First of all, these latter distinctions are presentist projections. For us moderns a material cultural item may have a certain denotation, but for ancients the same item probably possessed connotations that would slip out of our interpretive net. I have attempted to select terms that carried both religious denotations and connotations within the given cultural context. This was an exercise in judgment that no doubt needs refinement. Here I should also note that I did not include some terms describing official or administrative duties. However, an argument could easily be made that such terminology should be part of the religious wordstock given how the line between sacred and secular institutions was lacking and would not develop until late in the BA.

Analyzing the Data

The sections below examine the lexical weight of religiosity versus psychologicality in dictionaries (glossaries), texts, proper names, and different historical periods. Most analyses of the data begin with a ratio (usually Religious Lexemes to Psycholexemes). If the initial hypothesis is true—that RL > PL—then a more rigorous statistical analysis is applied. Hypothesis logs (3.1 to 3.5) summarizing the results conclude each section.

Dictionaries/Glossaries

The RL > PL hypothesis was true for all the lists of lexemes I examined, i.e. five out of five times. A more rigorous Chi-Sq G of F analysis supported the hypotheses four out of five times and was extremely significant (App Calculations 3.1 through 3.10), i.e. a salient difference in the proportion of occurrences of terms was evident.

Hypothesis Log 3.1. Dictionaries: Hypothesis: Religious Lexemes (RL) Significantly Outnumber Psycholexemes (PL).

RL > PL in ETCSL DICTIONARY? *Refer to* App Calculation 3.1. ETCSL DICTIONARY: No. of RL to PL and Their Ratio	Yes	
RL > PL in ETCSL DICTIONARY? *Refer to* App Calculation 3.2. ETCSL DICTIONARY: Chi-Sq G of F	▶	Yes
RL > PL in ePSD DICTIONARY? *Refer to* App Calculation 3.3. ePSD DICTIONARY: No. of RL to PL and Their Ratio	Yes	
RL > PL in ePSD DICTIONARY? *Refer to* App Calculation 3.4. ePSD DICTIONARY: Chi-Sq G of F	▶	Yes
RL > PL in HG Hittite D DICTIONARY? *Refer to* App Calculation 3.5. HG Hittite D DICTIONARY: No. of RL to PL and Their Ratio	Yes	
RL > PL in HG Hittite D DICTIONARY? *Refer to* App Calculation 3.6. HG Hittite DICTIONARY: Chi-Sq G of F	▶	No
RL > PL in LRC-UTA Hittite DICTIONARY? *Refer to* App Calculation 3.7. LRC-UTA Hittite DICTIONARY: No. of RL to PL and Their Ratio	Yes	
RL > PL in LRC-UTA Hittite DICTIONARY? *Refer to* App Calculation 3.8. LRC-UTA Hittite DICTIONARY: Chi-Sq G of F	▶	Yes
RL > PL in Mycenaean/Linear B DICTIONARY? *Refer to* App Calculation 3.9. Mycenaean/Linear B DICTIONARY: No. of RL to PL and Their Ratio	Yes	
RL > PL in Mycenaean/Linear B DICTIONARY? *Refer to* App Calculation 3.10. Mycenaean/Linear B DICTIONARY: Chi-Sq G of F	▶	Yes
	5/5	4/5

3. Bronze Age Super-Religiosity

Graph 3.1. Religious Lexemes (RL) and Psycholexemes (PL) in Dictionaries: Totals from App Calculations 3.1, 3.3, 3.5, 3.7, to 3.9.

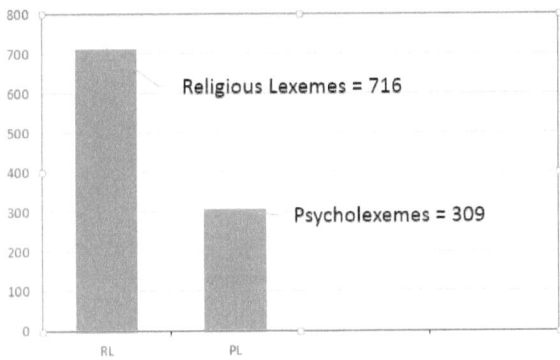

Texts

The RL > PL hypothesis was true for ETCSL and ePSD in two out of two times. In order to discern if a significant difference exists between RL and PL in the ETCSL and ePSD texts, Chi-Sq G of F was used. The hypothesis was accepted two out of two times and was extremely significant (App Calculations 3.11 through 3.14).

Hypothesis Log 3.2. Texts: Hypothesis: Religious Lexemes (RL) Significantly Outnumber Psycholexemes (PL).

RL > PL in ETCSL Texts? *Refer to* App Calculation 3.11. ETCSL Texts: No. of RL to PL and Their Ratio	Yes	
RL > PL in ETCSL Texts? *Refer to* App Calculation 3.12. ETCSL TEXTS: Chi-Sq G of F	▶	Yes
RL > PL in ePSD Texts? *Refer to* App Calculation 3.13. ePSD Texts: No. of RL to PL and Their Ratio	Yes	
RL > PL in ePSD Texts? *Refer to* App Calculation 3.14. ePSD TEXTS: Chi-Sq G of F	▶	Yes
	2/2	2/2

Graph 3.2. Religious Lexemes and Psycholexemes in Texts: Totals from App Calculations 3.11 and 3.13.

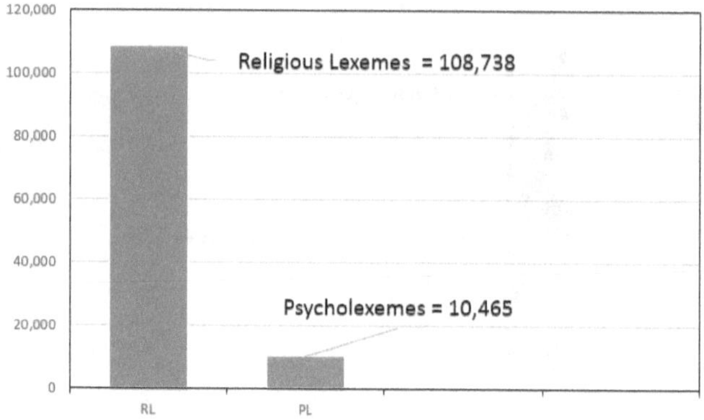

Religious Lexemes = 108,738

Psycholexemes = 10,465

Proper Names

A survey of the types of proper names and their frequency from ETCSL supports the argument that super-religiosity infused BA civilizations. Religious names (RN)—divine, temple, royal (given that "royal" denoted the sacred, this type of name is included under the religious rubric)—far outweigh what can be referred to as non-religious names (NR) (RN > NR hypothesis). Religious names account for 66.19% of all proper names, while the percentage of their frequency constitutes 78.02%. A Chi-Square Goodness of Fit analysis supported the research hypotheses which were accepted two out of two times and was extremely significant (App Calculations 3.15 through 3.18).

Hypothesis Log 3.3. Proper Names: Hypothesis: Religious Lexemes (RL) Significantly Outnumber Psycholexemes (PL).

RL > PL in ETCSL NAMES? *Refer to* App Calculation 3.15. ETCSL NAMES: Ratios of Religious and Non-Religious	Yes	
RL > PL in ETCSL NAMES? *Refer to* App Calculation 3.16. ETCSL NAMES: No. of Chi-Sq G of F	▶	Yes
RL > PL in ETCSL NAMES? *Refer to* App Calculation 3.17. ETCSL NAMES: Ratios of Frequencies of Religious and Non-Religious	Yes	
RL > PL in ETCSL NAMES? *Refer to* App Calculation 3.18. ETCSL NAMES: Frequencies. Chi-Sq G of F	▶	Yes
	2/2	2/2

Graph 3.3. Religious Names (RN) and Non-Religious Names (NR): Totals from App Calculations 3.15 and 3.17.

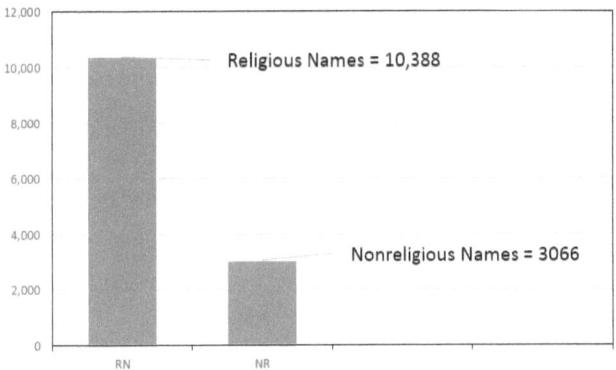

Negative Emotionality and the Right Hemisphere

Jaynes noted that the right hemisphere (the side generating divine "voices") "commonly triggers the emotional reactions of displeasure from the limbic system and brainstem" (1976: 116). Others have made similar connections: though not conclusive, evidence strongly suggests that unconscious negative emotional processing is a right hemispheric affair (Kimura et al. 2004; Sato and Aoki 2006). As a result it should not be surprising that great attention to lamentation and regret characterizes ancient literary traditions (cf. Jaynes 1976: 116). In addition, in this situation many of the earliest MWs, originating in the brain's then dominant right side and perceived to be spoken by supernatural entities, would also carry a negative emotional valence (EV).[10] We might note here that evidence for negative emotional saliency is seen in ancient Chinese (Carr 1983; see next chapters).

If Jaynes's thinking on negative emotionality is correct, then such negative sentiments should be greater than positive emotions in BA texts (NE > PE hypothesis). As can be seen below the NE > PE hypothesis was supported four out of seven times. A Chi-Sq G of F analysis further supported the research hypothesis, which was accepted in four out of four times and was extremely significant (a small number of terms referred to emotions with both negative and positive valences; in such cases they cancelled each other out) (App Calculations 3.19 to 3.29).

Hypothesis Log 3.4. Negative Emotions (NE) Significantly Outnumber Positive Emotions (PE).

NE > PE in ETCSL? *Refer to* App Calculation 3.19. ETCSL: No. of Negative Emotions	No	
NE > PE in ETCSL? *Refer to* App Calculation 3.20. ETCSL: Frequency of Negative Emotions	No	
NE > PE in ePSD? *Refer to* App Calculation 3.21. ePSD: No. of Negative Emotions	Yes	
NE > PE in ePSD? *Refer to* App Calculation 3.22. ePSD: No. of Negative Emotions. Chi-Sq G of F	▶	Yes
NE > PE in ePSD? *Refer to* App Calculation 3.23. ePSD: Frequency of Negative Emotions	Yes	
NE > PE in ePSD? *Refer to* App Calculation 3.24. ePSD: No. of Negative Emotions	▶	Yes
NE > PE in HG Hittite? *Refer to* App Calculation 3.25. HG Hittite: No. of Negative Emotions	Yes	
NE > PE in HG Hittite? *Refer to* App Calculation 3.26. HG Hittite: No. of Negative Emotions. Chi-Sq G of F	▶	Yes
NE > PE in LRC-UTA Hittite? *Refer to* App Calculation 3.27. LRC-UTA Hittite: No of Negative Emotions	Yes	
NE > PE in LRC-UTA Hittite? *Refer to* App Calculation 3.28. LRC-UTA Hittite: No. of Negative Emotions. Chi-Sq G of F	▶	Yes
NE > PE in Egyptian? *Refer to* App Calculation 3.29. Egyptian (Dickson): No. of Negative Emotions	No	
	4/7	4/4

Graph 3.4. Negative Emotions (NE) and Positive Emotions (PE) Terms: Totals from App Calculations 3.19, 3.21, 3.23, 3.25, 3.27, and 3.29.

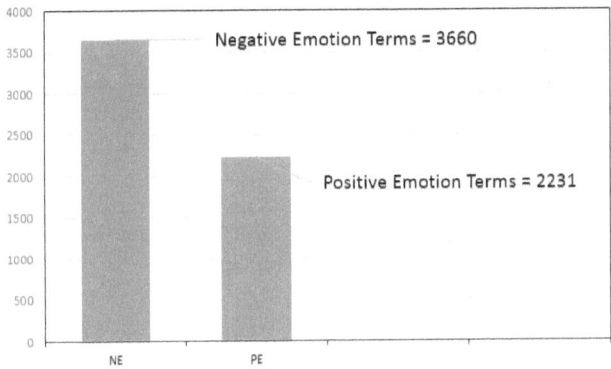

Mind-Words by Period

If the EmPL hypothesis is true, then the number of MWs appearing in latter periods will be greater than those appearing in previous periods. A Chi-Sq G of F analysis supported the two hypotheses (Hypothesis Log 3.5) whose statistical significance was extremely significant (App Calculations 3.30 and 3.31).

The hypotheses postulated in this section are problematic since (as of now) the number of texts in each period is unknown (also, due to uncertain dating, some periods overlap).[11] Nevertheless, some major patterns can still be discerned, e.g. the explosive growth of MWs beginning in the fifth and sixth periods when an interiorized psychologicality was presumably replacing bicamerality. We should also note that in the second period (Early Dynasty IIIb), the word *ed* appears 241 times, thereby greatly inflating the frequency of MWs for the second period. Though it is debatable whether *ed* should be included, since it might mean to go up or down, demolish, scratch, "rage," or to be rabid, for the sake of consistency I counted it as a MW ("rage") (Tables 3.1 and 3.2).

Table 3.1. ePSD: No. and Frequency of MWs by Period.

Period	Year Range: BCE	No. of Years	No. of MWs	Frequency of MWs
(1) Early Dynasty IIIa	2600–2500/2450	125[a]	4	5
(2) Early Dynasty IIIb	2500/2450–2350	100[b]	30	488
(3) Old Akkadian	2340–2200	140	22	166
(4) Lagash II	2200–2100	100	17	54
(5) Ur III	2112–2004	108	44	865
(6) Old Babylonian	2000–1600	400	145	5397

Source: See http://www.livius.org/misc/mesopotamian-chronology. This periodization follows the middle chronology.

[a] 125 = mean of 100 and 150.
[b] 100 = mean of 50 and 150.

Table 3.2. ePSD: Lexical Weight of No. and Frequency of MWs by Period.

Period	MWs as %age of Years	%age	Frequency of MWs as %age of Years	%age
(1) Early Dynasty IIIa	4 of 125	3.20%	5 of 125	4.00%
(2) Early Dynasty IIIb	30 of 100	30.00%	488 of 100	488.00%
(3) Old Akkadian	22 of 140	15.71%	166 of 140	118.57%
(4) Lagash II	17 of 100	17.00%	54 of 100	54.00%
(5) Ur III	44 of 108	40.74%	865 of 108	800.93%
(6) Old Babylonian	145 of 400	36.25%	5397 of 400	1349.25%

Hypothesis Log 3.5. Do the Distributions of the Number and Frequency of MWs Significantly Differ by Period?

Significant Distribution of MWs ePSD by Period? *Refer to* Table 3.1. ePSD: No. and Frequency of MWs by Period *Refer to* App Calculation 3.30. ePSD: No. of MWs by Periods. Chi-Sq G of F	Yes
Significant Distribution of MWs ePSD by Period? *Refer to* Table 3.2. ePSD: Lexical Weight of No. of Frequency of MWs by Period *Refer to* App Calculation 3.31. ePSD: Frequency of MWs by Period. Chi-Sq G of F	Yes
	2/2

Graph 3.5. Percentage of MWs by Period: Values from Table 3.2.

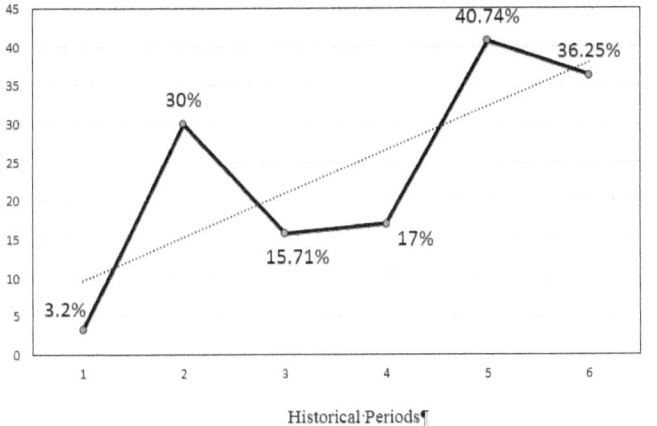

Graph 3.6. Frequency of MWs by Period: Values from Table 3.2.

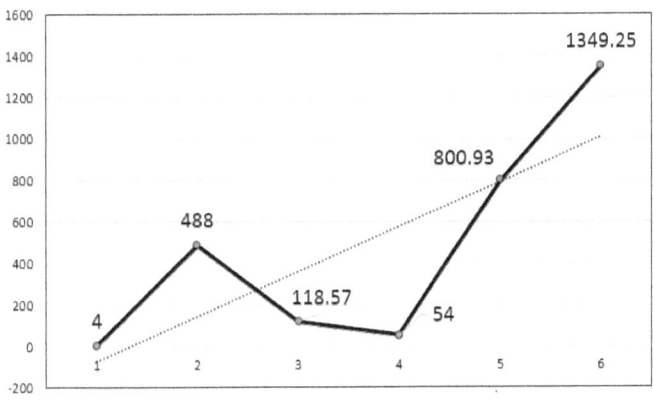

The Metaphoricity of Bronze Age Psycholexemes

Jaynes argued that psychological idioms, originally describing physiological and perceptual sensations, are built over time from the outside in, i.e. from the exterior physical world to the interior of the person. This process, obviously, can only be traced using written records, and for any number of reasons may be more apparent in certain linguistic trajectories. Relying on evidence from ancient Greek, Jaynes provided a framework for the historical evolution of linguistic terms describing psychological processes (1976).

Charts 3.1 to 3.6 provide examples of Sumerian psychological terms with clear metaphoric roots. Note especially the expressions with heart (*šag*; or inner body; it also means by extension in, inside), ear (*ĝeštug*), eye (*igi*), and head (*saĝ*). *Ur*, which besides liver might mean spleen or heart, is another bodily organ used in psychological expressions.[12] Some expressions are not completely clear in terms of ultimate origins (e.g. terms with *ni* meaning "fear"), but are partially metaphoric.[13] Of the 138 PL lexemes compiled for Middle Egyptian, 32 (23.19%) have "heart" (31 for *ib*, 1 for *HAty*). For Hittite, only one term out of 75 items designates "heart" (1.33%).

Chart 3.1. Sumerian Psychological Expressions with "Heart."

šag bala	ponder[a]	heart + turn
šag dab	hurt, angry, worried	heart + seize
šag dab	think, conceive an idea	heart + seize
šag dar	heartbroken	heart + split
šag de	decide	heart + bring
šag dug	cheerful	heart + good
šag gur	feel wonderful	heart + thick
šag huĝ	soothe	heart + hire
šag hul	be happy	heart + rejoice
šag kušu	soothe	heart + tired
šag sag	afflicted	heart + beat
šag sag	feel better	heart + good
šag šed	soothe	heart + cold
šag sig	plot	heart + place
šag sur	have diarrhea	heart + press
zi šag ĝal	provide with life	life + heart + be

[a] *šag bala* also means "procreate."

Chart 3.2. Sumerian Psychological Expressions with "Ear."

ĝeštug	reason, plan; (to be) wise; wisdom, understanding; ear	ear
ĝeštug deg	to ponder	ear + collect
ĝeštug ĝar	to pay attention, to listen	ear + place
ĝeštug gub	to pay attention, to plan	ear + stand
ĝeštug šum	to listen; to give wisdom	ear + give
ĝeštug ulu	to forget	ear + wind
ĝizzal	wisdom; understanding; ear; hearing	ear

Chart 3.3. Sumerian Psychological Expressions with "Eye."

igi gid	to look with disfavor	eye + long
igi suh	to be angry	eye + extract
igi tur gid	to look contemptuously at someone	eye + small + long

Chart 3.4. Sumerian Psychological Expressions with "Head."

saĝ gid	to be(come) angry	head + long
saĝ kešed	to take care, attend carefully to something	head + bind
saĝki gid	to be(come) angry	forehead + long

Chart 3.5. Sumerian Psychological Expressions with "Liver."

ur₅ aka	to gasp	liver + to do
ur₅-da	to be mindful, careful; to hear	liver + with
ur₅ gúr	to bow down (in grief)	liver + to bow down, submit
ur₅ sa6	to be/make comfortable, happy	liver + to satisfy
ur₅ ša4	to roar, bellow	liver + to mourn
ur sag	ameliorate	liver + good
ur ug	despair	liver + to die

Chart 3.6. Sumerian Metaphoric and Partially Metaphoric Psychological Expressions.

dib	to burn, wrath	burn
di kud	to judge	lawsuit + cut
er pad	to weep	tears + find
ešbar kiĝ	to decide	decide + seek
gabal du	to be hostile, to challenge	fight + build
ĝiškim til	to trust	sign + live
gu bar	to dislike, hate	neck + cvve a
gu du	to neglect	neck + build
hili	sex appeal; (to be) luxuriant; to have pleasure	luxuriant
hili kar	to love, be fond of, attracted to	luxuriant + flee
hili teĝ	to love, be fond of, attracted to	luxuriant + approach
hulu gig	to hate	bad + sick
inim sig	to express an idea, desire	word + place
isiš ĝar	to wail	sorrow + place
kaš bar	to make a decision	decision + cvve[a]
lipiš	anger, rage	inner body, heart
lipiš-bala	anger	innards + turn
ni dub	to relax	self + tremble
ni gur	to feel proud	self + thick
ni ri	to inspire fear	fear + cry
ni sig	to plot	fear + place
ni teĝ	to fear, to become afraid	fear + approach
ni ur	to be scared	fear + convulsed
nir ĝal	to trust	trust + be
šu bar	to release; to forget	hand + cvvea
šu pela	to defile; to reduce	hand + defile
su zig	to fear, to have goose bumps	flesh + bumps
sumug	darkness; calamity, fear	darkness
u dug	to admire; to regard, observe	admiration + speak

[a] Compound verb verbal element.

Voices and Visions

Like other BA civilizations for which we have written records, gods conversing among themselves and even supernatural entities visiting and communing with mortals is not unusual. How many of these are accounts of actual hallucinated experiences or merely semi-believed myths, legends, or fables is open to debate. However, given their ubiquity and impact on decisions both major and minor, it is time to entertain the idea that hallucinated voices and visions were a crucial element in our ancient past. Two examples, the first of a deity visiting a regent, follow:[14]

- On that day the maiden Inana, holy Inana [goddess], directed her steps all by herself towards Enki's [god] abzu [primeval sea or a ritual water container in a temple] in Eridug [city]. On that day, he of exceptional knowledge, who knows the divine powers in heaven and earth, who from his own dwelling already knows the intentions of the gods, Enki, the king of the abzu, who, even before holy Inana had approached within six miles of { the abzu } { (1 ms. has instead:) the temple } in Eridug, knew all about her enterprise — Enki spoke to his man, gave him instructions: "Come here, my man, listen to my words." (1 line fragmentary) (approx. 2 lines missing) (Inana and Enki: c.1.3.1).
- He performed extispicy on a kid and his omen was favourable. He cast grain on to …… and its appearance was right. Gudea [ruler] lay down for a dream oracle, and while he was sleeping a message came to him: in the vision he saw his master's house already built, the E-ninnu [temple] separating heaven and earth. This made him extremely happy (The building of Ningirsu's [god] temple (Gudea, cylinders A and B): c.2.1.7).

"Nocturnal Visions"

Especially intriguing are "nocturnal visions" (*mašĝik*). These may be what Jaynes called "bicameral dreams" which constitute a type of vision. Postbicameral "conscious dreams," on the other hand, are vicarial and translocative, i.e. one is doing something other than lying in one's bed and is able to move around and go to wherever a dream takes one. Also note that "dream books" are better thought of as omen texts (Jaynes 2012: 205). Below are two examples of what ETCSL refers to as "nocturnal visions":

- Naram-Suen [king] saw in a nocturnal vision that Enlil [god] would not let the kingdom of Agade occupy a pleasant, lasting residence, that he would make its future altogether unfavourable, that he would make its temples shake and would { scatter its treasures } { (1 ms. has instead:) destroy its treasuries }. He realised what the dream was about, but did not put into words, and did not discuss it with anyone. { (1 ms. adds 2 lines:) ... temples shake ... perform (?) extispicy regarding (?) his temple .... } (The cursing of Agade: c.2.1.5).

- On that day, in a nocturnal vision Gudea saw his master, Lord Ninĝirsu. Ninĝirsu spoke to him of his house, of its building. He showed him an E-ninnu with full grandeur. Outstanding though his mind was, the message remained to be understood for him. "Well, I have to tell her about this! Well, I have to tell her about this! I will ask her to stand by me in this matter. Profound things (?) came suddenly to me, the shepherd, but the meaning of what the nocturnal vision brought to me I do not understand. So I will take my dream to my mother and I will ask my dream-interpreter, an expert on her own, my divine sister from Sirara [temple], Nanše [goddess], to reveal its meaning to me" (The building of Ninĝirsu's temple (Gudea, cylinders A and B): c.2.1.7).

"Supernatural Brilliance"

When confronted by their gods, the ancient Mesopotamians "imagined a sort of eruption of terror which they believed emanated from the gods, as well as an extraordinary density of being." A "prodigious luminosity" resided in the divine personages. They wore their "supernatural brilliance" like a cloak of light, or placed it on "their bodies or their heads like a sparkling jewel, which shone around them, lighting and enchanting everything with a 'supernatural shine,' marvelous as well as terrible." The gods were "simultaneously admirable, by virtue of their splendor, and apt to repel humans by forcing them to kneel before such a strong ray of light, such a source of energy, which they emitted, proportional to their ontological density, as if light and luminosity in that land served as ideograms for what we call 'the being'" (Bottéro 2001: 38). Kings shared this supernatural radiance with the gods, which was called *melammu*. This Sumerian word is a compound of *me* (power) + *lam* (incandescent). *Melammu*, I submit, describes features of visual hallucination (cf. Yahweh appearing as a burning bush in front of Moses and similar biblical accounts). A survey of ETCSL and ePSD demonstrates a relatively salient number of terms meaning "shining" and "brilliant" (Charts 3.7 and 3.8). Of course, not all appearances of such terms evidence visual hallucinations, but below I provide examples of supernatural experiences from ETCSL (with the referencing number for the compositions):

- My lady, on your acquiring the stature of heaven, maiden Inana [goddess],[15] on your becoming as magnificent as the earth, on your coming forth like Utu [sun god] the king and stretching your arms wide, on your walking in heaven and wearing fearsome terror, on your wearing daylight and brilliance on earth (Inana and Ebiḫ: c.1.3.2).
- Their ruler (i.e. Enmerkar), riding on a storm, Utu's [sun god] son, the good bright metal, stepped down from heaven to the great earth. His head shines with brilliance, the barbed arrows flash past him like lightning; at his side the bronze pointed axe of his emblem shines for him, he strides forward keenly with the pointed axe, like a dog set on consuming a corpse (Lugalbanda in the mountain cave: c.1.8.2.1).
- The bull that eats up the black soup, the astral holy bull-calf (i.e. the moon), came to watch over him. He shines (?) in the heavens like the morning star, he spreads bright light in the night—Suen [god] is greeted as the new moon; Father Nanna [god] gives the direction for the rising Utu [sun god]. The glorious lord whom the crown befits, Suen, the beloved son of Enlil, { the god } { (1 ms. has instead:) the lord } reached the zenith splendidly. His brilliance like { holy Šara } { (1 ms. has instead:) holy Utu } { (1 ms. has instead:) lapis lazuli }, his starry radiance illuminated for him the mountain cave (Lugalbanda in the mountain cave: c.1.8.2.1).
- In those battles, where weapon clashes on weapon, Utu [sun god] shines on me (A praise poem of Šulgi (Šulgi B): c.2.4.2.02).
- The god of light, renewing his light! He is forceful, he is the king of heaven and earth! He ...... in the pure sky, he shines forth towards the earth (An adab [song] to Suen for Ibbi-Suen (Ibbi-Suen C): c.2.4.5.3).
- Lord Ašimbabbar shines forth towards the earth (An adab [song] to Suen for Ibbi-Suen (Ibbi-Suen C): c.2.4.5.3).
- Lord whose divine powers cannot be dispersed, who emits an awe-inspiring radiance, great crown! Youthful Suen, light elevated by Enlil to shine forth in the firmament, wide-spreading majestic light (A tigi [musical instrument] to Suen for Ibbi-Suen (Ibbi-Suen A): c.2.4.5.1).
- Nanna has made the righteous crown shine forth radiantly (A praise poem of Šulgi (Šulgi B): c.2.4.2.02).
- May you [King Šulgi] raise your head in terrifying splendour! May no man stand his ground before your fierce gaze! May your royal crown shine radiantly! (A praise poem of Šulgi (Šulgi D): c.2.4.2.04).

- Your lady Inana [goddess], the singular woman, the dragon who speaks hostile words to … who shines in brightness (The temple hymns: c.4.80.1).
- An [sky god] has determined a good destiny for you. Son of Enlil king of the lands, may your splendour shine forth! My lord Ninazu, may your splendour shine forth, may your splendour shine forth! May your wife, the maiden, the good woman, Lady Ningirida, say to you: "Your house, your city!" as she steps before you in prayer, god of the Land, my lord Ninazu! (A balbale [kind of poem] to Ninazu (Ninazu A): c.4.17.1).

Chart 3.7. ETCSL Expressions for "Brilliance, Etc."

Sumerian	English	Frequency
bu_7	to shine	2
ḫa-ad	to shine	2
kun_2	to shine	4
LUL-LUL	to shine (?)	3
šuba	shining	29
kug	shining	1,255
še-er-zid	radiance	27
mul	to radiate	63
si	brilliance	6
si-$muš_3$	brilliance	15
sud-$aĝ_2$	brilliance	31
ud-$ĝal_2$	illuminating	1

Chart 3.8. ePSD Expressions for "Brilliance, Etc."

Sumerian	English	Frequency
ašme	radiance; sun-disk ornament	8
bur	light; to glow, shine	78
dadag	(to be) bright; to clean	108
dalla	(to be) bright; (to be) impetuous, fierce	68
dalla e	to appear, shine	112
di	to shine	1
dilibad	shining	1
dirig	(to be) very great, supreme, excellent; more than; (to be) powerful, competent; (to be) big, huge; (to be) abundant; on, over, above; against; radiance; to project, stick up, build high; (to be) surplus	2,166
gug	(to be) bright	3
had	(to be) bright; to shine; (to be) pure; (to be) clear	18
ilim	radiance; deathly silence	8
iši	radiance	3
		Cont.

Sumerian	English	Frequency
kar	to blow; to light up, shine; to rise	52
kug	metal, silver; (to be) bright, shiny	3,875
kun	to shine brightly	4
lum	(to be) full, replete, satisfied (with); (to be) grown (tall); to fruit; (to be) fructified; to shine	107
mašĝik	(nocturnal) vision	1
melim	frightening splendor	159
mul	star; to shine, radiate (light); arrow; to radiate (branches)	129
nigal	awe-inspiring radiance	1
ni gal gur	clad in awesome luminosity	16
ni gur	clad in awesome luminosity	35
ni huš gur	clad in awesome luminosity	6
nim ĝir	to flash like lightning	19
nimur alkali	potash; coal; ashes; charcoal	1
pirig	bright	1
saĝ mu	to shine	7
šer	reddening, sunburn; to be) bright; brilliance, ray	29
šerzid	radiance	28
sikil	(to be) pure	457
simuš	brilliance, radiance	20
sudaĝ	a precious metal; (to be) shiny (a divine epithet)	6
sulim	awesome radiance	31
šun	to shine	1
suzi	awesome radiance	1
tam	(to be) bright; (to be) pure; to purify; (to be) clean	16
udĝal	illuminating	1
ul	to become bright, shine	1
zabar	(to be) bright, pure; arrowhead; weapon; metal mirror; (to be) shiny; measuring vessel made of bronze; a metal bowl; bronze	810
zaham	to shine	2
zal	to shine	2
zalag	(to be) pure; (fire) light; (to be) bright, to shine	135

Conclusion: Linguistic Remainders and Reminders of Earlier Mentalities

This preliminary study of BA written languages has attempted to offer support for the EmPL hypothesis. This is part of a larger agenda — to provide evidence for bicameral mentality. The aforementioned ratios and statistical analyses favored hypotheses thirteen out of sixteen times (81.25%) and fifteen out of fifteen times (100%), respectively. This is strong validation of at least the EmPL, if not bicamerality. And these arguments, as we shall see in the next two chapters, apply well beyond the ancient Near East.

Endnotes

1. One might be tempted to search for an inverse relationship between religious and psychological wordstocks, i.e. as a culture's psychological lexicon increases, its religious lexicon decreases. A review of lexicons after 1000 BCE will not indicate such a difference, given that words, like archeological layerings, accumulate over time.
2. Additional research needs to be done on BA written traditions. Arguably, lacking a well-developed conscious interiority, characters in literary accounts would be "flat," an expression borrowed from the English novelist E.M. Forster (1879-1970) who made a distinction between "flat" and "round" characters. The former were "types" and caricatures who were two-dimensional, possessed a single quality, and did not undergo development. Round characters possessed depth, were more complex, and sometimes surprised the reader in how they changed and developed over time (1963). Forster was examining literary works of the eighteenth and nineteenth centuries, but his distinction applies, I think, to other periods with even more force, i.e. flat characters would be *de rigueur* in BA written works.
3. Other languages that might offer important clues are Chinese, Mesoamerican writing systems (Olmec and Maya scripts), Ugaritic, Luwian, Hurrian, and Eblaite. Undeciphered BA languages include proto-Elamite script, Linear Elamite, Indus script, Cretan hieroglyphs, Linear A, and Cypro-Minoan.
4. http://etcsl.orinst.ox.ac.uk/
5. http://psd.museum.upenn.edu/epsd1/index.html
6. http://www.assyrianlanguages.org/hittite/en_lexique_hittite.htm
7. http://www.utexas.edu/cola/centers/lrc/eieol/hitol-0-X.html
8. https://archive.org/details/DictionaryOfMiddleEgyptian
9. http://www.projethomere.com/ressources/linearb.pdf. The Hittites, who spoke an Indo-European language, governed central and eastern Anatolia in Turkey and parts of what are today Syria and Lebanon from about 1800 until 1200 BCE. Mycenaean/Linear B was the first Greek writing system used in the Greek-speaking regions of the Aegean Sea. It was used between the fourteenth and twelfth centuries BCE.
10. In the dictionaries of ePSD and ETCSL, "lament" appears 0.38% and about 1%, respectively, while its frequency in ePSD is 0.13% (168 out of 131,106).
11. Note that 26 PLs from Dataset App D.5, "ePSD Dictionary: PL, Their Frequencies Categorized by Period, and EV" are not included in the "Mind-Words by Period" analysis as the ePSD did not categorize them by period.
12. Holloran also lists bulk, main body, foundation, loan, obligation, interest, surplus, profit, interest-bearing debt, repayment, slave-woman, to chew, to smell, to belch, burp, to roar, to clog, block, to imprison, to rub something in, to rent (1999).
13. Tables are based on ETCSL (Electronic Text Corpus of Sumerian Literature), ePSD, and Holloran (1999).

14 All examples are from ETCSL. Curly brackets are ETCSL insertions; square brackets are mine.
15 Alternative of Inanna. Goddess of love, fertility, and warfare.

Chapter 4

Ancient China
Social Complexity, Cognitive Adaptation, and Linguistic Change

"The grand and vigorous function of metaphor is the generation of new language as it is needed, as human culture becomes more and more complex." —Julian Jaynes

A perusal through any etymological dictionary readily shows that psychological lexicons are metaphoric; this is true for *all* languages. What we should be more concerned with is the theoretical implications of this fact—*why* they are metaphoric. Such an inquiry demands a "big picture" of the psychology of a cultural historical topic. In this chapter and the next I use Chinese as an illustration of how linguo-concepts reflect changing mentalities. I first introduce some basic linguistic aspects of Chinese necessary to appreciate my arguments. Next, I apply the BCI to ancient China and offer evidence that psychological linguo-concepts reflect growing social complexity and its concomitant neuro-cultural changes. Then I offer linguistic evidence for cognitive transitions. In the next chapter, which is a continuation of this one, I provide examples of the psychological lexicon of modern Mandarin. The empirical evidence I rely on comes from etymology and standard dictionaries.

Basic Linguistic Aspects of Chinese Languages

Before proposing a categorization of Mandarin MWs and their written representations, some qualifications are in order. First, note that one logograph does not necessarily correspond to one word; in modern Mandarin two logographs often constitute one word. Second, depending on one's classificatory scheme, seven to thirteen Chinese languages are now spoken (and many of these are mutually unintelligible). Moreover, numerous regional dialects exist. However, they all share the same written language (though non-standard written or colloquial Chinese might use "dialectal logographs").[1]

Given the complexity of the issues involved, I restrict my analysis to the most commonly spoken Chinese language, Mandarin.[2] Sociohistorical scaffolding is obviously a diachronic process. However, my focus is on this language's present-day psychohistorical stratum — or the synchronic product, as it were — of centuries-long sedimentization. Though the spoken languages of Chinese have developed at different rates, written Chinese has changed much less and thus offers a storehouse of informative linguo-conceptual vestiges.

Logograph Formation

Much debate surrounds the best way to account for the evolution of Chinese logographs. But for my purposes, I utilize five categories.[3] Note that for this work I will use "traditional" logographs rather than their simplified versions.[4]

(1) *Pictographs* (or *pictograms*). These depict objects, though over time these depictions have greatly changed (such as for the sun, moon, or goat).

(2) *Ideographs* (or *ideograms*). These indicate abstract meanings. Some are easy to discern, such as one, two, or three, while others are more culturally specific.

(3) *Complex Graphs*. These describe logographs that combine two or more pictographic or ideographic logographs in order to convey a meaning. For example, *nong2*, meaning agriculture, originally consisted of elements meaning "field" and "plough."

(4) *Phonosemantics* (or *semantic-phonetics, pictophonetics, radical-phonetics*). The most common type of logograph, these possess at least two components: a phonetic and a semantic element. While the former indicates pronunciation, the latter provides (or at least hints) at the logograph's meaning. This latter component is a signific (variously called a radical or classifier). 214 recurring signific components (water, person, bamboo, etc.) have been traditionally used to organize Chinese dictionaries. Significantly for my purposes, most MWs have one of the two forms of the radical for "heart." This is a clear indication of how salient bodily organs and embodiment have been in the evolution of the psychological lexicon of written Chinese.

(5) *Phonetic loans* (or *loan-graphs*). These describe logographs which were borrowed to write a word that lacked a logograph but shared the same pronunciation with the borrowed logograph.[5] The meanings of the homophonous words were unrelated.

4. Ancient China

Romanization

In this work I use Pinyin Romanization. Mandarin is a tonal language so it is also necessary to indicate its tones.[6] This is done by suffixing a number to each word: 1 for "high"; 2 for "rising"; 3 for "low (dipping)"; and 4 for "falling" tone. Some words possess a neutral tone. These are not suffixed with a number. Many, but not all, of the Chinese terms I will discuss are compounds (usually two logographs) and some are actually four-logograph idioms.

The BCI Applied to Ancient China

My contentions will not make much sense unless the metaphoricity of MWs are historically grounded and socioculturally contextualized further. Using the BCI framework introduced earlier, Chart 4.1 lists select examples from China.

Chart 4.1. Examples from China: Patterns of Bicameral Mentality and Its Vestiges.

Key Trait	Function, Evidence, and Examples
Centrality of Ancestor Worship (CAW)	Pre-dates Shang-era; handed down as rich complex of mourning rites in post-bicameral times
Theocentered Social Order (TSO)	Shang rulers functioned as high priests, conducted divination ceremonies; post-bicameral kings and emperors ruled by theopolitical Mandate of Heaven
Objects of Hallucinatory Focus (OHF)	Late Shang- and early Zhou-era ceremonial bronze utensils with dragon motif; ancestral tablets
Authority-Radiating Ceremonial Complexes (ARCC)	Numerous post-bicameral burial mounds of Zhou period attest to earlier tradition of ARCC, e.g. King Ling's tomb (died 545 BCE) Most famous is that of the First Emperor of Qin dynasty (260–210 BCE)
"As If" Mortuary Practices (AIMP)	Shang-era royal burials of weapons, sacrificial vessels, carriages, horses, retinue
Supernatural Visitations (SV)	Personation during Zhou; numerous festivals, customs (CAW); appeasement of roaming malevolent ghosts
Intermediary Beings (IB)	Numerous intercessionary local gods, goddesses, demigods, saints
Indirect Divine Communication (IDC)	Shang-era pyromancy, plastromancy, scapulimancy, oracle bones; classic Book of Changes (Yijing) divinatory text
Multiple Souls	Po4 associated with grave, hun2 with ancestral tablets; at death po4 remains with the body to the grave, hun2 dwells in ancestral tablet, third part goes to be judged; souls require nourish-

	ment though eventually they depart for the next world
Undeveloped Psychological Lexicon (UPL) before ca. 1000 BCE	See this chapter
Metaphoric Mind-Words	See next chapter
No Philosophical Tradition before ca. 1000 BCE	De-anthropophomization of Shang-era "High God" (Di); evolves into more abstract, impersonal "Heaven" during Zhou Sustained philosophical probing explodes with Confucianism, Mohism, Legalism, other schools during mid-first millennium BCE
Neo-bicameralism (NB) after ca. 1000 BCE	Personation, spirit possession, vereration of ancestors (CAW), Chinese folk religion or Shenism (from shen2: sundry deities, spirits, etc.)

The next sections provide a sketch of how human mentality accommodated massive sociopolitical and techno-economic transformations in ancient China.

(1) Neolithic Bicamerality

A number of Neolithic cultures in China have been discovered (e.g. Jiahu and Peiligang) which developed pottery, constructed buildings, and buried their dead. As in other places, with agriculture came increased population, specialization, the storage of surpluses, and the centralization of socioeconomic power. In the late Neolithic period (5000 to 3000 BCE) the Yangshao culture established itself along the Yellow River, and by 3000 BCE the Longshan culture began to flourish. Some researchers claim that pictographs found in Ningxia, dating to about 6000–5000 BCE, are actually China's earliest form of writing.

(2) Literate-Urban Bicameral Societies

In the case of China the historical record is not as clear as it is in the Middle East and India, so periodizing China's "classic" bicameral phase is problematic (refer to Chart 4.1). But it is clear that during the Shang dynasty (ca. 1700–1046 BCE) ancestor worship was institutionalized and theopolitical authorization was provided by local deities.[7]

(3) The Breakdown of Bicamerality

Arguably the Shang era also witnessed a centuries-long transition from classic to semi-bicamerality.[8] One indication of a change in mentality was the explosion in divination. The ubiquitous "asking the ancestors and gods for advice" should not be regarded as a superstitious pastime; this was a salient, ubiquitous, and crucial practice of communication/command/control linking mortals with the deities and kings with the royal ancestors. It was a vital act of theopolitical decision-making. In the late-Shang dynasty queries would be written on the shoulder bones of oxen (scapula) or the front plates of turtle shells (plastrons). These in turn would be heated up and the resulting cracks interpreted. This oracle bone script was the earliest type of Chinese writing.

The gradual loss of voice-volitions led to attempts to force the gods and ancestors to speak through oracles, dream visitations, and "personation," arguably a type of spirit possession (perhaps in earlier periods the commandeering supernatural entity became—rather than just entered—an individual).[9]

Cognitive changes during Shang also demanded new linguo-concepts which borrowed from bodily experiences in order to construct an analogous world of interiorized "simulated behavior" that allowed for more efficient cognition. An increasingly complicated political economic landscape demanded a more sophisticated array of linguo-concepts allowing individuals to navigate denser social relations and to better coordinate the behavior of their members.

Carr detects evidence of bicamerality and its vestiges in two other etymological trajectories. First, he attempts to resolve many textual misreadings by analyzing "to dead father," i.e. "communicate with one's dead father" (*k'ôg) (1989). Originally, *k'ôg was the name of an ancestral sacrifice which involved "divination, 'striking' bells to beckon spirits, drinking sacrificial wine, and actual/imagined spiritual communication." According to Carr, *k'ôg followed the etymological trajectory of: (1) examine, especially divinations; think about → (2) complete/achieve (spirit communication) → (3) dead father (in charge of ancestral spirits) → (4) strike/beat (musical instruments to beckon the gods) → (5) cry out; wail (for the dead) → (6) old age; longevity (in the sense of life after death) (Carr 1989: 111). The second linguo-conceptual tracing concerns "big head" terms. He notes the Shang-era belief that "rulers and priests were big-headed, in the sense that they heard spiritual voices or were divinely inspired" (Carr 1985b: 18), and the related oracle graphs either meant: (1) elder, leader, ruler; or (2) god, spirit, ghost.

(4) Post-Bicamerality

In China the post-bicameral period corresponds with the Zhou dynasty (ca. 1046–256 BCE), which can be subdivided in different ways. It was during Zhou that the more abstract notion of the Mandate of Heaven developed to legitimize kingship and stabilize psychopolitical authorization. During the Spring and Autumn Period (722–476 BCE; a subdivision of the Zhou), China shattered into numerous statelets, though in principle the Zhou king was still the paramount power. Key features of what we now associate with Chinese culture took shape and an explosion of ideas, seen in the "Hundred Schools of Thought" — Confucianism, Taoism, Legalism, Mohism — were born. Indeed, if the king ruled as Heaven's deputy during Western Zhou (1046–771 BCE), it was during Eastern Zhou (which lasted until 256 BCE) that the supreme authority of the deities was challenged and individual virtue became the bedrock of a stable social order.

By Zhou times individuals possessed a consciousness with which we would be familiar. However, the *degree* of their conscious interiorization would probably strike us as not very developed. In his analysis of the Confucian *Analects* (composed sometime between 475 and 221 BCE), Fingarette notes that in passages where we would impose a psychological import, the language itself is not psychically internal or subjective; it is more behavioral and objective (1972: 44–45). "The metaphor of an inner psychic life, in all its ramifications so familiar to us, simply isn't present ... not even as a rejected possibility" (Fingarette 1972: 45).

Another subdivision of Zhou was the Warring States Period (476–211 BCE). During this time seven centers of power were able to consolidate their rule, and in 211 BCE the king of the Qin state declared himself the First Emperor (Qin Shi Huang) and ruled over the brief but immensely influential Qin Dynasty (221–206 BCE). With Qin begins China's long succession of imperial dynasties that would last until the fall of the Qing dynasty in 1912. The First Emperor unified China, centralized administration, and, mindful of the chaos characterizing earlier centuries, ensured strict communication/command/control by instituting Legalism, a rigid political philosophy that placed absolute authorization in the emperor.

As for the written language: besides shells and bones (during Shang), Chinese would be written on other materials, such as bamboo strips. Some of these have survived. However, the First Emperor ordered the destruction of many old documents, though in the early second century CE the *Shuowen Jiezi* dictionary (*Explaining and Analyzing Characters*) was composed that preserved many logographs. Moreover, several thousand cast bronze articles have come down to us that recorded major events during Zhou. These articles were inscribed with what are called "bronze characters." To increase communicative efficiency and stabilize the sociopolitical system during Qin, uniformity and regulation became the order of the day. This included the written language. A list of official logographs was drawn up. These were standardized into "seal script," from which evolved variants, one of which, "regular script," became the most widely used style by around the fifth century CE. It is regular script that most closely resembles modern Chinese logographs (Chart 4.2).

Chart 4.2. Major Scripts of Chinese Writing.*

Major Scripts	Historical Period	Notes
Oracle Bone	Shang: 1600–1046 BCE	Records of divinations for communication with royal ancestral spirits; writing for other purposes on wood and bamboo has not survived
Bronze	Zhou: 1045–256 BCE	Used on bronze ritual objects beginning in late Shang
Large Seal		
Small Seal	Qin: 221–206 BCE	Standardized and adopted as the formal script for all of China
Clerical	Han: 206 BCE–220 CE	Most widely used and recognized
Regular		
Running		Also called semi-cursive
Grass		Also called "cursive"
Simplified	Since 1949	Used in the People's Republic of China and Singapore

* The periods of usage of these scripts overlapped.

China's Ancient Cosmological Vision

The pursuit of knowledge in premodern times meant integration, not fragmenting the world into a multitude of disciplines equipped with their own specialized idioms and concepts. Premodern thinking fused realms of thought that we moderns separate, such as medico-religious, religio-Psychological, psycho-medical, etc.[10] As in other cosmologies, ancient Chinese understandings of what we call the mind were embedded in a complex of ideas about the body and the natural and supernatural worlds. Divisions that we make today between religion and medicine, Psychology and physiology, and political and personal control did not exist. The macrocosm, microcosm, and introcosm (the individual psyche) were aspects of the same unified reality, spun together in an organic web of correspondences and correlations. Colors, numbers, musical notes, planets, and things as disparate as ministries and styles of government were part of a multifaceted cosmological vision. Attributes of spatiality (e.g. cardinal points), the realm of nature (e.g. seasons, classes of beasts, and domestic animals), and psycho-physical functions and features (viscera, bodily parts, sense organs, tastes, smells, demeanor, vision, thoughts, speech, hearing) were categorized and listed (usually in groups of five).

I cannot do justice to China's rich and complicated cosmology, especially since it evolved and changed greatly over the centuries. However, in the following section I offer one rendering of a Chinese psycho-cosmic vision that resonated with other versions. This is pertinent to demonstrating how the most recent layer of Mandarin's linguo-concepts rests upon earlier psychohistorical strata.

The Heart is the Ruler of the Body

We can begin with the word *xin1*, or heart, though given its broader denotations related to both emotions and thought, a better translation is "heart-mind" (Yu 2003). *Xin1* is a pictographic representation of a physical heart, and as we will see below, it forms the most primary and elemental building block for Chinese linguo-concepts having to do with the psychological. The *xin1* oversaw the activities of an individual's psychophysiological existence and was regarded as the ruler of the body — indeed, the person — in the same way a king ruled his people. If individuals cultivate and control their hearts, then the family, state, and world could be properly governed (Yu 2007, 2009b).

Psycho-Physio-Spiritual Aspects of the Person

Under the control of heart were the *wu3shen2* or "five spirits" (*shen2, hun2, po4, yi4, zhi4*) which dwelt respectively in the heart, liver, lungs, spleen, and kidneys. The five *shen2* were implicated in the operations of thinking, perception, and bodily systems and substances. A phono-semantic, *shen2* has been variously translated as mind, spirit, supernatural being, consciousness, vitality, expression, soul, energy, god, or numen/numinous. The left side element of this logograph means manifest, show, demonstrate; we can speculate that whatever was manifested came from a supernatural source; it may have meant "ancestral spirit" (Keightley 1978: 17). The right side provides sound but also the additional meaning of "to state" or "report to a superior"; again we can speculate that it meant communing to a supernatural superior.

Among the psychological aspects of *shen2* is what might be called "mental *shen2*" (written with the same logograph as the *wu3shen2* or "five spirits"). It denotes thinking or memory, and is related to wakefulness. Other psychological aspects are *yi4*, meaning idea, image, wish, desire, intention, or expectation (complex graph; signific: Heart), and *zhi4*, denoting purpose, will, determination, or ambition (phono-semantic; signific: Heart). Among the spiritual aspects are the two souls. *Hun3* is the ethereal, spiritual, or immortal soul, i.e. it can be detached from the body at death. A phonosemantic with ghost, it appears in psychology-related expressions. It is associated with inspiration and visions. *Po4* is the corporeal, "animal," or mortal soul, i.e. it stays with the body after death. It is associated with sensations and feelings.

Another spiritual aspect that should be mentioned is *ling2*, which denotes spirit, soul, divine, mysterious, anything pertaining to the deceased, and the spiritual realm that is apprehended by its impact on the everyday world. It appears in the compounds *ling2hun2* (spirit + soul = soul, spirit) and *wang2ling2* (deceased + spirit = departed spirit). The top element of this logograph indicates falling rain, while the bottom part represents wizard, sorcerer, or shaman. Interestingly, this graph also has three mouths, hinting that perhaps spiritual entities "spoke" to mortals. Besides the spiritual, *ling2* is also associated with other meanings, such as clever, nimble, sharp, quick, alert, efficacious, effective (Dataset App F.1). We might also mention the "five basic emotions" or *wu3zhi4* listed in Chart 4.3. *Zhi4* is the logograph used in modern Mandarin for purpose, will, determination, ambition.

Chart 4.3. The Five Emotions.

Emotion	Modern Mandarin	Logograph	Etymological Formation of Emotion Logograph	Corresponding Organ
Joy	xi3	憙	complex graph: beating a drum & laughing; signific = mouth	Heart
Fear	kong3	恐	phonosemantic; signific = heart	Kidneys
Anger	nu4	怒	phonosemantic; signific = heart	Liver
Anxiety	you1	憂	complex graph: heart signific & element meaning worried face	Spleen
Grief	bei1	悲	phonosemantic; signific = heart	Lungs

Textual Evidence for Vestigial Bicamerality's Decline and the Emergence of a Psychological Idiom

Ruptures in textual traditions point to a transition from a waning bicameral mentality to a more interiorized religiosity. This is illustrated by the differences between the highly ritualistic Rig Vedas and super-subjective Upanishads in the Hindu tradition, or the moralistically-harsh codes of the Old Testament and the more inner-focused New Testament. Due to a lack of written records, the break is not as clear in

China. Nevertheless, the oldest Chinese classic, the *Book of Poetry* (*Shijing;* also known as the *Book of Songs* or *Book of Odes*) illuminates a major cognitive shift that is consistent with Jaynes's bicameral thesis. A four-part collection of 305 poems and hymns, the *Book of Poetry* covers almost half a millennium beginning in the eleventh century BCE. But significantly for our purposes this was a time when Chinese civilization, having just left behind the semi-bicameral Shang era, was entering the increasingly psychologically-interiorized Zhou period (Chart 4.4).

Chart 4.4. Four Parts of the *Book of Poetry.*

Name of Parts	Chinese Name	Translation	Contents
Odes of the Temple and Altar	Song	Eulogies	Hymns for religious ceremonies of the court
Greater Odes of the Kingdom	Da Ya	Major Court Hymns	Poems or songs of praise of the rulers
Minor Odes of the Kingdom	Xiao Ya	Lesser Court Hymns	Poems or songs concerning life of the nobility
Lessons from the State	Guo Feng	Airs of the States	Poems or folk songs from ordinary people

The hypothesis I propose is that vestiges of bicamerality should be evident in the earlier parts of the *Book of Poetry* but decline in later parts. The thoughtful reader might object that the later parts were not specifically concerned with spiritual matters. However, we must be wary of the presentist fallacy that neatly segregates the religious, political, and mundane. In the premodern world such distinctions were alien. Also, some of the numbers are admittedly small, and, taken by themselves, insignificant. However, if taken together in the aggregate, *general trends* are apparent. I am using the *Book of Poetry* as one sample, but when put together with other patterns of evidence, the pieces of a puzzle should fall in place.

Let us begin with an examination of supernatural concepts. "Ancestor" witnessed a steep decline in usage until it vanished by the eighth-to-seventh centuries. "Heaven" declined by almost 75%. Though their appearance fluctuates throughout the centuries, four other concepts disappear altogether in the last part of the *Book of Poetry* (Tables 4.1, 4.2, and 4.3).

Table 4.1. Usage of Supernatural Concepts through Time in the *Book of Poetry*.

Period	1	2	3	4
Centuries: BCE	11th to 10th Odes of the Temple and Altar	10th to 9th Greater Odes of the Kingdom	9th to 8th Minor Odes of the Kingdom	8th to 7th Lessons from the States
Logograph Count	3,007	6,587	9,488	10,688
Ancestor (zu3)	0.33% (10)	0.19% (13)	0.09% (9)	0.00% (0)
Heaven (tian1 minus Son of Heaven and Mandate of Heaven)	0.67% (20)	0.89% (59)	0.46% (44)	0.16% (17)
Mandate of Heaven (tian1ming4)	0.13% (4)	0.06% (3)	0.02% (2)	0.00% (0)
God (shang4di4)	0.17% (5)	0.24% (16)	0.03% (3)	0.00% (0)
Son of Heaven (tian1zi3)	0.07% (2)	0.14% (9)	0.11% (10)	0.00% (0)
Spirit, God (shen2)	0.03% (1)	0.15% (10)	0.12% (11)	0.00% (0)
Total	1.40% (42)	1.67% (110)	0.83% (79)	0.16% (17)

Sources: Dates are Dobson's estimates (1964, 1968). Numbers in parentheses indicate raw numbers. To obtain logograph counts, all punctuation, titles, and headings were stripped from texts. Note that classical Chinese is far more concise and compact than English. Percentages are rounded to the second decimal place.

An examination of Legge's translation reveals a more ambiguous situation. However, the declining frequency rates of five out of eight supernatural concepts arguably suggests a decline in spirituality (Table 4.2).

Table 4.2. Usage of Supernatural Concepts through Time in the *Book of Poetry*.

Period	1	2	3	4
Centuries: BCE	11th to 10th Odes of the Temple and Altar	10th to 9th Greater Odes of the Kingdom	9th to 8th Minor Odes of the Kingdom	8th to 7th Lessons from the States
Word Count: Legge's Translation	5,250	11,774	15,605	17,872
Temple	0.11% (6)	0.05% (6)	0.01% (2)	0.02% (4)
Ancestor/Ancestral	0.30% (16)	0.23% (27)	0.04% (6)	0.01% (1)
Heaven (minus "Son of Heaven")	0.44% (23)	0.55% (65)	0.28% (44)	0.09% (16)
Son of Heaven	0.02% (1)	0.07% (8)	0.07% (11)	0.00% (0)
Spiritual Beings	0.02% (1)	0.01% (1)	0.01% (1)	0.00% (0)
God	0.19% (10)	0.25% (29)	0.02% (3)	0.01% (1)

Personator	0.00% (0)	0.10% (12)	0.00% (0)	0.00% (0)
Divined/Divine/Diviner	0.00% (0)	0.02% (2)	0.05% (2 + 3 + 3 = 8)	0.01% (1)
Total	1.08% (57)	1.28% (150)	0.48% (75)	0.14% (23)

Sources: For this table and the next the analysis of English words is based on translations by James Legge (http://search.lib.virginia.edu/catalog/uva-lib:476613/). To obtain word counts, all punctuation, titles, and headings were stripped from texts.

The Layered Psychological Lexicon of the Book of Poetry

An investigation of the different linguo-conceptual layers of the *Book of Poetry* strongly suggests changes in mentality (Table 4.3). In the *Book of Poetry* from the eleventh to seventh centuries BCE a decrease in spiritual concepts is apparent: ancestor/ancestral (95%); god (96%); temple (82%); and heaven (80%; minus "Son of Heaven"). In his analysis of the *Book of Poetry*, Carr in fact noted that, as the centuries passed, more attention was afforded the human heart and less to spiritual entities (Carr 1983: 7). Some increases in MW usage are admittedly more statistically salient than others—10.14-fold for "heart"/*xin1*, 22-fold for know/understand, 20.5-fold for "heart," 1.55-fold for thought/think, 17-fold for "feel," 4-fold for wish, 12-fold for "know," and 2.5-fold for mind. In any case, the overall trend should be clear: more psychological interiorization is evident through the centuries (the discrepancy between "heart"/*xin1* and "heart" is due to Legge's interpretive translation).

Table 4.3. Usage of Key Mind–Words through Time in the *Book of Poetry*.

Period	1	2	3	4
Centuries: BCE	11th to 10th *Odes of the Temple and Altar*	10th to 9th *Greater Odes of the Kingdom*	9th to 8th *Minor Odes of the Kingdom*	8th to 7th *Lessons from the States*
Logograph Count	3,007	6,587	9,488	10,688
Word Count: Legge's Translation	5,250	11,774	15,605	17,872
Heart (*xin1*)	0.07% (2)	0.30% (20)	0.76% (72)	0.71% (76)
Know/Understand (*zhi1*)	0.00% (0)	0.12% (8)	0.16% (15)	0.22% (24)
Heart	0.02% (1)	0.12% (14)	0.42% (66)	0.41% (74)
Thought/Think	0.29% (8 + 7 = 15)	0.11% (3 + 10 = 13)	0.23% (7 + 29 = 36)	0.45% (14 + 66 = 80)
Feel	0.02% (1)	0.03% (4)	0.05% (8)	0.34% (60)
Wish	0.02% (1)	0.02% (2)	0.08% (12)	0.08% (14)
Know	0.00% (0)	0.04% (5)	0.06% (9)	0.12% (21)

| Mind | 0.02% (1) | 0.06% (7) | 0.03% (4) | 0.05% (9) |
| Total | 0.44% (21) | 0.80% (73) | 1.79% (222) | 2.38% (358) |

Graph 4.1. Chinese Supernatural Words and MWs. Figures for Supernatural Words are Means of Totals from Tables 4.1 and 4.2. Figures for MWs are Totals from Table 4.3. Note the significant gap between supernatural words and MWs for periods 1 and 4, respectively: 0.8 and 2.23, a 2.79-fold increase.

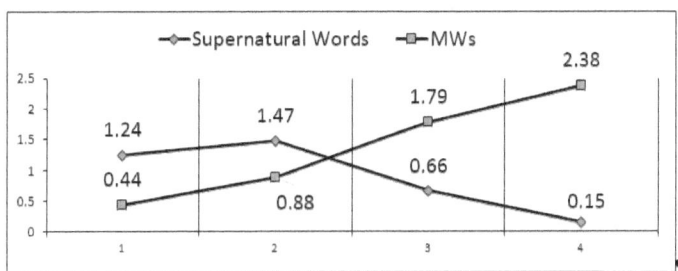

In his own analysis Carr also points out that in comparison with the frequency in the *Song*, "heart-mind" (*xin1*) occurs four times more often in the *Da Ya* and ten times more often in the *Xiao Ya* and *Guo Feng* (Carr 1983: 7). And as another sign of increasing interiorization, "think" and "know" words "show a steady diachronic increase in usage": 28 in the *Song*, 79 in the *Da Ya*, 93 in the *Xiao Ya*, and 99 in the *Guo Feng* (Carr 1983: 22).

Carr makes several points that bolster the argument that psychological idioms develop along the lines of Jaynes's four-phase trajectory explicated in Chapter 2. First, about one third of the words describing mental activity in the *Book of Poetry* possess other meanings, i.e. the psychological idiom did not seem well developed. Some are graphic loans (using a logograph with the same phonetic but a different radical), while others are phonetic loans (using a logograph with the same pronunciation to write a word without a logograph) (Carr 1983: 15). Second, most words meaning "think" actually have the sense of to "brood": "There would seem to be almost no words that meant 'think' in the abstract logical sense" (Carr 1983: 17). Third, physical pain is almost synonymous with mental anguish, and though the heart signific does appear, the sickness signific is used to write most words for grief, strongly suggesting that an interiorized psychological realm, segregated from the physical, was undeveloped (Carr 1983: 6, 12).

Statistical Analysis: Correlations between Periods and Types of Words

I propose four hypotheses related to decreasing usage of supernatural terms and increasing psychological interiorization:

Hypothesis Log 4.1. Decreasing Supernatural Terms and Increasing MWs.

Refer to App Calculation 4.1. Correlations between Periods and Types of Words	
The usage of supernatural words (totals from Table 4.1) will decrease as the centuries pass (i.e. the 4 periods)	No
The usage of supernatural words (totals from Table 4.2) will decrease as the centuries pass	No
The usage of MWs (totals) will increase as the centuries pass	Yes
As usage of supernatural words (means of totals from Tables 4.1 + 4.2) decrease, the usage of MWs increases	Yes
	2/4

The Pearson Product-Moment Correlation Coefficient produces ambiguous but highly suggestive results. Strong correlations exist between the passage of time and supernatural and MWs. Though two out of four correlations are not significant, two correlations are: (3) 4 periods and MWs and (4) MWs and supernatural. In other words, the hypothesis that, with each passing century, the number of psychological terms increased significantly, holds ($r = -0.9860$; a very strong negative correlation) (App Calculation 4.1).

To what degree is chance a factor in explaining the patterns of supernatural words and MWs across time? I utilize the Chi-Square test statistic and propose that the observed distribution of supernatural words and MWs across the four periods do not occur by chance. This proposition can be broken down into three hypotheses. As evidenced in App Calculations 4.2 through 4.4, the results are statistically significant, probably meaning that an underlying pattern is at work, i.e. as psychological interiorization increased, supernatural concepts eroded.

Hypothesis Log 4.2. Did Supernatural Concepts Decrease over the Centuries?

The distribution of supernatural words across the 4 periods is not random: *Refer to* App Calculation 4.2. Supernatural Words: Totals from Table 4.1. Chi-Sq G of F	Yes
The distribution of supernatural words across the 4 periods is not random: *Refer to* App Calculation 4.3. Supernatural Words: Totals from Table 4.2. Chi-Sq G of F	Yes
The distribution of MWs (totals) across the 4 periods is not random: *Refer to* App Calculation 4.4. MWs. Chi-Sq G of F	Yes
	3/3

The Language of the Unhappy Gods

Being responsible for keeping unruly and misbehaving mortals in line can make even a god feel depressed. So it should not be surprising if the earliest MWs, originating in the brain's then dominant (or domineering?) right side and spoken by officious deities, annoyed ancestors, irritated revenants, or entombed but still bellowing rulers, were often negatively charged. As pointed out in Chapter 3, Jaynes made a linkage between negative emotionality and a period when the right hemisphere was more dominant than it is today (1976: 116).

Linguistic evidence from ancient China supporting the notion of the "unhappy gods" is seen in Carr's analysis of the *Shijing*. He noted that of the 103 words written with the heart signific that refer to psychological states, 60% have negative meanings while less than 12% denote "happy" in any sense (1983: 6, 8). Additional evidence is seen in the early second century *Shuowen Jiezi* dictionary: of the twelve "series" of words that appear with the heart signific describing cognition or feeling, only three describe positive emotions (PE) (27.27%) ("thinking" is emotionally neutral).[11] Even more striking, almost 90% of items (excluding "thinking") in all series can be characterized as negative emotions (NE) (Table 4.4). App Calculation 4.5 summarizes results supporting the hypothesis that the distribution between NE and PE items is significantly uneven.

Table 4.4. Cognition and Emotion Terms in the *Shuowen Jiezi*.

	Series for Cognition or Feeling	No. of Items in Series	% of No. of Items in Each Series	% of No. of Items in Each Series: NE	% of No. of Items in Each Series: PE
1.	Worry	22	23.65%	24.71%	
2.	Resentment	12	12.90%	13.48%	
3.	Dejection	12	12.90%	13.48%	
4.	Fear	11	11.82%	12.35%	
5.	Dissatisfaction/Resentment	9	9.67%	10.11%	
6.	Shame/Humiliation	6	6.45%	6.74%	
7.	Anxiousness/Eagerness	6	6.45%	6.74%	
8.	Fear (minor*)	2	2.15%	2.25%	
9.	Affection	4	4.30%	4.49%	4.49%
10.	Thinking	4	4.30%	–	–
11.	Joy	3	3.22%	3.37%	3.37%
12.	Peaceful	2	2.15%	2.24%	2.24%
		$\sum = 93$	$\sum = 100\%$	$\sum = 89.9\%$	$\sum = 10.1\%$

* "Minor" means less than 3 items in the series.

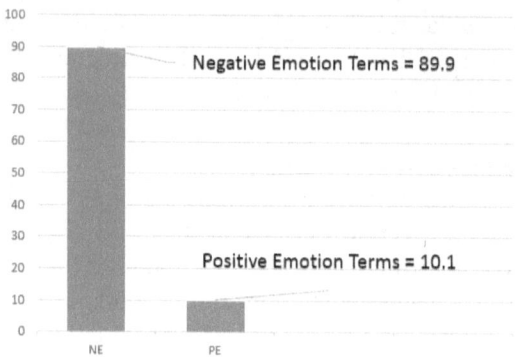

Graph 4.2. Negative Emotion (NE) and Positive Emotion (PE) Terms in the *Shuowen Jiezi*. From Table 4.4.

As further evidence that the earliest psychological lexicon derived from the brain's god-governed right side, App Calculations 4.6 and 4.7 greatly support the hypothesis that the majority of heart-signific logographs from Dataset App F.2 indicate negative sentiments.

Hypothesis Log 4.3. Negative Emotion Words Significantly Outnumber Positive Emotion Words.

Refer to Table 4.4. Cognition and Emotion Terms in the *Shuowen Jiezi*	
NE Words > PE Words in *Shuowen Jiezi* *Refer to* App Calculation 4.5. NE Words Outnumber PE Words in *Shuowen Jiezi*. Chi-Sq G of F	Yes
NE with Heart Signific Logographs Words > PE Words *Refer to* App Calculation 4.6. Logographs with Heart Signific Representing NE Words Outnumber PE Words	Yes
NE with Heart Signific Logographs Words > PE Words *Refer to* App Calculation 4.7. Logographs with Heart Signific Representing NE Words Outnumber PE Words. Chi-Sq G of F	Yes
	3/3

Now that the psychohistorical framework has been set, in the next chapter I offer examples of the psychological lexicon of modern Mandarin, the latest layer, as it were, of thousands of years of social adaptation and concomitant linguo-conceptualization.

Endnotes

1. Also, a number of Chinese languages have developed their own alphabetical system.
2. "Standard Chinese" is based on Mandarin (more specifically, its Beijing dialect) and is the official tongue of the People's Republic of China and Taiwan (Republic of China). It is also one of four officially-recognized languages of Singapore.
3. The origins of some logographs are unclear. Educated Chinese probably can read from 4,000 to 6,000 logographs, though there may be as many as 23,000 logographs. However, some dictionaries have listed as many as 50,000, though most of these would be rare, obscure, variants, or archaic logographs.
4. Simplified logographs were introduced in the 1950s in the People's Republic of China as part of attempts to reform and modernize the language. Note that not all logographs were simplified.
5. A subcategory of phonetic loans are re-clarified phonosemantics; in some cases, the logograph's original meaning is no longer associated with the logograph or has been lost or the original meaning is now expressed by a modification of the original logograph.
6. In spoken Mandarin, tones can change depending on their relation to the tone of adjacent words. Some Chinese languages have as many as eight to ten tones.
7. Predating Shang was the Xia Dynasty (ca. 2100–1600 BCE). The archeological evidence remains very scant, but markings on shells and pottery from this era may be the forerunners of what became Shang-era writing.
8. See Jaynes's speculative but intriguing commentary on artifacts from the Shang dynasty (2006).
9. Through etymological analysis, Carr has attempted to solve the puzzle of personation (its origins and why it ended) by applying Jaynesian Psychology (1985a; see also Carr 2006).
10. A defining feature of modernity is how these knowledge forms would be teased apart into new linguo-conceptual domains and scholarly disciplines beginning in certain parts of Europe in the 1600s. This disentangling picked up speed in the 1700s and then exploded with startling velocity by the mid-1800s. During this time entirely new lexicons were invented in response to industrialization and advances in the natural and human sciences.
11. Other mind-related terms listed in the *Shuowen Jiezi* that also have the heart signific are intelligence (3 items), stupidity (5 items), lack of diligence (5 items), effort (3 to 5), movement (3 items), and indulgence (2 items). I am relying on Bottéro and Harbsmeier (2008). Altogether the *Shuowen Jiezi* lists 275 words with the heart signific.

Chapter 5

The Metaphors of Mind-Words in Modern Mandarin

"Abstract words are ancient coins whose concrete images in the busy give-and-take of talk have worn away with use." — Julian Jaynes

Mandarin's Most Recent Stratum of Mind-Words

This chapter continues the previous one by offering examples of modern Mandarin's psycholexemes. Its purpose is to show how certain patterns of psychohistorical development and metaphoricity are apparent in the most recent stratum of Chinese linguo-conceptualization.

Typology of Modern Mandarin MWs

Creating a corpus of Mandarin MWs was accomplished by simply referring to standard dictionaries (note that modern Mandarin MWs may or may not be composed of one logograph; many have two logographs). I then divided the terms into three main categories: those that have their origins in (1) embodied experiences related to the heart; (2) embodied experiences without the heart; and (3) external entities (unless otherwise specified, all logographs are phonosemantic; several have etymological formations that are not clear). These categories were further subdivided.

(1) Embodied Experiences with "Heart"

- "Heart." By far the most salient mind-related word in Chinese is "heart" (*xin1*). Appearing in 249 compounds (Dataset App F.3), by metaphoric extension *xin1* means mind, intention, or thought. Though most words with *xin1* are mental terms, its original sense of a physical organ is still retained in *xin1zang4* (physical heart) and in medical terms having to do with "cardio." As in other MWs relying on bodily parts, *xin1* is paired with adjectives or verbs that describe

the heart or its activity. *Xin1* also appears in some terms that have to do with non-psychological but sensate meanings, such as heartburn (*shao1xin1*).¹
- Heart Significs. Dataset App F.2 lists 170 logographs with the heart signific (the heart component is written differently depending on the logograph). These logographs, with a few exceptions, refer to psychological processes, events, or personality characteristics. Note that many of these logographs usually appear in compounds and some are literary and not commonly used.

The following logographs possess the heart signific, but as their usage is salient, I list them separately.

- *Ai4*. Meaning love, this logograph represents a person walking with a heart. The word may have once meant "to walk on tip toe" or "gracious gait."
- *Bei1*. Meaning sorrow, grief; sorry, or sad.
- *Gan3*. This pictograph means feel, sense, move, touch, be grateful, or be affected. It possesses the heart signific suggesting the meaning and the other component indicating sound.
- *Kong3*. Meaning fear; fearful, apprehensive.
- *Mu4*. This logograph means to long for, desire, or admire.
- *Nian2*. This complex graph indicates to miss, worry, or display affection (as well as read; to study; to attend [school]; to read aloud). It has the heart signific, but also a component meaning now ("keep the present in mind" or "keep the mind in the present").
- *Nu4*. Meaning to be angry or furious, this logograph has the signific heart and the phonetic component for female slave.
- *Qing2*. Used in many terms, this logograph means feelings, emotions, sentiments, love, affection, passion.
- *Si1*. This means think, consider, ponder, long for, or thought. A complex graph, it brings together two organs often associated with the psychological: brain (replaced with logograph for field) and heart (*xin1*).
- *Xiang3*. This term means think, suppose, reckon, want to, would like to, remember with longing, or miss.
- *Yi4*. Meaning "sound of heart," this complex graph, with the semantic components of heart (signific) and sound/speech, means "speech of the heart" or "sound of the heart." It may mean wish, desire, intention, mind, feeling, inner heart, think of, long for, affection, and miss. In addition to its psychological associations, *yi4* denotes "meaning" as in "significance" (*you3yi4si*) or "indication" as in sketch map (*sheng1yi4tu2*), signal, hint, motion (*shi4yi4*), or some-

thing of interest, as in profound meaning (*shen1yi4*) or plaything, toy (*wan2yir4*). *Sheng1yi4* means tendency to grow, life, and vitality.
- *You1*. This complex graph, meaning sad, mournful, or anxious, possesses the semantic components for "going with a worried face."
- *Yu4*. This logograph means desire, appetite, passion, lust, greed. However, the etymology of this logograph is a bit complicated. The heart signific indicates meaning, while the component that indicates sound also means desire, want, or long for and is composed of the component "lack" (for meaning, i.e. to desire) and "valley" for the sound (*yu4*). *Yu4* appears in the compound *yu4wang4* (desire, longing, appetite, craving).
- *Wang4*. Meaning to forget; though the phonetic component signifies death or perish, it may be interpreted as in the heart (mind) an idea perishes.
- *Zhi4*. Meaning to make up one's mind to pursue some object, will, purpose, determination, a desire, ambition, interest, or wish.

(2) Other Embodied Experiences without "Heart"

Internal Organs and Bodily Parts besides the Heart

In addition to the heart, other organs metaphorically indicate psychological processes and personality dispositions. Gallbladder (*dan3*), chest (*xiong1*; which might also be translated as bosom, thorax, mind, or heart), and brain (*nao3*) figure prominently (Dataset App F.4). We should also note nose (*zi4*), which can stand for personal, private, in person, or personally.

Bodily Activities (Dataset App F.5)

- *Chi1*. In Mandarin "eat" has the extended meaning of absorb, soak up, suffer, incur, or "acquiring ideas is eating" (Yu 2003: 143). This is an example of how physico-bodily activity is pressed into service to describe something psychological.
- *Ji4*. Meaning record, write down, this logograph has the speech signific.
- *Ren4*. To recognize, know, understand. Its signific—a mouth with a tongue hanging out denoting speech, words, speak, say—provides the meaning while the other component gives sound.
- *Shi2*. Another logograph with the speech signific, *shi2* means know, knowledge, learning. The other component provides the sound.
- *Zhi1*. This complex graph means know, be aware, realize (as well as inform, notify, tell, knowledge, administer, be in charge of). Though its signific is an arrow, I have included this logograph under bodily

activity since its other component is mouth. An interpretation might be "(speak) from mouth like an arrow."

Perception (Datasets App F.5 and App F.6)

- *Chu4.* This means touch or contact but, metaphorically extended, it means to move somebody or stir up their feelings. The basic meaning *chu4dong4* is to move something, but it also means to emotionally move someone (*dong4*: move). *Chu4mu4 jing1xin1* means startling, shocking (*mu4*: eye; *jing1*: frighten [logograph with heart signific]; *xin1*: heart).
- *Dong4.* This logograph carries the strength signific and means move, action, movement, but can have psychological meaning as in *dong4yao2* (indecisive) or *dong4ren2* (touching).
- *Jian4.* A complex graph ("person with a big eye") also means to see or sight. "Seeing" is commonly used metaphorically in different languages that concern mental processes.[2]
- *Jiao1.* The signific for this logograph is person; it means burned, scorched (bird roasted by fire?), and, by extension, worried or anxious.
- *Jue2.* Though categorized as a phonosemantic (signific: "see"), the etymology of *jue2* is unclear. *Jue2* basically means to wake up, but it has been semantically extended to mean sense, feel, conscious, become aware. Interestingly, *jue2* shares the same logograph with *jiao4*, which means to sleep, the opposite of *jue2*'s basic sense of "awake."
- *Kan4.* This complex graph of "hand over the eye looking into the distance" means to see. Note that the sense of sight is used to construct "quasi-perceptions" or "introceptive" (as opposed to perceptive experiences; see McVeigh 2013).
- *Ku3.* This means bitter but can also mean hardship, suffering, misery, painstakingly. Its signific is grass.
- *Man3.* Meaning full and possessing the water signific, *man3* has the extended metaphoric sense of satisfied.
- *Nan4.* Meaning hard, difficult, arduous, or unable, the signific is a bird.
- *Re4.* This logograph possesses the grass signific, and means heat or to burn.

(3) External Entities

- *Cosmic Energy. Qi4* appears in various compounds and might mean gas, air, breath, smell, odor, weather, spirit, or morale. However, as a central concept in Chinese cosmology, philosophy, and medico-religious traditions, it should be understood as the "cosmic ether" or "vital energy" uniting the macrocosm with the microcosm (incidentally, the most important and common term describing psychological events and dispositions in Japanese is *ki*, quite similar in meaning to *qi4*; see McVeigh 1996) (Dataset App F.5).

External-Bodily, Entities, and Other Terms (Datasets App F.5 and App F.7)

- *Ai1*. This logograph means sad, mournful, pitiful, or pity (from cloths and mouth, perhaps indicating crying).
- *An1*. This logograph means peace, calm, and is a complex graph with the components woman and building, presumably indicating tranquility when a woman is in a house.
- *Ba1*. This logograph, a pictographic of a snake, means hope, wait, anxiously, cling to, stick, be close. It appears in the phrase *ba1bude*, meaning eager for, long for, look forward to (*bu* = no; *de* = obtain).
- *Cai1*. This logograph, with the signific dog, means guess, conjecture.
- *Dong4*. This logograph possess the signific water and means hole, cavern, cavity (and by extension "penetrate").
- *Fa1*. This logograph is a general-use verb with many meanings, such as send, emit, develop, discharge, open up, express, rise, ferment, and bring into existence, but is also utilized in terms about showing one's feelings and other MWs.[3]
- *Fan2*. The formation of *fan2* may be either phonosemantic (fire signific) or a complex graph: head burning with fire. It means to feel vexed or to bother, trouble, or annoy.
- *Jing1*. A pictographic of rice (the other component provides sound), this logograph means refined, essence, extract, semen, clever, skilled, goblin, spirit, demon, or a fundamental substance which maintains the functioning of the body and life essence.
- *Jing1*. This logograph has the horse signific and means surprised, frightened, be scared (perhaps horses are easily startled?).
- *Le4*. This logograph is a complex graph of a musical instrument with strings and a pluck on a wooden base. It means happy, cheerful, joyful, take pleasure in, glad, or amused.
- *Liao4*. Meaning material stuff, it also means expect or anticipate. Its origins are either: (1) complex graph (measuring with a Chinese peck) or (2) phonosemantic (rice) suggests the meaning while the other component provides sound.
- *Shen2*. This pictographic logograph means god, divinity, spirit, or supernatural being, but is used in expressions having to do with being smart, clever, or mind.

- *Wang4*. This logograph means to gaze (into the distance), look towards, or look at. Its extended meanings include to hope, expect, look forward, or visit. Two etymological explanations are given. The first, a complex graph, is a person gazing at the moon. The second, a phonosemantic, is of the moon (signific) while the other element provides sound.
- *Xi1*. This complex graph, meaning rare, hope, expect, to strive for, represents something crossed on a fabric.
- *Xi3*. A complex graph formed from (beating) a drum and mouth (signific), this logograph means happy, delighted, be fond of, enjoy.
- *Xing4*. A complex graph composed of two parts: (1) carry on one's shoulders/hands lifting something together; and (2) same, together with. It means to thrive, prosper, flourish, begin, but also appears in compounds indicating mood, desire to do something, interest, or excitement.
- *Yan4*. Meaning disgusted with, detest, be fed up, bored with, satiate, it is has cliff as its signific.
- *Yi2*. A complex graph, this represents, as mentioned above, an old man with hand on a cane asking for directions and means suspicious, doubt, disbelieve, to suspect.

A Heart-Centered Psychological Idiom

At this point I propose a general hypothesis: due to the predominance of the heart-centered cosmology in ancient China, the psychological lexicon of modern Mandarin should be heart-centric. The majority of MWs in present-day Mandarin will convey the semantic legacies of the internal, subjective, and synthetic stages of psycholinguistic development as postulated by Jaynes (1976). Though I cannot offer direct evidence, I submit that terms indicating psychologicality relying on external entities (the first or "objective" phase in Jaynes's scheme) have either been lost to time or are of relatively recent coinages.

I break the aforementioned general hypothesis down into several more specific hypotheses. The first one states that among the twenty most common MWs in modern Mandarin, those with the heart element will be the most common. Table 5.1 provides a very rough gauge of which mind-related terms are commonly used.[4] We can observe that eleven out of twenty of the terms listed either mean "heart" (*xin1*) or possess the heart signific (55%); if the bodily terms "gall bladder" and "chest/bosom/heart" are included, it rises to 65%. Statistically these figures are not impressive. However, the next hypothesis carries more significance: *given the saliency of heart-related concepts for denoting psychologicality,* the number of their associated compounds will be higher than other mind-related logographs among the eleven most common logographs with the heart element.

Calculating the mean of the number of compounds for these eleven logographs give us 64.09 which is noticeably higher than 8.38 for the population of the 307 MW logographs (i.e. 318 minus the number of compounds of the eleven most common logographs) (Table 5.2).

Table 5.1. Top 20 Mind-Word Logographs.

Logograph	Pinyin	Rank among Top 20 MW Logographs[a]	Rank among All Logographs	Individual Raw Frequency	Meaning
心	xin1	1.00	90	392,228	heart, mind
想	xiang3	1.10	99	368,819	think, believe
意	yi4	1.15	104	360,232	idea, meaning, wish, desire
情	qing2	1.33	120	312,900	feeling, emotion, passion, situation
知	zhi1	1.36	123	306,384	know, be aware
認	ren4	2.36	213	191,866	recognize, know, admit
感	gan3	2.70	243	178,383	feel, move, touch, affect
思	si1	3.31	298	144,503	think, consider
望	wang4	3.62	326	133,145	hope, expect
覺	jue2	3.63	327	132,041	thinking, awake, aware
識	shi2	3.77	340	125,220	know, knowledge
念	nian4	5.30	477	85,953	think, read aloud
志	zhi4	6.02	542	75,904	will
巴	ba1	6.06	546	74,917	hope, wish
料	liao4	6.18	557	72,778	expect, anticipate, guess
憙	xi3	7.42	668	58,449	like, enjoy, happy, pleased
慾	yu4	11.61	1,045	28,856	desire, wish, longing, appetite
忘	wang4	11.73	1,056	27,961	forget, overlook, neglect
胆	dan3	15.02	1,352	17,486	gall bladder, courage, guts
胸	xiong1	15.06	1,356	17,392	chest/bosom/ heart/mind/ thorax

Source: From Jun Da's Modern Chinese Character Frequency List (http://lingua.mtsu.edu/chinese-computing). Based on 9,933 logographs and the CEDICT (Chinese–English Dictionary [http://www.mandarintools.com/cedict.html]) and the online HSK word list (http://www.hskhsk.com/word-lists.html). Total number of characters in the corpus: 193,504,018. The number of compounds/idioms were compiled from http://dictionary.writtenchinese.com and http://www.chinese-dictionary.org.

a Rank among all logographs divided by 90.

Table 5.2. Eleven Most Common Logographs with the Heart Element Compared to Other MW Logographs.

11 Most Common MW Logographs		Pinyin	No. of Compounds	Compounds of Other MW Logographs from Dataset App F.8	
1.	心	xin1	268	12.	
2.	想	xiang3	80		
3.	意	yi4	143		
4.	情	qing2	17		
5.	感	gan3	21		
6.	思	si1	66		
7.	念	nian4	32		
8.	志	zhi4	3		
9.	意	xi3	20		
10.	欲	yu4	10		
11.	忘	wang4	45	318.	
			$N = 11$ $\sum = 705$ $M = 64.09$		$N = 307$ $\sum = 2573$ $M = 8.38$

Heart-related Words and Other Mind-Words

The following discussion puts into perspective modern Mandarin's heat-centered psychological lexicon in relation to other MWs. Table 5.3 classifies MW logographs and lists their amount and percentages. Table 5.4 shows the abbreviations for the subcategories used in Table 5.3 (from Dataset App F.8).

Table 5.3. The No. of Mind-Word Logographs by Category.

Category	Subcategory	Subtotals (%)	Total	%
Internal Embodied Experiences	"Heart" (xin1)	1 (0.3144)		
	Heart Signific	167 (52.51)		
			168	52.83
Internal Embodied Experiences without Heart Signific	Other Organs & Body Parts	22 (6.91)		
	Bodily Activities	24 (7.54)		
	Perception	35 (11.00)		
			81	25.47
Internal Entities	Cosmic Energy (qi4)	1 (0.3144)		
	Immortal Soul (hun3)	1 (0.3144)		
	Mortal Soul (po4)	1 (0.3144)		
			3	0.9433
External Entities	Ext-Bodily & Entities	64 (20.12)		
	Spirit-God (shen2)	1 (0.3144)		
	Spirit-Soul (ling2)	1 (0.3144)		
			66	20.75
Total		318 (100%)	318	100%

Table 5.4. Abbreviations for Types of MW Logographs.

Category	Subcategory	Abbreviation
Internal Embodied Experiences	"Heart" (xin1)	HEART
	Heart Signific	HEART SIG
Internal Embodied Experiences without Heart Signific	Other Organs & Bodily Parts	NO HEART-Organs
	Bodily Activities	NO HEART-Bodily
	Perception	NO HEART-Percep
Internal Entities	Cosmic Energy (qi4)	INTER-Cosmic
	Immortal Soul (hun3)	INTER-Immortal
	Mortal Soul (po4)	INTER-Mortal
External Entities	Ext-Bodily & Entities	EXT-Bodily
	Spirit-God (shen2)	EXT-Spirit-God
	Spirit-Soul (ling2)	EXT-Spirit-Soul

Heart (xin1) and logographs with the heart signific are salient. To demonstrate the greater proportionality of heart-related concepts, I first add together the subcategories to form three clusters, i.e. HEART, NO HEART, and EXTERNAL. These groupings can be compared to each other. Table 5.5 enumerates the resulting values: (1) the number of terms in the HEART cluster will significantly outnumber those of NO

HEART and EXTERNAL clusters, and (2) the number of MW compounds/idioms in the HEART cluster outnumber those in the NO HEART and EXTERNAL clusters.

Table 5.5. The No. of MWs and MW Compounds/Idioms by Cluster.

	HEART Heart (xin1) Heart Signific	NO HEART Other Organs & Bodily Parts Bodily Activities Perception Cosmic Energy (qi4) Immortal Soul (hun3) Mortal Soul (po4)	EXTERNAL Ext-Bodily & Entities Spirit-God (shen2) Spirit-Soul (ling2)
No. of Terms	168 (52.83)	84 (26.41)	66 (20.75)
No. of Compounds	1,863 (56.83)	836 (25.00)	579 (17.66)

To what degree is chance a factor in explaining the differences among the number of MWs and MW compounds/idioms in different categories? I utilize the Chi-Square test statistic and propose two hypotheses: the observed distribution of terms and compounds across the three categories of HEART, NO HEART, and EXTERNAL do not occur by chance. As seen in App Calculations 5.1 and 5.2, the results are statistically significant, showing that the distributions are salient.

Hypothesis Log 5.1. Are There Salient Differences between the Number of MWs and between Their Compounds?

Salient Differences among No. of MWs *Refer to* App Calculation 5.1. Differences among No. of MWs Are Salient. Chi-Sq G of F	Yes
Salient Differences among MWs Compounds/Idioms *Refer to* App Calculation 5.2. Differences among MWs Compounds/Idioms Are Salient. Chi-Sq G of F	Yes
	2/2

If HEART and NO HEART are added together to form a larger cluster characterized by terms that are person-centered and embodied (as opposed to terms describing entities outside the person, i.e. EXTERNAL), this new cluster constitutes 79.24% of all MWs and 81.83% of all MW compounds/idioms (Table 5.6).

Table 5.6. Person-Centered and Embodied HEART and NO-HEART Terms.

	HEART + NO HEART = INTERNAL	EXTERNAL Ext-Bodily & Entities Spirit-God (shen2) Spirit-Soul (ling2)
No. of Terms	168 (52.83) + 84 (26.41) = 252 (79.24)	66 (20.75)
No. of Compounds	1,863 (56.83) + 836 (25.00) = 2,699 (81.83)	579 (17.66)

To what degree is chance a factor in explaining the differences among INTERNAL (i.e. embodied) and EXTERNAL categories? I utilize the Chi-Square test statistic and propose two hypotheses: the first concerns the distribution of terms while the second tests compounds across INTERNAL and EXTERNAL categories. As seen in App Calculations 5.3 and 5.4, the results are statistically significant, showing that the distributions are salient and do not occur by chance.

Hypothesis Log 5.2. Internal Terms Significantly Outnumber External Terms.

Salient Distribution of Terms across INTERNAL and EXTERNAL Categories *Refer to* App Calculation 5.3. Observed Distribution of Terms across INTERNAL and EXTERNAL Categories Exists	Yes
Salient Distribution of Compounds across INTERNAL and EXTERNAL Categories: *Refer to* App Calculation 5.4. Observed Distribution of Compounds across INTERNAL and EXTERNAL Categories Exists	Yes
	2/2

Graph 5.1. Types of MWs. Figures Are Means of Number of MWs and MW Compounds. From Table 5.6.

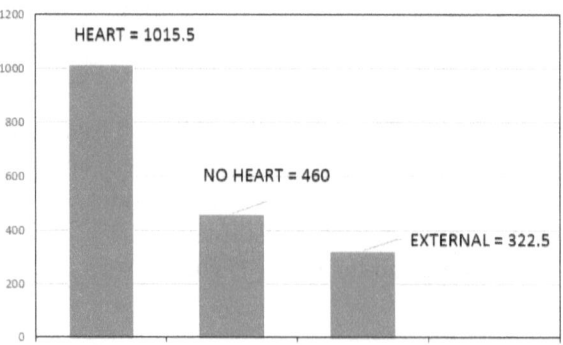

Graph 5.2. EXTERNAL vs. INTERNAL (HEART plus NO HEART) Terms. Figures Are Means of Number of Terms and Compounds. From Table 5.6.

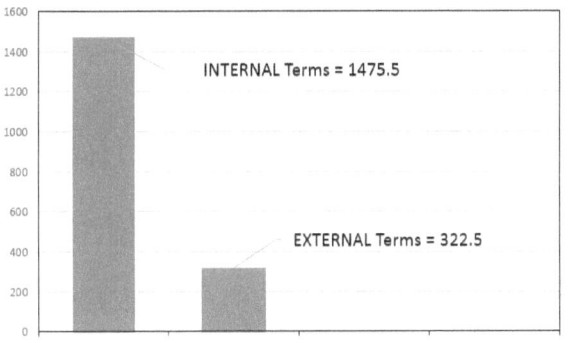

Endnotes

1. Also note that this bodily organ has been extended from its bodily associations to mean anything central, centered, or innermost: magnetic core (*ci2xin1*); lampwick (*deng1xin1*); earth's core (*di4xin1*); heliocentric theory (*ri4xin1shuo1*); concentric (*tong2xin1*); kernel, core (*he2xin1*); and pavilion in the middle of the lake (*hu2xin1ting2*).
2. See Yu (2003) for metaphors of "thinking is seeing."
3. See Yu (2003) for metaphors of "thinking is moving."
4. This frequency list has to be approached very cautiously since it shows single logographs, not compounds, and most spoken Mandarin words are compounds. I disqualified certain words because, though they may function as psychological descriptors, they also might mean something non-psychological in different compounds. Some were simply too ambiguous for inclusion, such as the logograph for *yao1* and *yao4*. Though written the same, the former means demand, ask, request, coerce, while the latter means important, vital, want, going to, must. Finally note that heart (*xin1*), which is ranked 90th (which is number one for my purposes), appears in a number of medical expressions denoting the physical heart itself and terms with "cardio."

Chapter 6

Hallucinations as Superceptions
Hearing Voices as Adaptive Behavior

"Why is 'hearing voices' universal throughout all cultures?" — Julian Jaynes

I had just gone to bed when I heard my father's voice sharply call out my name. I sat up and within a second realized that something was strangely amiss, as I was the only one in the house that night. The voice — clear, unmistakable, and with an echo-like resonance — originated from the living room down the hall from my bedroom. Though this was the first and only time that I distinctly hallucinated a voice (I was probably about eighteen years old), two other similar experiences have stayed with me. A colleague was supposed to pick me up for a dinner engagement at a hotel where I was staying in Durham, North Carolina. Ten, twenty, forty-five minutes passed. I gradually grew impatient and finally annoyed. And then a sentence — "Your life is not your own" — popped into my head, reminding me that in our daily lives our control over events is limited. Not exactly spoken in an audible voice but with a force that was more than a passing thought, the words felt as if they came from somewhere other than my own mind. These very same words would visit me again about a year later, but under very different circumstances.

I must have been 35,000 feet over northern Canada, flying from Tokyo to Newark, NJ. Turbulence was buffeting and rocking an otherwise uneventful and mind-numbingly boring thirteen-hour flight, when suddenly I could have sworn I heard banshee-like noises — screaming winds — coming from outside. Then bumps turned into forceful jolts and the plane began to violently jerk, shudder, and vibrate. I had flown through choppy weather many times before, even severe turbulence, but nothing prepared me for the sickening feeling of being belted into an aircraft that was plummeting like a rock out of the sky. It was as if my body defied gravity; my stomach strained against the seatbelt attached to a plane that was rapidly descending. Thuds, bangs, screams, and other alarming noises filled the cabin. The shaking was so intense that the oxygen masks dropped from the ceiling. And then half-way through the ordeal, that quasi-vocalization—"Your life is not your own"—again nonchalantly rambled across my mind. The words were not reassuring. I suppose a part of my self was just being philosophical under what seemed, at the time, a very dire situation. The experience of a voice, though not orotund, spontaneously arising from the depths of my psyche made me wonder to what degree we have control over the endless train of thoughts that parade across our mental landscape.

Purpose:
Explaining the Mystery of Hallucinations

What does the saliency of hallucinations among the general, non-clinical population indicate? Are hallucinations a matter of loose wires or vestigial neurostructures that under the right circumstances are reactivated? To answer these questions, I first define hallucinations, distinguishing them from pseudohallucinations and illusions. Many assume that hallucinations in and of themselves are psychopathological, but we need to be cautious in confusing causation with what might be called symptoms. The analysis of hallucinations requires highlighting three issues: (1) their prevalence among the non-clinical population; (2) confusing a root cause with accompanying conditions or triggers; and (3) the innateness of hallucinations. As I argue below, hallucinations are expressions of "aptic structures" that once served a socially adaptive function; these are evolved, innate neurological networks plus environmental stimuli that afford certain aptitudes (Jaynes 1976). I integrate what we do know about the basics of the neurology of language, the adaptive advantages of the asymmetrical dual brain, right-side brain activity, and hallucinations. I conclude by noting how some therapists acknowledge that hallucinations are not inherently psychopathological, and that "voice-hearers" should be encouraged to confront their voices as an aspect of their selves. I also suggest that, in order to understand hallucinations, a new terminology is required and that mental imagery, though in some respects quite different from hallucinations, is essentially hallucinatory and the successor to what Jaynes termed bicameral mentality. Taken together, hallucinations and mental imagery (inner quasi-perceptions) constitute "superceptions."

Hallucinations, Pseudohallucinations, and Illusions

The word "hallucination"[1] — or "waking sensory experience having no identified external physical stimulus" (Stevenson 1983: 1609) — was coined by the physician Jean-Étienne Dominique Esquirol (1772–1840) in 1817. He also distinguished between this phenomena and illusions. The DSM-V defines hallucinations as a "perception-like experience with the clarity and impact of a true perception but without the external stimulation of the relevant sensory organ" (American Psychiatric Association 2013). The experient may or may not have insight into the non-veridical nature of the hallucination.

Hallucinations and illusions are sometimes used interchangeably in the literature. They should not be. The latter transpire when an external stimulus is misinterpreted or misperceived. Hallucinations, however, often occur without perceptual triggers. They are not just sensory distortions and do not require external objective sensation. Notably, hallucinations are superimposed over sensory experience, i.e. they happen concurrently with real perceptions. The key features of hallucinations include: (1) appearing as if in objective space (in the physical world, not "in the mind"), i.e. they are externalized or projected, as if they come from outside the person; (2) having the same realistic qualities as actual physical objects; (3) not subject to volitional manipulation; and (4) they are a normal sensory experience from the experient's point of view; the belief that something was veridically perceived is not corrected even in light of other information after the hallucinatory experience.[2] The difference between illusions and hallucinations is actually not always clear-cut, and, in some instances, hallucinations may be triggered by illusions. Pseudohallucinations, sharing features of both hallucinations and illusions, are an intermediate category of experience. However, pseudohallucinations are recognized as not being a veridical experience, i.e. the experient possesses insight into the unreality of the hallucination. Most likely, illusions, pseudohallucinations, and hallucinations form a continuum. Indeed, some contend that hallucinations and pseudohallucinations are not two separate entities but rather sit on a spectrum (Weller and Wiedemann 1989).[3]

Hallucinations can be either elementary, composed of simple percepts, or complex. They may be experienced through one sensory mode (auditory, visual, haptic, gustatory) or multimodal.[4] Auditory verbal hallucinations (AVHs), the most commonly reported in the research literature, may be perceived in the distance, in one's ears, or in one's head or body. AVHs have been characterized as "second person" (a voice directly address the experient); "commanding" (gives authoritative instructions to the experient); "running commentary"; "third person" (two or more voices talk about the experient); or "thought echo" (voices anticipate or repeat the experient's thoughts). Besides audiovisual superceptions, individuals have also described "thought insertion," "thought broadcasting" (or "thought diffusion"), "thought blocking," or "thought extraction." These may qualify as hallucinatory experiences.

The Ubiquity of Hallucinations among the General Population

A surprisingly large number of "normals" experience hallucinations without any detrimental effects. Here we should note that it is likely that many individuals who have hallucinations, due to its association with stigma and mental illness, do not report their experiences. Given that non-clinical populations commonly report hallucinatory experiences, "perhaps the real question should be why are a minority [of those reporting AVHs] pathological?" (Pearson et al. 2008: 637).

Very much related to the ubiquity of hallucinations is their saliency that is evident in ancient religious texts (Jaynes 1976). In this chapter I will not investigate the historical aspect of the problem, but it should at least be mentioned as it involves how pivotal and widespread hallucinations have been throughout human history.

Investigating the prevalence of hallucinations among the general population presents a host of challenges. For one thing, due to an association with mental illness, the very word "hallucination" carries strong negative associations. Consequently, those who have hallucinations may be disinclined from reporting their experiences. Stevenson, who defines hallucinations as "unshared sensory experiences" (1983), asks if we need a new word to replace "hallucination" in order to neutralize its negative meanings. He suggests "idiophany," from the Greek for "private" (*idios*) and "appear" (*phainomai*).[5]

Problems of definition and assessment plague investigations of how common hallucinations are among non-clinical populations,[6] but reported prevalence rates for hallucinations in the general population range from 10% to as high as 25% or from 4.2% to 20.01% (Jardri et al. 2012). Interest in hallucinations has been a topic of modern Psychological research since the late 1800s. Francis Galton argued that hallucinations occurred at the extreme end of a continuum, with mental imagery in the middle, and a complete absence of imagery at the other end (1883). Between 1889 to 1892 Sidgwick et al. (1894) surveyed 17,000 adults in England, Russia, and Brazil and reported prevalence rates of 8% and 12% among men and women, respectively (9.9% and 6.9% adjusted for sleep-related phenomena). 3.6% claimed they heard human voices.[7] To their credit, the researchers went to great efforts to eliminate false positives. More modern studies have reported relatively high rates. West (1948) noted 8.0% (N = 1519), and in what might be termed the first modern study, McKellar (1968) found that 25% (N = 125) of normals experienced hallucinations at least once in their lives. In a more recent study, Johns et al. determined that 4% of normal "white respondents" (N = 2,800) hallucinated (1998).

In a review of seventeen surveys from nine countries, Beavan, Read, and Cartwright (2011) note that hallucinations are not only experienced by psychiatric patients; voice-hearing is neither rare nor a meaningless symptom of mental illness. Though making comparisons is problematic because of differences in definitions and methodologies, Beavan, Read, and Cartwright (2011) reviewed 17 studies conducted between 1894 and 2007. Prevalence rates range from 0.6% to 84%, with a mean of 19.5% (SD = 24.71). They suggest that their findings support the movement away from pathological models of hallucinations to appreciating how voice-hearing is occurring in the general population. They also contend that hallucinations possess meaning for the voice-hearer.

In a large-scale study that investigated the prevalence of visual, auditory, olfactory, and somatic hallucinations, Tien (1991) used data from the National Institute of Mental Health's Epidemiologic Catchment Area Program (between 1980 and 1984). The ECA surveyed New Haven, Baltimore, Durham, St. Louis, and Los Angeles, and relied on the NIMH Diagnostic Interview Schedule (DIS) from the DSM-III. Prevalence rates were 13.0% (N = 18,572), 11.1% (follow-up data one year later, N = 15,258), and 4.6% (new incidence at follow-up, N = 13,622). 1.5% to 3.2% claimed they experienced AVHs. Gender differences were apparent: visual hallucinations were higher in males (about 20 per 1000 per year) than females (about 13 per 1000 per year). For males, auditory hallucinations peaked at age 25–30, while for females the peak was at age 40–50. The most consistent finding was an increase in hallucinations due to age-related disorders (e.g. sensory loss).

In another large-scale investigation, Ohayon sampled the general population of the United Kingdom, Germany, and Italy aged 15 years or older (N = 13,057) to delineate the variety of experiences (visual, auditory, olfactory, haptic, gustatory, out-of-body experiences, hypnagogic, and hypnopompic hallucinations) (2000). Ohayon found that 38.7% reported hallucinatory experiences (19.6% less than once in a month; 6.4% monthly; 2.7% once a week; and 2.4% more than once a week). Though many hallucinatory experiences were associated with mental illness or other pathologies, the prevalence of hallucinations in non-clinical populations is "not negligible." Ohayon also notes that daytime auditory and visual hallucinations are correlated with a greater risk of psychiatric disorders (2000).

Hill and Linden (2013) examined 14 studies[8] and found that voices are more positive, less frequent, less disruptive, and less distressing among non-clinical populations and that in clinical populations voice-hearing seems linked to negative life experiences. They also suggest that the brain circuitry of hallucinations involve the same specific sensory pathways that are recruited for the analysis of external stimuli.

Hallucinations among University Students

Several studies indicate relatively high numbers of university students experiencing hallucinations. Some studies report students who heard voices were not troubled by the experiences, though those diagnosed with schizophrenia were greatly distressed by the voices (Bentall and Slade 1985; Young et al. 1986; Kendell 1985). Posey and Losch (1983) claim that their study of college students supports Jaynes's hypotheses about bicamerality. They report that 71% (N = 374) claimed to have had brief auditory hallucinations during wakeful situations (interviews and Minnesota Multiphasic Inventory results suggested these accounts are not pathological). They describe five types of hallucinatory experiences: (1) hypnagogic and hypnopompic events; (2) hearing a voice call one's name when alone; (3) hearing one's thoughts spoken aloud; (4) hearing a comforting or advising voice; and (5) holding a conversation with a voice.

Feelgood and Rantzen (1994) administered the Launay-Slade Hallucination Scale (LSHS; designed to measure the predisposition to hallucinate among non-clinical populations) to university students (N = 136) who were also requested to complete an auditory task that utilized non-hypnotic suggestion and ambiguous stimuli. The "high LSHS group" reported a significantly greater number of meaningful visual and auditory experiences in response to ambiguous stimulation. Though one could argue that higher vividness of imagery among the high LSHS scorers may not be genuine hallucinations, Feelgood and Rantzen (1994) contend that they are in fact hallucinations.

Barrett and Etheridge (1992) conducted two studies. They used the verbal hallucination scale developed by Posey and Losch (1983) plus several instruments to assess social conformity. The first study was among 19 male and 586 females college students (N = 605), of which a "large minority" reported hallucinations that were not related to psychopathology. On some of the questions their findings were consistent with Posey and Losch's (1983) as well as Pearson et al.'s (2008) research (N = 496) (Table 6.1).

Table 6.1. Comparison of Research Findings on Two Items.

	Barrett & Etheridge (1992)	Posey & Losch (1983)	Pearson et al. (2008)
Heard one's own thoughts spoken aloud	37.1%	38.9%	41.1% & 49.1%, adolescent & adults, respectively
Heard one's own name when alone in the house	32.8%	36%	31.2% & 30.8%, adolescent & adults, respectively

López-Rodrigo et al. (1997) contend that hallucinations exists on one end of a continuum of normal conscious experience that include vivid imagery and daydreams. They asked college students (N = 222) to fill in the Hallucination Questionnaire (Barrett and Etheridge 1993; 1994), the Betts QMI Vividness of Imagery Scale (Richardson 1969), and Millon's Clinical Multiaxial Inventory (MCMI-II; Millon 1983). Compared to non-hallucinators, hallucinators experience more vivid imagery and score higher on most Millon's Inventory scales. However, a normal distribution of the hallucinatory experiences was not apparent, which raises questions about the dimensionality of hallucinations.

Using the Revised Hallucination Scale (RHS), Cangas, Langer, and Moriana (2011) analyzed a non-clinical population of Spanish university students (N = 265) in order to describe the participants' meaning of their associated beliefs. Four factors, made up of six types of beliefs (personal difficulties, psychological explanations, dreamlike experiences, vivid thoughts, perceptive distortions, and personal desires), explain 52.8% of the variance.

The figures in Table 6.2, which list percentages of individuals from the general population who experienced hallucinations, are borrowed from Beavan, Read, and Cartwright (2011) with two more additional studies. Among 72,347 individuals from all studies, 10.90% (7,888.22 individuals) experienced hallucinations. That almost eleven percent of the population claim to have experienced hallucinations is an intriguing datum. The mean of the percentages of those who hallucinated for the 19 studies is 20.94.

Table 6.2. Studies of Hallucinations in the General Population.

Study	No. of Participants	% Who Hallucinated	No. Who Hallucinated
Sidgwick et al. (1894)	17,000	3.6%	612.00
West (1948)	1,519	8.0%	121.52
McKellar (1968)	125	25.0%	31.25
Johns et al. (1998)	2,800	4.0%	112.00
Tien (1991)	18,572	1.5%–3.2% [2.4%][a]	445.73
Ohayon (2000)	13,057	38.7%	5053.05
Posey & Losch (1983)	374	71.0%	265.54
Rees (1971)	293	13.3%	38.97
Jocano (1971)	2,000	13.3%	266.00
Bentall & Slade (1985)	136	15.4%	20.94
Young et al. (1986)	204	13.2%	26.93
Barrett & Etheridge (1992)	345	45.0%	155.25
Grimby (1993)	50	30.0%	15.00
Verdoux et al. (1998)	462	16.0%	73.92
Millham & Easton (1998)	55	84.0%	46.20
Johns et al. (2002)	7,849	1.1%	86.34
Dhossche et al. (2002)	796	2.3%	18.31
Caspi et al. (2005)	803	3.4%	27.30
Shevlin, Dorahy, & Adamson (2007)	5,907	8.3%	490.28
	Σ = 72,347	Σ = 398 N = 19 M = 20.94	Σ = 7,888.22 10.90% total

[a] Mean of 1.5% and 3.2% = 2.4%.

Hallucinations and Imaginary Playmates

Some researchers discern a possible linkage between hallucinations and imaginary playmates, though commentary on this linkage deserves another chapter. But here it suffices to mention the connections and point to a number of recent studies.[9] Bass (1983) adopts a psychoanalytic approach and focuses on the normal development of ego in an adult's imaginary companion (see also Connolly 1991). Taylor, Cartwright, and Carlson (1993) point out that, though many recognize the unreality of their imaginary (hallucinated) playmates, some do not and that these may constitute full-blown hallucinations. Trujillo et al. (1996) discern a normal to pathologic continuum of boys with imaginary companions and dissociative identity disorder/multiple personality disorder. Pearson et al. (2001) found that 46.2% of normal children aged 5 to 12 years (N = 1800) had imaginary companions, a phenomenon that is more common among girls than boys and not restricted to the very young.[10] Pearson, Burrow, FitzGerald, Green, Lee, and Wise (2001) also suggest that hallucinatory experiences may be linked to imaginary companions.

Confusing Cause with Accompanying Conditions and Triggers

Various causes have been given for hallucinations: schizophrenia, schizoaffective disorder, dementia; affective and mood disorders; borderline personality; dissociative disorders; disorders of sense organs (e.g. negative scotoma); sensory deprivation (e.g. black patch disease in cataract surgery, enucleation); structural lesions of the visual pathways; lesions (tumors; infarcts); epilepsy; migraines; disorders of the central nervous system (e.g. temporal lobe epilepsy); hallucinogens, alcohol, and abuse of other substances; Parkinson's disease; hearing impairment; and strong suggestion while under hypnosis (Weller and Wiedemann 1989). Intense emotions, fatigue, and exhaustion have also been associated with hallucinations.

Bentall (1990) reviews various explanations of hallucinations: conditioning (learned behavior); seepage of normally pre-conscious material into consciousness; failure of disinhibitory processes; abnormally vivid mental imagery; subvocalization theories ("inner speech" is experienced as alien experience). He suggests that hallucinations result from a failure of the metacognitive skills involved in discriminating between self-generated and external sources of information or between imaginary and real events (Bentall 1990). Larøi et al. (2012) enumerate the characteristic features of AVHs in clinical and non-clinical groups, noting that they are not a unitary entity and heterogeneous. Therefore, multiple models are needed and they call for careful phenomenological investigations. Jones (2010) reviews different theories of AVHs, such as inner speech and intrusions from memory. He examines the phenomenological fit of cognitive and neurological models and asks if we need multiple models and subcategorizations of AVHs since different neurocognitive mechanisms might underlie their presentation. McCarthy-Jones et al. (2012) provide a phenomenological survey of the types, qualities, and content of hallucinated voices among a psychiatric population diagnosed with schizophrenia (N = 199; 81%). They note that different underlying neurocognitive mechanisms demand different clinical interventions and therapies.

Diederen et al. (2011: 1079–80) list four theoretical models. The first is the most influential: AVHs result when the experient fails to recognize that such phenomena are self-generated "inner speech." The focus for this hypothesis is the activation of left frontal and temporoparietal areas during AVHs, which has consistently been implicated in linguistic production and perception. For example, in a thorough review of methods, subjects, experimental designs, and neurological activation patterns associated with hallucinations, Allen et al. (2008) present a neuroanatomic model that accounts for "erroneous precepts" and dysfunction in the prefrontal premotor cingulate, subcortical, and cerebellar regions that seem to contribute to hallucinatory experiences. This dysfunction involves "top-down" and "bottom-up" networks that lead to an "experience of externality." However, they do not explain why the human neurological apparatus is able to produce hallucinations in the first place. At a more general level, the "failure-to-recognize-self-generated-inner-speech" model cannot explain activation of right hemisphere frontal and temporoparietal regions that are regularly observed in AVHs. Moreover, what exactly is "inner speech"?

A second model hypothesizes that AVHs result from the release of language activity in the right hemisphere, which is usually inhibited in the normal brain. While right hemisphere frontal and temporoparietal areas are not considered classic language regions, studies have shown that the right hemisphere can generate non-propositional or "automatic" language, such as overly learned sequences of low linguistic complexity. In a third model AVHs result from aberrant activation of the primary auditory cortex (in their own study, Diederen et al. [2011] found no support for this theory). In the final model, AVHs emerge from memory, leading to the re-experience of previously encoded information. Perhaps memory recollections that precede AVHs trigger activations in language-related areas are responsible for the experience of the actual AVHs. However, no activation of regions implicating memory processing has been evident, at least according to Diederen et al. (2011).

Loose Wires or Innate Structures?

I submit that the aforementioned accounts of the "why" of hallucinations fall under the category of "loose-wiring." Besides confusing hallucinations with distorted sensory perceptions, many of the aforementioned "causes" are just descriptions or accounts of circumstances or accompanying conditions under which hallucinations transpire or are triggered; *they are not explanations.*[11] Not a few studies acknowledge that non-clinical populations do experience hallucinations, but the underlying assumption seems to be that, while hallucinations may be benign in certain circumstances, they result from some type of dysfunction.[12] Other researchers utilize a non-clinical population as a control group in order to better understand the pathological aspects of hallucinations. In principle there is nothing wrong with this. After all, to the extent that hallucinations interfere with daily functioning or harass an individual they are, of course, abnormal (Appendix G).

I propose that we must carefully differentiate between (1) elicitors (which may or may not be psychopathological) and (2) the innate ability to experience hallucinations. An analogy might be assuming that since speech is part of coprolalia, speech itself is abnormal. I contend that hallucinations in and of themselves are not abnormal and can be understood as operating in two modes. In the first or "potential" mode they are culturally "turned off": latent, dormant, and inactive, the sociocultural environment discourages their expression. In the second or "engaged" mode, they become, due to any number of reasons, "turned on." When activated, they usually manifest themselves without harmful effects. However, psychopathological conditions can exacerbate the presentations of engaged hallucinations. However, such negatory hallucinations are not the cause of dysfunction, but rather a symptom.

Hallucinations are most likely engaged neurological networks that result from "aptic structures." These are the basis of innate, evolved aptitudes *plus* the results of experience (i.e. enculturation). For Jaynes these organizations of the brain are "meant to replace such problematic words as instincts." Aptic structures "make the organism apt to behave in a certain way under certain conditions" (Jaynes 1976: 31). Language is probably an array of aptic structures.

The Basics of the Neurology of Language

Neurologically, human language is produced and processed in the "dominant" left hemisphere. Left-hemisphere dominance for language is evident in 95% of right-handed people. Matters are more complicated for left-handed people, among whom 60% have left-hemisphere dominance but about 19% have right-hemisphere dominance for language, while about 20% have bilateral language functions. The corpus callosum links the two hemispheres, while the anterior commissure connects the two temporal lobes. A number of brain regions are involved in language production and comprehension, the best known being Broca's area, Wernicke's area (the arcuate fasciculus links Broca's and Wernicke's areas), the supplementary motor cortex, and the auditory cortex.

The first, Broca's area, is involved in articulation, vocabulary, inflection, grammar, and directs muscle movements involved in speech. The second, Wernicke's area, is involved in vocabulary, syntax, meaning, and speech comprehension. There is some debate concerning the exact location of Wernicke's area, but generally this region adjoins the auditory complex on the Sylvian fissure (where the temporal and parietal lobes meet and is represented as the posterior part of

Brodmann area 22). The third area is the supplementary motor cortex and is mostly involved in articulation (Chart 6.1).

Chart 6.1. Key Language Areas of the Brain.

Major Area	Name of Regions	Brodmann's Areas
Broca's	Left frontal lobe, in inferior frontal gyrus	
	Pars opercularis	44: Afferent connections from motor, somatosensory, inferior parietal regions
	Pars triangularis	45: Receives afferent connections from prefrontal cortex, superior temporal gyrus, superior temporal sulcus
Wernicke's	Left temporal lobe, posterior section of superior temporal gyrus; encircles auditory cortex on Sylvian fissure	22 (posterior part): some branches extend around posterior section of lateral sulcus in parietal lobe
Auditory Cortex	Bilateral, superior temporal plane, comprising parts of Heschl's gyrus & superior temporal gyrus	41, 42, partially 22
Supplementart Motor Cortex	Bilateral, top of left frontal lobe	6

Research by Binder et al. (1997) demonstrated the complexity of pinning down the language areas of the brain. They found evidence of localization that is less consistent with the classic models of language production: (1) the existence of left hemisphere temporoparietal language areas outside the traditional Wernicke's area, namely, in the middle temporal, inferior temporal, fusiform, and angular gyri (approximately Brodmann areas 21, 20, 36, 37, and 39, respectively); (2) extensive left prefrontal language areas outside the classic Broca's area; and (3) clear participation of these left frontal areas in a task emphasizing "receptive" language functions. The large temporoparietal regions in the left hemisphere, then, probably play a significant role in comprehension at a linguistic-semantic level. These areas include, but may not be limited to, the angular gyrus, middle temporal gyrus, inferior temporal gyrus, and fusiform gyrus.

For our purposes it is the homologs of Broca's and Wernicke's areas in the right hemisphere that deserve focus. Note that while both hemispheres can understand language, only the left can speak. Moreover, the right hemisphere is superior to the left for processing aspects of linguistics that are indispensable for understanding emotional intent, e.g. inflectional nuances such as intensity, stress, melody, intonation, timbre, and cadence. It is at this point that some attention to cerebral asymmetry will provide perspective on the function of language and hallucinations.

Adaptive Advantages of the Asymmetrical Dual Brain

Studies investigating AVHs typically utilize functional magnetic resonance imaging (fMRI) to detect activation in the language production/perception regions of the left hemisphere during hallucinations. However, activation of right hemispheric regions should be contextualized within what is known about the duality of the brain. For centuries it has been recognized that the human brain possesses two parts. But in 1844 the English physician Arthur Wigan (1785–1847) published *The Duality of the Mind* (1985) in which he argued that if we have two brains (hemispheres), then we have two minds. These two neurological components "must occasionally be discrepant when influenced by disease, either direct, sympathetic, or reflex" (1884: 201–02). It would not be until the pioneering "split-brain" research of the 1950s (Gazzaniga 1970; Sperry 1974) that the significance of Wigan's thinking became appreciated. It was experimentally shown that if the corpus callosum was severed (the neurological bridge that transfers sensory, perceptual, motor, and gnostic information between the two hemispheres), surprising aspects of interhemispheric communication were revealed — the left specializes in logical, analytic functions, while the right concentrates on analogical, holistic processes.

One person, one brain, one mind. The relation between these three entities seems obviously straightforward. But in fact, given that input from paired external organs which is dually processed by two hemispheres, a mystery surrounds the question as to why we do not perceive objects doubly (Puccetti 1993: 675). Usually, though it certainly seems that two hemispheres subserve a single mind, experiments on those who have had their corpus callosum severed demonstrate that, for certain purposes, it makes little sense to assume that we only have one mind. Split-brain research shows that each hemisphere, despite having access to sensory information from only the contralateral half of space, nevertheless somehow perceives a whole stimulus and functions as if it is programmed to "believe" that it possesses rules to guide its construction of a model of the world. Each hemisphere, then, completes the stimulus it receives by hallucinating the missing portion of the perceptual field (Levy 1977: 267).

We are a "complex minded entity" (Puccetti 1993: 679). Could it be that the two hemispheres are the "biological substrate of *two persons,* each of which has *one mind*" (Puccetti 1993: 679, emphasis in original)? Was there a time when each individual possessed two "persons" who communicated with each other? Note that some neuroscientists and philosophers postulate a non-unitary concept of mind, e.g. a "society of mind," "modularity," and "cognitive homunculi" (Cavanna et al. 2007).

Why might different parts of our neurological apparatus be dedicated to certain tasks, especially given Mother Nature's predilection to build redundancy into organisms? The answer is to be found in the evolutionary and comparative study of animal behavior and the role of the nervous system (i.e. neuroethology). As Vallortigara and Rogers point out, capacities are generally not lateralized in the animal kingdom. However, for some species lateralization enhances cognitive capacities. More specifically, asymmetrical brains can increase the chances of survival for a species.[13] For neuroethological reasons, the preferential use of the left or right visual hemifield during activities such as the search for food, agonistic responses, and escape from predators can be advantageous (2005). Such specialization has been found in fish, reptiles, birds, as well as mammals. The left hemisphere focuses on classifying information and governs mundane, routine activities, while the right hemisphere controls responses to emergencies, novelty, and unexpected events.

In his discussion of the adaptive consequences of cerebral asymmetry, Levy (1977) argues that the functional asymmetry of the human brain is a biological adaptation that developed in a social milieu. Beginning with the very basics, he notes that in the brains of bilateria—organisms with two-sided symmetry, i.e. they have a front and back, as well as an upside and downside—bimorphic structures mirror organs on the left and right, reflecting the general bilateral symmetry of the body as a whole. More specifically in the case of higher-order mammalians, Levy believes that cerebral asymmetry is capable of dealing not just with the immediate environment, but also with unseen distal spatial regions, as well as being able to plan better since not only can the organism learn from the past, but the future can be imagined (1997: 266–67). Even more specifically, human brain asymmetry appears to be a recent evolutionary attempt at "de-duplication" of function. This allows the utilization of all 1300 cc of the brain mass, instead of just half that much, to construct our spatio-temporal worlds (Levy 1997: 269). In other words, the lateral asymmetry of the brain almost doubles its cognitive power. Evolutionary forces have reduced unnecessary redundancy and extended space for new functions (Gazzaniga 2005a). This asymmetry arose as a response to specifically social selective pressures. Mutually interdependent, each hemisphere served to increase the fitness of the species by the contribution of specific skills (Levy 1997: 271).

Despite cerebral specialization, interhemispheric communication must transpire in order for the organism to function as one entity. The corpus callosum plays an integrative role, serving as the great communication link between redundant systems. "Lateral specialization reflects the emergence of new skills" and the retention of others; in other words, pre-existing capabilities could be jettisoned as new functions developed in one hemisphere (Gazzaniga 2005b: 1294).

Right-Side Brain Activity and Hallucinations

If Jaynes is correct that the right hemisphere houses aptic structures evolved to produce hallucinations now disengaged by the force of socialization, then we should still be able to detect cerebral activity on the right side of the brain during hallucinations. Cavanna et al. (2007) note that functional neuroimaging findings seem to confirm the theory that the right middle temporal gyrus is the source of hallucinations in at least some schizophrenic patients. The findings are suggestive but inconsistent. This may be due to individual variation, timing of the scan to the exact onset of the hallucinations, motion artifacts, the effects of anti-psychotic medication, or other confounding variables (Kuijsten 2009). In this section I look at the evidence that hallucinations and right-side brain activity correlate. But first, to set the stage, some discussion of the relation between the two hemispheres is in order.

Neurocultural Organization and Interhemispheric Integration

In a piece on neuroimaging, auditory hallucinations, and the bicameral mind, Sher (2000) cites Olin (1999) to support his views on Jaynes, who argued that neuroimaging studies have confirmed Jaynes's theories. Olin borrowed findings from Lennox et al. (1999) and Dierks et al. (1999) to make his case. Building upon split-brain research and inspired by Jaynes's theories, Nasrallah offered evidence for how unintegrated right hemispheric cognition is interpreted as an "alien intruder" in schizophrenics (1985). His arguments concern, I contend, how culture can socialize us to either inhibit or disinhibit communication among different components of our mental machinery, thereby forming different patterns of neurocultural organization adapted to a historical period.

In bicameral times, right hemispheric speech areas sent voice-volitions, via the anterior commissure, to the corresponding areas in the left hemisphere. The default relation between the two hemispheres was one of disinhibition. Due to sociopolitical forces, this disinhibitory state had to be overcome, and individuals gradually learned a new, more efficient post-bicameral neurocultural arrangement. In post-bicameral settings individuals are raised to believe that within their bodies (usually the chest or head) exists a "space" occupied by an executive, unitary self. An important part of this belief system is how culture trains the left hemisphere to not register the reception and transmission of thoughts, intentions, and feelings between itself and the right hemisphere. This inhibition of aptic structures designed to produce hallucinations maintains the unity of the right and left hemispheres. The result of this new mentality is that the left hemisphere (for most of us) is linguistically-dominant; it is the verbally expressive "spokesperson" self that has been taught that it alone is in charge (note that now the right hemisphere can understand but cannot produce speech). In fact perceptuo-cognitive inputs from both the left and right hemispheres constitute part of the same self, regardless of what the "spokesperson" left hemisphere may tell itself.

Under certain conditions, the culturally-imposed inhibition of communication of right-hemispheric activity breaks down. In schizophrenia (and in benign dissociative states, such as most forms of spirit possession), defective interhemispheric integration occurs (which is probably neurochemical in nature). This leads to disinhibition of the awareness by the left hemisphere that it is being "influenced" by an unknown "external force," which is in fact the right hemisphere. An individual can function with "two anatomically communicating but neurochemically unintegrated" spheres of consciousness (Nasrallah 1985: 275) (though note that the two hemispheres, even in split-brain patients, are extensively connected at the subcortical level).

Nasrallah argues that schizophrenia is associated with a left-hemispheric dysfunction, a weakening of hemisphereic dominance, and a shift of laterality. It involves the experience of "nonself" and "alien" information from an external source. The consequences are Schneiderian first rank symptoms:[14] (1) delusion of influence from outside; (2) somatic passivity; (3) thought withdrawal; (4) thought insertion; (5) thought broadcasting; (6) "made" feelings; (7) "made" impulses; (8) "made" volitional acts; (9) delusional perception; and (10) specific auditory hallucinations (audible thoughts, voices arguing, voices commenting on actions) (cited in Nasrallah 1985: 275). Abnormal lateralization implicates vestiges of an earlier, adaptive mentality. Interestingly, in findings that correspond with Jaynes's views, Diederen et al. (2010) found that decreased language lateralization characterizes psychosis, *not* auditory hallucinations.

Mitchell and Crow (2005) review evidence that supports the view that right hemisphere language functions are central to social communication and argue that the primary problem in psychosis is the desegregation of right and left hemispheric functions.[15] As they point out, schizophrenics perform poorly on tests of discourse planning/ comprehension, understanding humor, sarcasm, metaphors, indirect requests, and the generation/comprehension of emotional prosody. These right-hemispheric specializations are crucial to appreciating communicative intent and thus facilitate social interaction. Speculating that schizophrenia and language have a common origin in genetic changes some 100,000 to 150,000 years ago that configured this feature, they offer a bi-hemispheric theory of the neurology of language, stressing the part played by the *Homo sapiens*-specific "cerebral torque" in which the right frontal and left posterior poles of the two hemispheres are larger. This neuroanatomical feature of the human brain has implications for the origins of language and the typical symptoms of schizophrenia. According to this model, each of the four quadrants possesses a distinct function: the "phonological loop has motor and sensory components focusing on Broca's and Wernicke's areas, respectively, and the visuospatial sketchpad likewise has a sensory component in right occipito-temporo-parietal cortex and a motor component in right dorso-lateral prefrontal cortex" (Mitchell and Crow 2005: 973). Information typically flows from left occipito-temporo-parietal to right occipito-temporo-parietal to right dorso-lateral prefrontal to left dorso-lateral prefrontal. But any "back-flow" or leakage of neural activity from the right dorso-lateral prefrontal cortex into right occipito-temporo-pareital cortex possibly ends up presenting abnormal input to the left hemisphere.

In an examination of cognitive and neural processes in non-clinical auditory hallucinations, Barkus et al. (2007) administered the Oxford Liverpool Inventory of Feelings and Experiences (O-LIFE) to assess schizotypy and the Launay-Slade Hallucination Scale (LSHS) to 1,206 individuals. From this group were selected 63 participants who completed the Schizotypal Personality Questionnaire (SPQ) and a semi-structured interview to assess substance use and the presence or history of major depression or psychotic disorder. The participants, based on their scores, were divided into three groups: high (N = 30), medium (N = 15), or low (N = 18) on hallucination proneness. The groups then completed an auditory signal detection task designed to elicit verbal hallucinations. From the high-hallucination prone group subjects (N = 8) who produced a large number of false alarm responses (interpreted as non-clinical hallucinations) were selected to repeat the task during functional MRI.

For the signal detection experiment, four results were determined for each participant: (1) hit—positive responses when a voice is present;

(2) correct rejections — negative responses when a voice was not present; (3) misses — negative responses when a voice was presented; (4) false alarms — positive responses when a voice was not present (the phenomena under investigation). Results showed that participants highly prone to hallucinations reported more false perceptions of voices under conditions of stimulus ambiguity during the signal detection test. Two subtractions were made: (1) false alarms minus correct rejections — to examine areas activated by hallucination-like phenomena; (2) false alarms minus hits — to examine areas activated by hallucination-like phenomena in addition to areas activated by hearing a voice which was present. One-sample t-test was used. Z scores above 3.09 were taken to be significant (approximating to p = 0.001 level of uncorrected significance). For false alarms minus correct rejections, right-side activations were 75%; for false alarms minus hits, right-side activations were 37.5%. If false alarms minus correct rejections and false alarms minus hits are added together, activation on the right side is 50%.

Barkus et al. (2007) concluded that those in the non-clinical population who reported AVHs during functional MRI displayed cerebral activity patterns similar to those of schizophrenics experiencing AVHs. The four areas of activation included: right middle temporal gyrus, bilateral fusiform gyrus, and the right putamen. Significantly, areas on the right side of the brain were activated 50% of the time, though this number increases to 75% for "false alarms minus correct rejections" (Table 6.3). Barkus et al. (2007) also noted that for individuals to be prone to false perceptions more than high schizotypy scores are required. As they point out, from the study in question it was not possible to determine what the additional factors might be. Could it be something we all share? Aptic structures that have been culturally disengaged?

Table 6.3. Activity in Brain Regions and False Alarms.[a]

Brain Region	R = Right, L = Left
False alarms minus correct rejections	
Middle temporal gyrus	R
Fusiform gyrus[b]	L, R
Putamen[c]	
	R
False alarms minus hits	
Superior frontal gyrus	R, L
Middle frontal gyrus	L
Cingulate gyrus	R

Superior temporal gyrus	L, L
Middle temporal gyrus	L
Cerebellum	R

ᵃ Borrowed and modified from Barkus et al. (2007: 79).
ᵇ Part of the temporal lobe and occipital lobe (Brodmann area 37).
ᶜ A round structure located at the base of the forebrain (telencephalon).

Using PET (positron-emission tomography) scans, Buchsbaum et al. (1982) examined cerebral glucography (local cerebral uptake of deoxyglucose labeled with fluorine 18) in schizophrenics (N = 8) and in age-matched normal volunteers (N = 6). The schizophrenics showed lower ratios in the frontal cortex (suggesting relatively lower glucose use than the control subjects) as well as increased glucose uptake in the right temporal lobe, indicating increased brain activity in this part of the brain among schizophrenics with AVHs.

While it is assumed that AVHs are a key characteristic of schizophrenia, they also occur in non-psychotic individuals in the absence of a psychiatric or neurological disorder or substance abuse. In order to discern if AVHs elicit similar brain activation in psychotic and non-psychotic individuals, Diederen et al. (2011) utilized a conjunction analysis using 3T (fMRI) scanning. Subjects included non-psychotic subjects with AVHs (N = 21) and matched psychotic patients (N = 21) (10 = schizophrenia; 2 = schizoaffective disorders; 9 = psychosis not otherwise specified). During the experience of AVHs a number of areas of activation were observed for the psychotic and non-psychotic subjects: bilateral inferior frontal gyri, insula, superior temporal gyri, supramarginal gyri and postcentral gyri, left precentral gyrus, inferior parietal lobule, superior temporal pole, and right cerebellum. Interestingly, significant differences in AVH-related neural activity were not evident between the groups. A 2-sample t-test was employed to discover possible differences in AVH-related activation between the groups. No significant differences in activation during AVHs between the groups was revealed. Also, no significant differences in lateralization indices were observed between non-psychotic individuals (mean = –0.09; SD = 0.29; range = 1.36) and the psychotic individuals (mean = –0.04; SD = 0.18; range = 1.67). The researchers concluded that the AVH-related activation of multiple common areas in psychotic and non-psychotic individuals implicates the involvement of the same cortical network in both groups. 3 out of the 7 brain regions that displayed activation were on the right side (42.85%) during AVHs (Table 6.4).

Table 6.4. Brain Region Activated during AVHs.[a]

Side	Brain Region Activated
Left	Postcentral gyrus/supramarginal gyrus
Left	Precentral gyrus/superior temporal gyrus
Left	Inferior parietal lobule
Right	Superior temporal gyrus/inferior frontal gyrus/insula
Left	Inferior frontal gyrus/insula/superior temporal gyrus/superior temporal pole
Right	Postcentral gyrus/supramarginal gyrus
Right	Cerebellum

[a] From Diederen et al. (2011: 1079).

For Dierks et al. (1999), AVHs, supposedly a common trait of mental illness, can inform us about what they refer to as "internally generated sensory perceptions" that are attributed to external sources. In a study of paranoid schizophrenic patients (N = 3) and relying on functional MRI, the researchers discerned activation in Heschl's gyrus (transverse temporal gyri; in the primary auditory cortex within the lateral sulcus, Brodmann's area 41) during AVHs. Right-side brain regions were activated 11 out 23 times (47.83%) (Table 6.5).

Table 6.5. Brain Areas Activated during AVHs.[a]

Patients	Frontal Operculum	Posterior Superior Temporal Gyrus	Middle Temporal Gyrus	Hippocampus	Amygdala	Sensorimotor Cortex
1: Session 1	Left		Left	Left		Right
1: Session 2	Left	Left		Left	Left	
	Right			Right	Right	Right
2			Right		Right	Right
3	Left	Left	Left	Left	Left	
				Right	Right	Right

[a] Dierks et al. (1999: 619).

Dierks et al. (1999) speculated that increased activity in the primary auditory cortex during AVHs may account for why hallucinations, unlike auditory imagery or "inner speech," are experienced as real. The prominent activation of classic speech production areas is suggestive of processes related to inner speech. However, important differences should be noted: inner speech is not perceived to arise from external influences and does not activate Heshcl's gyrus.

Using fMRI scans to determine areas of hallucinatory activation, Sommer et al. (2007) applied low-frequency repetitive transcranial magnetic stimulation (rTMS) to the left temporoparietal areas of a medication-resistant group (effect size of 0.76).[16] The group consisted of male schizophrenia patients (N = 15). Twelve treatments were successful. Hallucinatory activation was predominantly within the left temporoparietal areas for four patients. For five patients it was in the right-sided temporopareital areas, and for three it was located deep within the contralateral homolog of Broca's area. Thus, most patients (8 out of 12; 66.7%) had predominantly right-sided hallucinatory activity.

In an article published in *Schizophrenia Bulletin* (Sommer et al., 2010), scores from around 4,000 respondents to a website questionnaire (a version of the Launay-Slade Hallucination Scale) led to the identification of a group of 103 people who had genuine voice-hearing experiences but no psychopathology. The 42 people who were scanned in the new study were selected from this larger sample, and matched to data from an existing fMRI dataset from psychiatric patients with a range of disorders (including schizophrenia, schizoaffective disorder, and psychosis not otherwise specified). To be included, participants had to have had at least four AVH experiences during the 8-minute scan period, with a minimum total duration of fifty seconds. Participants indicated when they were hearing a voice by squeezing a balloon and releasing it when the voice stopped. The results of these analyses were rather simple: in both groups, the areas that were expected to activate mostly did activate. There were no differences in activation *between* the groups, however, leading the researchers to conclude that non-clinical and clinical AVHs do not differ in terms of their underlying neural activation.

In an article whose title succinctly expresses their findings— "Auditory Verbal Hallucinations Predominantly Activate the *Right* Inferior Frontal Area"—Sommer et al. (2008, emphasis in original) used fMRI to measure cerebral activation among psychotic patients (N = 24) (schizophrenia, schizoaffective disorder, or psychotic disorder not otherwise specified). The researchers carried out two experiments. In the first, scanning occurred while subjects experienced AVHs. Activation was evident in the right homolog of Broca's area, bilateral insula, bilateral supramarginal gyri, and right superior temporal gyrus. 10 out of 21 activations (47.6%) were on the right side. Interestingly, Broca's area and the left superior temporal gyrus were not activated. In the second experiment, scanning occurred while they silently generated words. Activation occurred in Broca's and Wernicke's areas and to a lesser degree their right-sided homologs, bilateral insula, and anterior cingulate gyri. 13 out of 27 activations (48.1%) were on the right side.

The main difference that Sommer et al. (2008) found between cerebral activity during AVHs and activity during normal inner speech appears to be lateralization. The predominant engagement of the right inferior frontal area during AVH may be related to the typical low semantic complexity and negative emotionality. The mean lateralization index was −0.11 (SD 0.41) during AVHs and 0.14 (SD 0.34) for the word generation task. Paired sample t-tests revealed significantly lower lateralization ($t(23) = -2.4$, $p < 0.02$). In a conjunction analysis brain areas on the right side were activated 9 out of 15 times (60.0%).

Activity during AVHs was uncorrelated with language lateralization; rather, lateralization was related to the degree to which the content of the AVHs possessed negative emotionality. Sommer et al. (2008) noted that the predominant engagement of the right inferior frontal area during AVHs may be related to low semantic complexity and negative emotionality.

Van de Ven et al. (2005) used spatial independent component analysis (sICA)[17] to extract the activity patterns associated with AVHs in schizophrenia patients (N = 6). Viewed bilaterally, activation of the auditory cortex (components of interest) occurred 60.0% on the right side during hallucinations (not including the posterior temporal plane) (Table 6.6). If bilateral activations are eliminated (i.e. only unilateral instances are considered), right-side activation occurred 66.7% of the time during AVHs.

Table 6.6. Activation of Auditory Cortex and the Posterior Temporal Plane.[a]

Patient	Components of Interests	Other Areas
1	HG = Left, Right	PTP = Left
	SMC = Right	
2	SMC = Right	
3	HG = Left, Right	PTP = Left
	SMC = Right	
4	HG/STG = Right	
	SMC = Left	
5	SMC = Left	

[a] Based on Van de Ven et al. (2005: 651); abbreviated.
HG = Heschl's gyrus; SMC = sensorimotor cortex; STG = superior temporal gyrus; PTP = posterior temporal plane.

Table 6.7 summarizes the frequency of right-side activity during AVHs as reported in a number of selected studies.

Table 6.7. Summary: Frequency of Right-Side Activity During AVHs Reported in Selected Studies.

Study	Number of Participants	Frequency of Right-Side Activity
Barkus et al. (2007)	8	50.0%
Buchsbaum et al. (1982)	14	100.0%
Diederen et al. (2011)	42	42.9%
Dierks et al. (1999)	3	47.8%
Sommer et al. (2007)	15	66.7%
Sommer et al. (2008)	24	47.6%
		60.0% (conjunction analysis)
Van de Ven et al. (2005)	6	66.7%
		Mean = 60.21% (SD = 17.26)
		If conjunction analysis not included, Mean = 60.24% (SD = 18.45)

Other Relevant Studies

Ćurčić-Blake et al. (2012) attempted to discern connectivity models between left hemispheric speech-processing areas and their right hemispheric homologs. They investigated reduced information flow to Broca's area in schizophrenia patients with AVHs. Besides Broca's area, they examined the interaction among three other linguistic regions: Wernicke's area (in left hemisphere) and the homologs of Broca's and Wernicke's areas in the right hemisphere (Chart 6.2). Subjects included a healthy control group (presumably those who do not experience hallucinations) (N = 18) and two groups of schizophrenics without (N = 14) and with hallucinations (N = 21). The subjects were asked to perform a task requiring inner speech processing during functional brain scanning (fMRI). The researchers used dynamic causal modeling to track the flow of information (this allows for directional inference). Bayesian model averaging was used to estimate the connectivity strengths and evaluate group differences.

Results indicated that those with AVHs had activation of the left superior temporal gyrus[18] (including Wernicke's area), the left inferior frontal gyrus (including Broca's area) (97% certainty), and the homologs of both areas (i.e. on the right side) (93% and 94% certainty). They also showed significant reduced connectivity from Wernicke's to Broca's area and a reduction in connectivity from the homologs of Broca's and Wernicke's areas. Patients without AVHs were found to be intermediate. These results indicate that, in schizophrenics with AVHs, the input from temporal to frontal language areas is reduced. This suggests that activity in Broca's area may be less constrained by perceptual information sent by the temporal cortex. Asynchronization between Broca's area and its homolog may lead to the erroneous interpretation of emotional speech activity from the right hemisphere, i.e. that it is coming from an external source (cf. Nasrallah 1985). Ćurčić-Blake et al. speculated that disconnectivity between *both* interhemispheric transfer *and* frontal and temporal areas might underlie AVHs in schizophrenia.

Chart 6.2. Interactions among Four Primary Linguistic Areas.

Left Hemipshere Broca's	↔	Right Hemisphere Broca's Homolog
↕		↕
Wernicke's	↔	Wernicke's Homolog

Bentaleb et al. (2002) noted that two theories for AVHs have received empirical support: they arise (1) from misinterpreted inner speech or (2) from aberrant activation of the primary auditory cortex. To test these hypotheses, they used fMRI to measure the brain activity of a schizophrenic woman in the temporal and inferior frontal regions during AVHs and while listening to external speech. This woman usually experienced continuous AVHs but these disappeared when she listened to loud external speech. A matched control subject's brain activity was recorded under the same conditions. They found higher metabolic activity in the left primary auditory cortex[19] and the right middle temporal gyrus during AVHs and believe that these areas possibly interact during AVHs. They concluded that the two theories are not mutually exclusive.

Psychotic patients typically display decreased language lateralization. However, Diederen et al. (2010) investigated whether dysfunction is associated psychosis in general or with certain symptoms of psychosis, such as AVHs. Subjects included patients with a psychotic disorder (N = 35), 35 non-psychotic subjects with AVHs (N = 35), and healthy control subjects (N = 35). All groups covertly performed a paced verbal fluency task while being scanned (3T fMRI). In order to measure performance, subjects were asked to generate words overtly in an additional task. Language lateralization indices were calculated and group-wise brain activation during verbal fluency was compared for the three groups. Task performance did not differ significantly among the groups. Lateralization indices are defined as the difference in "thresholded" signal intensity changes in the left versus the right hemisphere (in the selected language areas) divided by the sum of "thresholded" signal intensity changes. +1 indicates strong left-hemispheric dominance, while −1 indicates strong right-hemispheric dominance. As expected, relative to the other two groups, decreased language lateralization was significantly reduced for the patient group.

The latter group also presented significantly more activity in the right precentral gyrus, left insula, and the right superior parietal lobule compared to the other groups. Interestingly, lateralization indices were not very different between the AVHs-non-psychotic group and the healthy control groups, and no significant differences in neural activity during verbal fluency between the two non-psychotic groups were discerned. Diederen et al. (2010) conclude that language lateralization was not significantly reduced in the AVHs-non-psychotic group and presently a relationship between AVHs and reduced language lateralization cannot be demonstrated.

Ocklenburg et al. (2013), in an effort to integrate studies investigating language lateralization in schizophrenics, provided indirect evidence of right-side activity during AVHs. Using dichotic listening testing, they conducted two meta-analyses. The first looked at 21 different studies, comparing schizophrenics (N = 700) with healthy controls (N = 707). The results showed schizophrenics had weaker language lateralization compared to healthy controls. However, the effect size was small: $g = -0.26$ (95% confidence interval -0.36 to -0.15), significantly different from zero ($Z = -4.69$; $p < 0.00001$). The schizophrenic population, then, cannot be considered a homogenous group in relation to language lateralization. In the second analyses of 8 different studies, schizophrenics experiencing AVHs (N = 179) were compared with non-hallucinating controls (N = 228). In this analyses the effect size was significantly larger: $g = -0.45$ (95% confidence interval -0.65 to -0.25), significantly different from zero ($Z = -4.45$; $p < 0.00001$). Compared to non-hallucinating controls, schizophrenics who have AVHs show a significantly reduced right-ear advantage in the dichotic listening tasks.[20] The researchers concluded that reduced language lateralization is a weak trait marker for schizophrenia. However, reduced language lateralization is a strong trait marker for those experiencing AVHs within the schizophrenic population.

Concluding Thoughts

Affinities between Hallucinations and Introspection

I have attempted to show that though redundancy characterizes many crucial biological features, the lateralization of human speech is consistent with a common trait of bilateria, i.e. capabilities on one side of the brain are freed up so as to allow its focus on pressing environmental matters. In the case of pre-conscious humans, this would involve social situations in which predictable routines, for whatever reason, broke down and guiding, commanding, admonishing, or inspiring divine voices intervened. Though not completely convincing, suggestive evidence exists that auditory hallucinations originate in the right temporal lobe in regions corresponding to the language areas in the left temporal lobe. The hemispheres are "communicating," but in surprising ways they are "unintegrated" neurological components. About three thousand years ago massive sociocultural changes redesigned our socioneurology, replacing voice-volitions with another form of hallucinatory experience, i.e. the quasi-perceptions of mental imagery (conscious interiority). Even patterns of inhibition and disinhibition are matters of culture and socialization.

Practical and Therapeutic Implications

Numerous articles have been written on AVHs as if they are inherently psychopathological (Bentall, Haddock, and Slade 1994). However, enough evidence exists to argue that AVHs in themselves may not be *neurologically* pathological (i.e. they arise from built-in aptic structures), though they can be *psychologically* pathological (they might accompany or indicate serious dysfunction). If so, what are the therapeutic implications of acknowledging that AVHs in and of themselves are not pathological? A number of others have acknowledged that AVHs can be potentially positive: Beavan (2011); Chin, Hayward, and Drinna (2008); Hayward et al. (2008); and Pérez-Álvarez et al. (2008).

Romme and Escher (1996) submit that hearing voices has a functional role in aiding people to cope with the problems of daily life. They noticed key differences between good copers and bad copers. The latter experienced more negative "imperative voices," i.e. a power structure existed between the voices and person, with the voices viewed as stronger than one's self. Romme and Escher also found that non-patients were more likely to be married, received more support than patients, and were more likely to discuss their voices with other people than patients. They found no connection between the characteristics of hearing voices and specific psychiatric illnesses, indicating that voice-hearing is not the result only of psychopathology.

Romme et al. (1992) sent questionnaires to 460 people with chronic hallucinations who responded to a request on a television show. They received 254 replies, of which 186 could be used for analysis (it was determined that 13 were probably not experiencing hallucinations). They found that 115 reported an inability to cope with voices, 97 were in psychiatric care, and copers were significantly less often in psychiatric care (24%) than non-copers (49%). They discovered that successful copers used four strategies for dealing with AVHs: (1) distraction; (2) ignoring the voices; (3) selective listening; and (4) setting limits on their influence.

Corstens, Longden, and May (2012) introduce a therapeutic approach called "Talking with Voices" that is derived from the theory and practice of Voice Dialogue (Stone and Stone 1989, authors of *Embracing Ourselves: The Voice Dialogue Training Manual*). The Stones (1989) postulated that selves are composed of "sub-personalities" that require re-integration. Corstens, Longden, and May (2012) explain how the therapist acts a "facilitator" who directly engages with the different selves (e.g. primary or dominant selves that push away "disowned selves") in order to raise awareness of the meaning and origin of voices. As Jones and Coffey (2012) contend, in their thematic analysis of the personal meanings behind AVHs, a biologically-based psychiatry with its medico-physical explanations is inadequate for acknowledging the actual experiences of voice-hearers.

Endnotes

1. From the Latin "to wander in the mind," which came from the Greek, *alusso*, "to be uneasy."
2. Cultural traditions, of course, play a role in how hallucinations are defined. See Luhrmann (2011), Luhrmann et al. (2014), and Larøi et al. (2014). Al-Issa (1995) examines the differences between "Western" and "non-Western" views of hallucinations. In the former, or "rational" societies, a clear distinction between reality and fantasy encourages negative attitudes toward hallucinations resulting in people being unfamiliar with their own imagination. But in "less rational" cultures the distinction between reality and fantasy is more "flexible" and individuals are socialized to accept their hallucinations. An appreciation of such views towards anomalous experiences might aid mental health providers in distinguishing pathological from culturally-sanctioned hallucinations.
3. Much of my treatment of the categorization of hallucinations and illusions relies on Kaplan and Sadock's *Synopsis of Psychiatry: Behavioral Sciences and Clinical Psychiatry* (1991).
4. Some are "reflex" in which a stimulus in one sensory modality causes a hallucination in another, while others are "functional," i.e. a stimulus causes a hallucination in the same sensory modality, but both the stimulus and the hallucination are experienced.
5. Suggested to Stevenson by David Kovacs, a scholar of classics at the University of Virginia.
6. E.g. see Kokoszka (1992) who investigated "altered states of consciousness" in normal populations, e.g. hallucinations, peak experiences, mystical states, hypnotic-like experiences, and out-of-body experiences. Kokoszka pointed out that such phenomena are too common to be ignored by Psychology.
7. It should be noted that Sidgwick et al.'s study was under the auspices of the Society for Psychical Research and sought to prove the existence of telepathy.
8. Andrew et al. (2008); Daalman et al. (2011); Davies et al. (2001); Diederen et al. (2011); Hill et al. (in preparation a); Hill et al. (in preparation b); Honig et

al. (1998); Johns et al. (2002a,b); Jones et al. (2003); Leudar et al. (1997); Linden et al. (2011); Romme and Escher (1989); Sommer et al. (2010); Sorrell et al. (2010).

9   For a review of studies on imaginary playmates, see Klausen and Passman (2006).
10 On children who hear voices, see Escher, Romme, and Buiks (1998) and Pearson (1998).
11 In the case of visual hallucinations, for example, causes may be irritative phenomena, release phenomena, or processing disturbances within the visual pathways (Weller and Wiedermann 1989).
12 Two useful works that provide an overview of the subject are Watkins, *Hearing Voices: A Common Human Experience* (1998) and Romme and Escher, *Making Sense of Voices: A Guide for Mental Health Professionals Working with Voice-Hearers* (2000).
13 Lateralization is evident in vertebrate and even some invertebrate species (Halpern et al. 2005).
14 From the German psychiatrist, Kurt Schneider (1887–1967).
15 They also point out that studies of stroke patients with lesions and dichotic listening and functional imaging studies of healthy people show that certain language functions are mediated by the right hemisphere rather than the left.
16 The Auditory Hallucination Scale (AHRS) and Positive and Negative Symptom Scale (PANSS) were utilized to make assessments.
17 sICA decomposes the functional dataset into a set of spatial maps without the use of any input function.
18 In a study by Jardri (2007) of a schizophrenic child, bilateral activation of the superior temporal gyri was evident (predominantly on the left hemisphere).
19 The primary auditory cortex is bilaterally located, near the upper sides of the temporal lobes on the superior temporal plane within the lateral fissure and comprising parts of Heschl's gyrus and the superior temporal gyrus. It includes planum polare and planum temporale and roughly corresponds to Brodmann's areas 41, 42, and part of 22.
20 The "right-ear advantage" in dichotic listening tests is usually defined as the difference between the number of correctly identified stimuli presented to the right ear compared to the number of correctly identified stimuli presented to the left ear.

Conclusion

Final Thoughts
Psychohistorical Ruptures and Stratigraphic Psychology

"The intellectual life of man, his culture and history and religion and science, is different from anything else we know of in the universe. That is fact. It is as if all life evolved to a certain point, and then in ourselves turned at a right angle and simply exploded in a different direction." – Julian Jaynes

I close this book with two points. Then I provide several reasons why some find the theories of Jaynes (and by implication the "other" Psychology) highly problematic. The first point concerns the high degree of neuroplasticity characterizing the human mind and evidence that our mentality has undergone momentous transformations. Many of us are uncomfortable with such a proposition, perhaps due to a basic metaphor of mind we unconsciously and habitually accept—the "mind-as-vase." In this metaphor, society deposits its cultural contents into a predetermined container, and it is the configuration of the container that shapes the cultural stuff. To conventional Psychologists, socialization is of secondary concern since it is the shape of the vase— i.e. the "central processing mechanism" (CPM)—that matters (cf. Shweder 1990). Thus, Psychology becomes a search for psychic unity and psychic structures, since it is assumed that though cultural information varies historically and from place to place, the basic shape of the container is the same. The mind is a receptacle into which society pours its values, ideas, concepts, and classificatory schemes.

Here allow me to suggest another, more helpful trope: mind-as-putty. This metaphor draws our attention to the socially-constructed aspect of mind, which can be molded into a number of shapes for culturally determined purposes. The putty material is the same, of course, for all individuals, but it can be formed into radically different configurations depending on the historical circumstances. Rather than searching just for universals, I argue, Psychology should be searching for psychic plasticity and psychic diversity, rather than some preset shape. Psychology should also be taking seriously what our past and ancient patterns of behaviors might teach us.

Sociohistorical Scaffolding, Linguistic Layering, and the Historicity of Mind-Words

The second point concerns the relation between temporal change and psyche. Very much related to the metaphoricity of inner experience is historicity. In any given language the idiom used to describe mental events rests upon earlier sociohistorical layers of linguistic expressions. Languages are scaffolds built upon scaffolds informed by experiences and the vagaries of history. As such, they retain vestiges of earlier historical periods.

The "Temporal Extension Thesis" and Linguo-Conceptual Remnants

Recently, thinkers such as Clark (2008), Clark and Chalmers (1998), Menary (2010), Sterelny (2004), and Wilson (2005) have argued that mind must be understood as something "extended," i.e. the mind is not contained by "skin and skull," but emerges from interactions with tools and the social environment. Indeed, the mind is not only embedded in and enhanced by technology; rather such externalities (e.g. memory storage devices) properly count as parts of psyche. The "extended mind thesis" (EMT) is, in a sense, a spatial extension of psychological processes. But I would complement EMT with a "temporal extension thesis" (TET) arguing that if we take seriously the inherently cultural aspect of psyche, we are forced to acknowledge its historicity; in other words, the mind is extended through time. Unless socialization transpires in a particular linguo-conceptual community (this is where culture comes in), mind cannot emerge. There is no reason to assume that psychological processes, as we experience them today, have been a constant throughout humankind's history. In the same way we understand political institutions, economic systems, and religious ideologies by peeling back their historical layerings and peering into their pastness, so should we approach the mind. And language is an excellent place to start. Such a stratigraphic psychology does not answer all questions about human mentality, of course, but it is a very useful antidote to essentializing and overly-naturalizing something that rests upon cultural historical scaffolding.

Biological and Cultural Inter-Evolution and Stratigraphic Psychology

It is essential to stress that for our purposes evolution and adaptation do not necessarily denote biological changes. As Jaynes makes clear, consciousness, while certainly grounded in human physicality and neurology, is not a product of biological evolution. It was the consequence of *cultural* change and psychohistorical ruptures; more precisely, it was the product of inter-evolution between biology and culture.

Evolution, of course, is about time, and for our present purposes we need to pay attention to the relation between temporal change and psyche. Here I introduce the notion of "stratigraphic psychology," i.e. the view that human mentality can radically change and that the study of sociocultural strata, accumulating through the centuries, constitute human sociopsychological adaptation. Different layers of a stratigraphic psychology are evident in the surprising typicality of civilizational patterns seen in the archeological record as enumerated in the Bicameral Civilizational Inventory, linguistic development, and vestiges of earlier mentalities. We should take seriously what ancient patterns of behaviors can teach Psychology.

Obstacles to Understanding Jaynes's "Other" Psychology

My argument has not been that *Völkerpsychologie* and its variations are specifically what Jaynes had in mind when his wrote *The Origin*, but, in a broad sense, Jaynes's own agenda profoundly resonates with a cultural-historical approach. Jaynes's arguments are disquieting, though very few accounts in Psychology have wielded such a sharp Occam's razor and explained so much with such startling parsimony. Below I list a number of intellectual pointers that require acknowledgment before we can assess Jaynes's contribution to Psychology (and by extension, cultural-historical approaches) (see McVeigh 2006b, 2007a,b).

(1) *The word "consciousness" itself, which is too vague to be of any practical use for research purposes.* It is used to mean perception, reasoning, self-awareness, self-reflection, and cognition of any kind, etc. A more precise, refined set of terms should be utilized to describe psychological phenomena.

(2) *The problem of assuming that conscious interiority is only an innate biological capability.* More useful approaches should, as much as possible, as argued by Shu-Chen Li in "Biocultural Orchestration of Development Plasticity Across Levels: The Interplay of Biology and Culture in Shaping the Mind and Behavior Across the Life Span" (2003). Admittedly, biocultural co-constructivism, being multidisciplinary, demands an uneasy alliance of very different realms of knowledge, but researchers should at least be aware of both the natural and social aspects of the human condition. Cultural changes of the psyche

may be much more profound than we have assumed (could it be that neurological evolution and psycho-cultural modifications are not that different in terms of functional impact?).

(3) *Not recognizing that conscious interiority, not unconscious processes, is the pressing problem demanding exploration.* Many of us assume that conscious awareness is a type of default cognition and that unconscious operations and events are somehow out of the ordinary. But early theorists recognized that what we are subjectively experiencing is a mere tip of the iceberg. Here some historical perspective is needed. In the British tradition, mind was equated with consciousness, while in the German tradition, where no such equation existed, unregistered mental processes became central to a fair amount of research (i.e. the "unconscious") (Danziger 1980: 242). Indeed, by the late 1800s, different versions of the unconscious emerged: the no-nonsense, laboratory-based experimentation researching sensory perception that failed to show up on the individual's conscious radar screen; Freudian and psychoanalytic; and more mystical understandings of a profound, mysterious and vitalistic power—e.g. von Hartmann (1884; see McVeigh 2010a,b).

(4) *Ignoring history as a source of evidence for psychic diversity and psychic plasticity.* The inherently historical and sociocultural nature of psychological processes can be understood as: (1) psychic plasticity during one's life course (a series of socializations, desocializations, and resocializations); (2) psychic plasticity across different cultures; and (3) the psychic plasticity of our species as conditioned by history. Certain periods may be characterized by ruptures that produce distinct mentalities functionally adapted to the vagaries of passing time.

(5) *Failing to integrate the natural and social sciences.* Utilizing measurement-focused quantitative as well as meaning-focused qualitative methods is no easy task. "Quantitative" and "qualitative" types are both guilty of dismissing useful tools for analysis. The former needs to acknowledge the value of in-depth empirical knowledge of history, languages, cultures, etc., while the latter should become more familiar with at least the basics of biology and neurology.

(6) *Political correctness.* While a graduate student at Princeton University, I asked if Jaynes could sit on my dissertation committee and was told that "he's not welcome in our Department" (Anthropology) because of his views. And a letter I received while in the field from Prof. Gananath Obeyesekere described Jaynes's ideas as "ethnocentric." Once, while I was standing in line in a campus cafeteria with an

English translation of Lucien Lévy-Bruhl's *La Mentalité primitive* on my tray, a young woman looked at the book and said "Oooh! I can't believe someone would write such a thing." She then rolled her eyes and tilted her head, as if to say "I don't know why you're reading something like that, but I'm sure you have your reasons." Any talk of stages or major changes in the history of the psyche smacks, for some, of politically incorrect anti-cultural relativism, despite earlier scholarly traditions (*l'histoire des mentalités*) that, arguably, explored such changes. In any case, political correctness is no friend to serious academic inquiry (Lilienfeld 2010: 284).

(7) *Defying categorization.* Part of the problem with Jaynes is that people do not know how to classify him. Never one for the latest vogue, Jaynes did not see a need to intellectually align himself with a "school." Highly pragmatic and eclectic, he followed evidence in a "just-the-facts-please" manner that left little time for trends. Well-steeped in intellectual history, he was wary of the latest scholarly fad or pompous "ism." He drew attention to the under-appreciated extraordinariness and singularity of conscious interiority as a phenomenon in its own right in human history. Diligently focused on the problem of conscious interiority, his dogged pursuit took him to some very strange but rewarding places.

Appendix A

Types of Ceptions

Perception	Superception			Coception
Reactivity	------------------Control Over Ceptive Experience--------------> --Interiorization: Increasingly Experienced "Inside" Person--> Auditory--Sensory Mode Becoming Dominant: Visuality			Alignment of Perception & Introception
	Extraception	Vesitigial Extraception and Perception	Introception[a]	
-Visual -Auditory -Kinesthetic -Olfactory -Haptic -Gustatory -Vestibular	-Bicameral Hallucinations	-Schizophrenic Hallucinations -Extracampine Experiences -AEP: Autoscopic Extraception -AEP: Heautoscopic & Out-of-Body Extraception -Sense of Presence -Eidetic Imagery -Apophenia -Pareidolia -Pseudo-Hallucinations -Hearing Voices -Phantom Limb -Dreaming -Lucid Dreaming -Hypnagogic Experiences -Hypnopompic Experiences	-Visual -Auditory -Kinesthetic -Olfactory -Haptic -Gustatory -Vestibular	-Visual -Auditory -Kinesthetic -Olfactory -Haptic -Gustatory -Vestibular

[a] Also called inner imagery, mental imagery ("mind's eye"), or quasi-perceptual experience.

Appendix B

Types of Adaptive Mentalities

Aspects of Human Condition	Types of Adaptive Mentalities			
	Pre-Bicamerality	Bicamerality		Interiority
	Upper Paleolithic -- Neolithic -- Early Town Polities -- Transitional Period -- 12th C. -- Axial Age: c. 800–200 BCE --> ------- Increasing Demographic Scale -------> ------- Increasing Economic Surplus -------> ------- Increasing Need for Extensive Communications ------->			
Techno-economics	- Hunting & gathering - Pre-agricultural - Stone tools	- Early Agricultural - Specialization - Early Literacy - Irrigation, Calendrics - Early Mathematics		- Agricultural - Increased Specialization - Increased Literacy - Proto-science, Improved Technologies - Mathematics
Ideational Style	Unknown	- Theopolitical, Mythopoetic		- Philosophical, Speculative
Cosmology Nature Time History Types of Space Nature of Deities		- Concrete Categories - Sacred, Anthropomorphized - Cyclical, Serial - Annals & Chronicles - Macrocosm, Microcosm - Commanding, Talkative - Immanent - In this World, Co-natural		- Abstract Categories - Desacralized, Impersonal - Linear - Narrative, First Histories - Macrocosm, Microcosm, Introcosm (Mental Space) - Silent, Reticent - Transcendent

Attitude toward Deities		- Superhuman - Polytheism, Specialized Functions - Existence Assumed, Unquestioned - Total Obedience, Submission	- Above & Beyond this World, Supernatural - Trans-Human - Monotheistic Trend, Generalized Function - Skepticism Toward, Interrogating - Doubt, Invention of "Belief"
Sociopolitical	- Kinship-based - Tribes - Clans	- Supra-kinship Based - Town-polities/Kingdoms, Centralization - God-kings/Priestly Class	- Supra-kinship Based - Empires, Increased Centralization - Developed States/More Specialists
Neurocultural	Unknown		
Source of Authorization for One's Behavior		- Gods'/Ancestors'/Rulers' Voices - Divine Authorization	- Voices Melded into Self - Self-authorization

Appendix C

Statistical Analyses for Chapter 3

App Calculation 3.1. ETCSL DICTIONARY: No. of RL to PL and Their Ratio.

	RL	PL	All Lexemes in Dictionary
	170 (5.55%)	50 (1.63%)	3064 (100%)
Ratio	3.40 : 1		

App Calculation 3.2. ETCSL DICTIONARY: Chi-Sq G of F.

Type	Observed	Expected	Diff	Diff Sq	Diff Sq/Exp Fr
RL	170	110	60.00	3600.00	32.73
PL	50	110	-60.00	3600.00	32.73

P-Value	Significant at	df	χ^2	Critical Value	ES	H_0:	H_1:
< 0.001	$p \leq 0.05$	1	65.46	3.84	0.5454	RL = PL	RL ≠ PL

App Calculation 3.3. ePSD DICTIONARY: No. of RL to PL and Their Ratio.[a]

	RL	PL	All Lexemes in Dictionary
	375 (6.11%)	174 (2.84%)	6137 (100%)
Ratio	2.16 : 1		

[a] The frequency for "heart" (šag) in ePSD is 10,808. As it is at this time not always obvious how this term is actually used in the texts (i.e. human organ, animal organ, or in psychological expressions), I only report expressions that clearly use it in PL.

App Calculation 3.4. ePSD DICTIONARY. RL to PL: Chi-Sq G of F.

Type	Observed	Expected	Diff	Diff Sq	Diff Sq/Exp Fr
RL	375	274.50	100.50	10100.25	36.80
PL	174	274.50	-100.50	10100.25	36.80

P-Value	Significant at	df	χ^2	Critical Value	ES	H_0:	H_1:
< 0.001	$p \leq 0.05$	1	73.59	3.84	0.3661	RL = PL	RL ≠ PL

App Calculation 3.5. HG Hittite DICTIONARY: No. of RL to PL and Their Ratio.

	RL	PL	All Lexemes in Dictionary
	99 (7.48%)	75 (5.66%)	324 (100%)
Ratio	1.32 : 1		

Appendix C

App Calculation 3.6. HG Hittite DICTIONARY. RL to PL: Chi-Sq G of F.

Type	Observed	Expected	Diff	Diff Sq	Diff Sq/Exp Fr
RL	99	87	12.00	144.00	1.66
PL	75	87	-12.00	144.00	1.66

P-Value	Significant at	df	χ^2	Critical Value	ES	H_0:	H_1:
< 0.069	$p \leq 0.05$	1	3.31	3.84	0.1379	RL = PL	RL ≠ PL

App Calculation 3.7. LRC-UTA Hittite Dictionary: No. of RL to PL and Their Ratio.

	RL	PL	All Lexemes in Dictionary
	56 (7.97%)	9 (1.28%)	703 (100%)
Ratio	6.22 : 1		

App Calculation 3.8. LRC-UTA Hittite DICTIONARY. RL to PL: Chi-Sq G of F.

Type	Observed	Expected	Diff	Diff Sq	Diff Sq/Exp Fr
RL	56	32.5	23.50	552.25	16.99
PL	9	32.5	-23.50	552.25	16.99

P-Value	Significant at	df	χ^2	Critical Value	ES	H_0:	H_1:
< 0.001	$p \leq 0.05$	1	33.99	3.84	0.7231	RL = PL	RL ≠ PL

App Calculation 3.9. Mycenaean/Linear B DICTIONARY: No. of RL to PL and Their Ratio.

	RL	PL	All Lexemes in Dictionary
	16 (5.33%)	1 (0.33%)	300 (100%)
Ratio	16 : 1		

App Calculation 3.10. Mycenaean/Linear B DICTIONARY. RL to PL: Chi-Sq G of F.

Type	Observed	Expected	Diff	Diff Sq	Diff Sq/Exp Fr
RL	16	8.5	7.50	56.25	6.62
PL	1	8.5	-7.50	56.25	6.62

P-Value	Significant at	df	χ^2	Critical Value	ES	H_0:	H_1:
< 0.001	$p \leq 0.05$	1	13.24	3.84	0.882	RL = PL	RL ≠ PL

App Calculation 3.11. ETCSL TEXTS: No. of RL to PL and Their Ratio.

	RL	PL	All Lexemes in Texts
	7201 (5.49%)	3464 (2.64%)	131,106 (100%)
Ratio	2.08 : 1		

App Calculation 3.12. ETCSL TEXTS. RL to PL: Chi-Sq G of F.

Type	Observed	Expected	Diff	Diff Sq	Diff Sq/Exp Fr
RL	7201	5332.5	1868.50	3491292.25	654.72
PL	3464	5332.5	-1868.50	3491292.25	654.72

P-Value	Significant at	df	χ^2	Critical Value	ES	H$_0$:	H$_1$:
< 0.001	p ≤ 0.05	1	1309.439	3.84	0.3503	RL = PL	RL ≠ PL

App Calculation 3.13. ePSD TEXTS: Frequencies of RL and PL and Their Ratio.[a]

	RL	PL
	101,537	7001
Ratio	14.50 : 1	

[a] Due to the very large corpus of to which the ePSD refers, the percentages of RL to PL in ePSD texts are currently unavailable.

App Calculation 3.14. ePSD TEXTS. RL to PL: Chi-Sq G of F.

Type	Observed	Expected	Diff	Diff Sq	Diff Sq/Exp Fr
RL	101,537	54269	47268.00	2234263824.00	41170.17
PL	7001	54269	-47268.00	2234263824.00	41170.17

P-Value	Significant at	df	χ^2	Critical Value	ES	H$_0$:	H$_1$:
< 0.001	p ≤ 0.05	1	82340.335	3.84	0.870	RL = PL	RL ≠ PL

App Calculation 3.15. ETCSL NAMES: Ratios of Religious and Non-Religious Names.

	No. of Religious Names	No. of Non-Religious Names
	607	310
Ratio	1.96 : 1	

App Calculation 3.16. ETCSL NAMES: RN to NR: No. of Chi-Sq G of F.

Type	Observed	Expected	Diff	Diff Sq	Diff Sq/Exp Fr
Religious	607	458.5	148.50	22052.25	48.10
Non-Religious	310	458.5	-148.50	-22052.25	48.10

P-Value	Significant at	df	χ^2	Critical Value	ES	H$_0$:	H$_1$:
< 0.001	p ≤ 0.05	1	96.193	3.84	0.323	RN = NR	RN ≠ NR

Appendix C

App Calculation 3.17. ePSD NAMES: Ratios of Frequencies of Religious and Non-Religious Names.

	Frequency of Religious Names	Frequency of Non-Religious Names
No.	9,781	2,756
Ratio	3.55 : 1	

App Calculation 3.18. ePSD NAMES: Frequencies. RN and NR: Chi-Sq G of F.

Type	Observed	Expected	Diff	Diff Sq	Diff Sq/Exp Fr
Religious	9781	6268.5	3512.50	12337656.25	1968.20
Non-Religious	2756	6268.5	-3512.50	12337656.25	1968.20

P-Value	Significant at	df	χ^2	Critical Value	ES	H_0:	H_1:
< 0.001	$p \leq 0.05$	1	3936.398	3.84	0.5603	RN = NR	RN ≠ NR

App Calculation 3.19. ETCSL: No. of Negative Emotions.

	No. of Neg Emotions (%)	No. of Pos Emotions (%)
No. of PL = 50 (100%)	13 (26.00%)	16 (32.00%)
Ratio	0.81 : 1	

App Calculation 3.20. ETCSL: Frequency of Negative Emotions.

	Frequency of Neg Emotions (%)	Frequency of Pos Emotions (%)
Frequency of PL = 3374 (100%)	253 (7.50%)	639 (18.94%)
Ratio	0.40 : 1	

App Calculation 3.21. ePSD: No. of Negative Emotions.

	No. of Neg Emotions (%)	No. of Pos Emotions (%)
No. of PL = 174 (100%)	65 (37.36%)	31 (17.82%)
Ratio	2.10 : 1	

App Calculation 3.22. ePSD: No. of Negative Emotions. Chi-Sq G of F.

Type	Observed	Expected	Diff	Diff Sq	Diff Sq/Exp Fr
Neg Emotions	65	48	17.00	289.00	6.02
Pos Emotions	31	48	-17.00	289.00	6.02

P-Value	Significant at	df	χ^2	Critical Value	ES	H_0:	H_1:
< 0.001	$p \leq 0.05$	1	12.04	3.84	0.354	NE = PE	NE ≠ PE

App Calculation 3.23. ePSD: Frequency of Negative Emotions.

	Frequency of Neg Emotions (%)	Frequency of Pos Emotions (%)
Frequency of PL= 7001 (100%)	3259 (46.55%)	1499 (21.41%)
Ratio	2.17 : 1	

App Calculation 3.24. ePSD: Frequency of Negative Emotions. Chi-Sq G of F.

Type	Observed	Expected	Diff	Diff Sq	Diff Sq/Exp Fr
Neg Emotions	3259	2379	880.00	774400.00	325.51
Pos Emotions	1499	2379	-880.00	774400.00	25.51

P-Value	Significant at	df	χ^2	Critical Value	ES	H_0:	H_1:
< 0.001	p ≤ 0.05	1	651.03	3.84	0.3699	NE = PE	NE ≠ PE

App Calculation 3.25. HG Hittite: No. of Negative Emotions.

	No. of Neg Emotions (%)	No. of Pos Emotions (%)
No. of PL = 75 (100%)	38 (50.67%)	13 (17.33%)
Ratio	2.92 : 1	

App Calculation 3.26. HG Hittite: No. of Negative Emotions. Chi-Sq G of F.

Type	Observed	Expected	Diff	Diff Sq	Diff Sq/Exp Fr
Neg Emotions	38	25.5	12.50	156.25	6.13
Pos Emotions	13	25.5	-12.50	156.25	6.13

P-Value	Significant at	df	χ^2	Critical Value	ES	H_0:	H_1:
< 0.001	p ≤ 0.05	1	12.26	3.84	0.490	NE = PE	NE ≠ PE

App Calculation 3.27. LRC-UTA Hittite: No. of Negative Emotions.

	No. of Neg Emotions (%)	No. of Pos Emotions (%)
No. of PL = 9 (100%)	4 (44.00%)	0 (0%)
Ratio	N/A	

App Calculation 3.28. LRC-UTA Hittite: No. of Negative Emotions. Chi-Sq G of F.

Type	Observed	Expected	Diff	Diff Sq	Diff Sq/Exp Fr
Neg Emotions	4	2	2.00	4.00	2.00
Pos Emotions	0	2	-2.00	4.00	2.00

P-Value	Significant at	df	χ^2	Critical Value	ES	H_0:	H_1:
< 0.046	p ≤ 0.05	1	4.00	3.84	1.00	NE = PE	NE ≠ PE

App Calculation 3.29. Egyptian (Dickson): No. of Negative Emotions.

	No. of Neg Emotions (%)	No. of Pos Emotions (%)
No. of PL = 138 (100%)	28 (20.29%)	33 (23.91%)
Ratio	0.85 : 1	

App Calculation 3.30. ePSD: No. of MWs by Period. Chi-Sq G of F.

Category	Observed Frequency[a]	Expected Frequency
(1) Early Dynasty IIIa	3	23.83
(2) Early Dynasty IIIb	30	23.83
(3) Old Akkadian	16	23.83
(4) Lagash II	17	23.83
(5) UR III	41	23.83
(6) Old Babylonian	36	23.83

[a] Percentages rounded off.

P-Value	Significant at	df	χ^2	Critical Value
< 0.0001	p ≤ 0.05	5	42.92	11.07

H_0:	$P_1 = P_2 = P_3 = P_4 = P_5 = P_6$
H_1:	$P_1 \neq P_2 \neq P_3 \neq P_4 \neq P_5 \neq P_6$

App Calculation 3.31. ePSD: Frequency of MWs by Period. Chi-Sq G of F.

Category	Observed Frequency[a]	Expected Frequency
(1) Early Dynasty IIIa	4	468.98
(2) Early Dynasty IIIb	488	468.98
(3) Old Akkadian	119	468.98
(4) Lagash II	54	468.98
(5) UR III	801	468.98
(6) Old Babylonian	1349	468.98

[a] Percentages rounded off.

P-Value	Significant at	df	χ^2	Critical Value
< 0.0001	p ≤ 0.05	5	2976.54	11.07

H_0:	$P_1 = P_2 = P_3 = P_4 = P_5 = P_6$
H_1:	$P_1 \neq P_2 \neq P_3 \neq P_4 \neq P_5 \neq P_6$

Appendix D

Datasets for Chapter 3

Table App D. List of Datasets.

Dataset App D	Source	No. of Terms	Frequencies
D.1	Total Entries of Dictionaries and Total Words of ETCSL Texts	N/A	N/A
D.2	ETCSL Dictionary: RL and Their Frequencies	170	7,291
D.3	ETCSL Dictionary: PL, Their Frequencies, and EV	50	3,374
D.4	ePSD Dictionary: RL and Their Frequencies	375	101,538
D.5	ePSD Dictionary: PL, Their Frequencies Categorized by Period, and EV	174	7,001
D.6	ePSD Dictionary: Sums and Frequencies of PL Categorized by Period	288[a]	7,001
D.7	ETCLS NAMES: Their Types and Their Frequency	917	12,537
D.8	HG Hittite Dictionary: RL	99	N/A
D.9	HG Hittite Dictionary: PL and EV	75	N/A
D.10	LRC-UTA Hittite Dictionary: RL	56	N/A
D.11	LRC-UTA Hittite Dictionary: PL and EV	9	N/A
D.12	Dickson: Middle Egyptian Dictionary of PL	138	N/A
D.13	Mycenaean/Linear B Dictionary: RL	16	N/A
D.14	Mycenaean/Linear B Dictionary: PL	1	N/A

[a] Categorized by period.

Dataset App D.1. Total Entries of Dictionaries and Total Words of ETCSL Texts.

ETCSL Dictionary: Total Entries	3,064
ePSD Dictionary: Total Entries	6,842
LRC-UTA Hittite Dictionary: Total Entries	703
HG Hittite Dictionary: Total Entries	1,324
ETCSL Text Frequencies of All Words	131,106
Dickson: Middle Egyptian Dictionary of PL	138
Mycenaean/Linear B Dictionary: Total Entries	300

Dataset App D.2. ETCSL Dictionary: RL and Their Frequencies.

	English	Sumerian	Frequency
1.	ancestor	bil_2-ga	1
2.	ancestor	pap-bil_2-ga	9
3.	birth goddess (?)	sig_7-ḫi	3
4.	border of heaven	an-zag	21
5.	cella	agrun	19
6.	chief minister	sukkal-maḫ	11
7.	(city) ruler	$ensi_2$	94
8.	cloister	$ĝa_2$-gi	1
9.	cloister	$ĝi_6$-par_4	70
10	corner of heaven	an-ub	1
11.	(cosmic) bond	di-ir-ga	7
12.	(cosmic) bond	uz_3-saĝ	10
13.	(cosmic) post	dim	1
14.	cult center (?)	gu_2-ne	2
15.	cult dais (?)	ki-us_2	2
16.	cult place	ki-šu	5
17.	cult place	ki-šu-peš	5
18.	cult place	ki-šu-tag	2
19.	cult place of Suen	ki-ĝarka	2
20.	cult) meal	ĝišbun	24
21.	curse	$aš_2$	42
22.	cylinder seal	kišib	14
23.	deity	diĝir	851
24.	destiny	nam	670
25.	destiny	nam-tar	58
26.	divine mother	diĝir-ama	1
27.	divine son	diĝir-dumu	1
28.	(divine) standard	šu-nir	23
29.	diviner	$maš_2$-šu-gid_2-gid_2	4
30.	divinity	nam-diĝir	26
31.	dream interpreter	ensi	10
32.	entirety of heaven	an-$šar_2$	3
33.	entrail omen	uzu-ga	2
34.	fear	nam-te	2
35.	festival, type of	a_2-ki-tum	2
36.	festival, type of	$eš_3$-$eš_3$	4
37.	festival	ezen	74
38.	figurine	dim_3-ma	8
39.	figurine	za-na	1
40.	food) offering	nidba	73
41.	funerary chapel	e_2-ninda-ki-sig_{10}	1
42.	funerary offering	ki-sig_{10}-ga	10
43.	ghost	gidim	30
44.	ghost	lil_2	86
45.	goddess	ama-inana	1

46.	grave	ki-mah	3
47.	grave	ki-tum$_2$	4
48.	guardian deity	alad	5
49.	guardian deity	an-gub-ba	2
50.	guardian deity	lamma	91
51.	haunted desert	edin-lil$_2$	7
52.	heaven	an	1,233
53.	heaven	utah	4
54.	heavenly star	mul-an	33
55.	high (priestly) office	nam-en	101
56.	high priest(ess)	en	40
57.	incantation	mu$_7$-mu$_7$	16
58.	incantation	nam-šub	9
59.	incantation	tu$_6$	16
60.	incantation formula	ka-inim-ma	8
61.	incantation priest	ka-mu$_7$-ĝal$_2$	1
62.	incantation priest	lu$_2$-mu$_7$-mu$_7$	2
63.	interior of heaven	an-šag$_4$	44
64.	joy	giri$_{17}$-zal	154
65.	kingship	nam-lugal	230
66.	limit of heaven	an-bar	2
67.	lord	en	1,146
68.	minister	lagar$_3$	2
69.	minister	sukkal	126
70.	necromancer	lu$_2$-gidim-ma	1
71.	noble	gir$_{15}$	4
72.	(offering) table	banšur	65
73.	(oracular) utterance	inim-ĝar	21
74.	outdoor shrine	ub-lil$_2$-la$_2$	2
75.	part of temple	aĝarka	1
76.	part of temple	a-lal$_3$	2
77.	place of (divine) decisions	ki-eš-bar	1
78.	place of creation	ki-ulutim$_2$	10
79.	polluted item	niĝ$_2$-u$_2$-zug$_4$	4
80.	polluter	u$_2$-zug$_4$	5
81.	pray	šudu$_3$-šudu$_3$	2
82.	prayer	sizkur$_2$	60
83.	prayer	šudu$_3$	88
84.	prayer	u$_3$-gul	18
85.	prince	nun	384
86.	purification	nam-luh	1
87.	reverent	ni$_2$-tuku	15
88.	rite	ĝarza	75
89.	ritual cleansing	ka-luh	2
90.	ritual cleansing	šu-luh	79
91.	ritual function	nam-ĝarza$_2$	1
92.	ruler	UN-gal	4
93.	sacred area	unu$_2$-ri-ban$_3$-da	2

Appendix D

94.	(sacred) goblet	eš$_2$-da	6
95.	seal bearer	kišib-la$_2$	2
96.	shrine	eš$_3$	273
97.	shrine	zag-ĝar-ra	1
98.	shrine associated with Inana	niĝin$_3$-ĝar	7
99.	sin	nam-tag	45
100.	sorcerer	maš-maš	20
101.	sorcerer's craft	nam-maš-maš	3
102.	statue	alan	63
103.	status as deity second to Enlil	nam-en-lil$_2$-ban^3-da	1
104.	status as principal deity	nam-en-lil$_2$	8
105.	summit shrine	e$_2$-suḫur	2
106.	temple administrator	saĝĝa	10
107.	temple cook	engiz	2
108.	temple oval	ib-gal	1
109.	temple terrace	gi-gun$_4$-na	23
110.	anoint	šeš$_2$	10
111.	cult performer, type of	gala-tur-ra	6
112.	cult performer, type of	kur-ĝar-ra	11
113.	cult performer, type of	lu$_2$-ĝiš-gi-saĝ-keše$_2$	1
114.	cult performer, type of	munus-ĝiš-gi	1
115.	cult performer, type of	pi-li-pi-li	6
116.	cult performer, type of	saĝ-ur-saĝ	10
117.	demon, type of	gal$_5$-la$_2$	66
118.	demon, type of	lil$_2$-la$_2$-en	1
119.	demon, type of	u$_{18}$-lu	1
120.	demon, type of	udug	37
121.	divination, type of	i$_3$-gid$_2$	1
122.	ecstatic, type of	lu$_2$-al-ed$_2$-de$_3$	3
123.	ecstatic, type of	lu$_2$-gub-ba	3
124.	ecstatic, type of	ni$_2$-su-ub	2
125.	festival, type of	eš$_3$-eš$_3$	4
126.	festival, type of	a$_2$-ki-tum	2
127.	offering, type of	bur-saĝ	2
128.	priest, type of	a-tu	1
129.	priest, type of	a-u$_3$-a	20
130.	priest, type of	abrig	3
131.	priest, type of	gudug	20
132.	priest, type of	išib	13
133.	priest, type of	lal$_3$	1
134.	priest, type of	lagar	7
135.	priest, type of	lu$_2$-maḫ	11
136.	priest, type of	nam-šita$_4$	1
137.	priest, type of	nu-eš$_3$	3
138.	priest, type of	pa$_4$-šeš	2
139.	priest, type of	sur$_9$	2
140.	priest, type of	susbu	5
141.	priest, type of	šag$_4$-gada-la$_2$	7

142.	priest, type of	šennu	1
143.	priest, type of	šim-mu$_2$	5
144.	priest, type of	šita	4
145.	priest, type of	šita-eš$_3$-a	1
146.	priest, type of	tu	1
147.	type of priestcraft	nam-egir$_3$-zid	2
148.	priestcraft, type of	nam-išib	15
149.	priestcraft, type of	nam-lu$_2$-mah	2
150.	priestcraft, type of	nam-lagar	3
151.	priestcraft, type of	nam-gudug	2
152.	priestcraft, type of	nam-lukur	1
153.	priestcraft, type of	nam-nin-diĝir	2
154.	priestess, type of	igi-du$_8$-a	1
155.	priestess, type of	lukur	6
156.	priestess, type of	munus lagar bad	1
157.	priestess, type of	munus lagar me	1
158.	priestess, type of	nin-diĝir	18
159.	priestess, type of	nu-bar	4
160.	priestess, type of	zirru	3
161.	ritual, type of	biluda	6
162.	shrine, type of	e$_2$-nun	4
163.	shrine, type of	barag-sig$_9$-ga	1
164.	shrine, type of	pa-pah	4
165.	shrine, type of	uz-ga	11
166.	shrine, type of	uzug	6
167.	temple official, type of	enkum	8
168.	underworld	irigal	18
169.	(nocturnal) vision	maš$_2$-ĝi$_6$	10
170.	ziggurat	u$_6$-nir	7

$\sum 7{,}291$

Dataset App D.3. ETCSL Dictionary: PL, Their Frequencies, and EV.

	English	Sumerian	Frequency	EV
1.	(sexual) arousal	šag$_4$-zig$_3$-ga	2	
2.	coveting	igi-tum$_3$	8	NE
3.	decision	eš-bar	56	
4.	decision	ka-aš	51	
5.	desire	al	63	
6.	desire	kurku$_2$	20	
7.	dream	ma-mu^2	42	
8.	envy	ninim	2	NE
9.	(excessive) concern	za-ra	2	NE
10.	expression of joy	a-al-la-ri	1	PE
11.	expression of sorrow	me-li-e-a	16	NE
12.	expression of) compassion	muš$_3$-am$_3$	9	PE
13.	fear(someness)	ni$_2$	391	

14.	(fore)thought	*umuš*	41	
15.	furious	*lipiš-tuku*	10	NE
16.	heart	*šag₄*	1,517	
17.	heartache	*šag₄-zaraḫ*	1	NE
18.	insight	*nam-igi-ĝal₂*	1	
19.	joy	*mud₅*	1	PE
20.	joy	*mud₅-me-ĝar*	2	PE
21.	joy	*niĝ₂-ḫul₂-la*	5	PE
22.	joy	*niĝ₂-ul*	3	PE
23.	jubilation	*niĝ₂-me-ĝar*	1	PE
24.	life-giving (encouraging?)	*zi-šag₄-ĝal₂*	28	PE
25.	pride	*teš₂*	25	PE
26.	proud	*teš₂-tuku*	1	PE
27.	rage	*urgu₂*	2	NE
28.	rejoicing	*asila*	31	PE
29.	smitten person	*saĝ-DU*	1	
30.	tears (of joy)	*i-si-iš*	34	PE
31.	to be angry	*sumur*	46	NE
32.	to be frightened	*ḫuluḫ*	39	NE
33.	to be happy	*ḫul₂*	419	PE
34.	to be joyful	*li*	3	PE
35.	to be nervous	*mud*	3	NE
36.	to forget	*u₁₈-lu*	7	
37.	to have pleasure	*ḫi-li*	5	PE
38.	to rage	*mir*	25	NE
39.	to swell (with joy)	*ul*	71	PE
40.	to weep	*šeš₂*	86	NE
41.	weeping	*šex*	13	NE
42.	wisdom	ĜEŠTUG₂.NISABA	1	
43.	wisdom	*nam-gal-an-zu*	1	
44.	wisdom	*nam-kug-zu*	11	
45.	wisdom	*nam-zu*	3	
46.	wise	*igi-ĝal₂*	22	
47.	wise	*igi-ĝal₂-tuku*	10	
48.	wise	*kug-zu*	49	
49.	wonder	*u₆*	120	
50.	liver [often used in psychological terms]	*ur₅*	73	

$\sum 3374$

Dataset App D.4. ePSD Dictionary: RL and Their Frequencies.

	Sumerian	English	Freq.	Note
1.	*abgal*	sage; priest	32	
2.	*abigal*	person associated with funerals	2	
3.	*abrig*	cultic functionary	13	
4.	*abum*	festival; mound for funerary use	25	

5.	abzaza	figurine	12	
6.	abzu	(cosmic) underground water; ritual water container in temple	314	
7.	aga	tiara, crown	118	
8.	agarka	part of temple	1	1a
9.	agrun	cella; bedroom; ritual building; the sanctuary of the goddess Ningal	33	
10.	aguba	cultic vessel for water	1	1a
11.	akiti	festival at New Year; month name	7	
12.	ala	demon	1	1a
13.	alad	spirit	4	
14.	alal	part of temple	15	
15.	alan	statue; form	399	
16.	guhšu	reed altar; (part of) container	2	
17.	amagal	grandmother; priestess	5	
18.	ama'inanak	goddess	1	1a
19.	amalug	priestess; goddess	7	
20.	an	sky, heaven; upper; crown (of tree)	1,598	
21.	anbad	heaven's heights	1	1a
22.	anbar	side of heaven	2	
23.	anguba	tutelary deity	3	
24.	anki	the universe, heaven and earth	6	
25.	ankišua	the extent of heaven and earth	6	
26.	annibatu	an ecstatic	1	1a
26.	anšag	the interior of heaven	44	
28.	ansala	cultic performer	1	1a
29.	anšar	the entirety of heaven	4	
30.	anubda	cosmographic or geographic term; quarter (of the universe)	1,748	
31.	anzag	horizon, border of heaven	22	
32.	anzil	abomination	7	
33.	anzud	mythological eagle	28	
34.	apap	birth canal; clay pipe; interment, burial; funerary ceremony	13	
35.	ara	times (with numbers); ways; way; omen; step (math.)	4,046	
36.	arali	earth, land; underworld	3	
37.	arua	votive offering	743	
38.	asag	demon; disease	23	
39.	ašte	chair, throne; seat, dwelling; shrine, chapel; unit of area	2	
40.	atu	doorkeeper (?); priest or cultic functionary	21	
41.	atua	type of priest	76	
42.	atua	lustration rite	6	
43.	a'ua	cultic musician (?)	1	1a

44.	az	(bear) figurine	248	
45.	azag	taboo, forbidden thing	6	
46.	banšurzaggula	cultic table	3	
47.	banšurzaggara	cultic table	1	
48.	barag	ruler, king; dais, seat	423	
49.	biluda	rituals, rites	15	
50.	bisagdubak	archivist	459	
51.	bizaza	(frog) figurine	16	
52.	bur	(food) offering, sacrifice; meal(time); (stone) bowl; priest	85	
53.	bur	cultic location	1	
54.	bur	priest	3	
55.	burgia	an offering	7	
56.	burzi	bowl	50	
57.	dab	to seize, take, hold; bind; envelop, overwhelm; choose (by extispicy); accept; take charge of		
58.	dalla	ring, crown	20	
59.	digir'ama	divine mother	1	
60.	digir	deity, god, goddess	1,837	
61.	digirdumu	divine son	1	
62.	dilmun	(to be) made manifest; heavy; important; ritually unclean, impure person; instruction	11	
63.	dima	small object, figurine	20	
64.	dimme	demon	2	
65.	dimmea	demon	1	
66.	dirida	(divine) instruction, order	1	1a
67.	du	throne platform for deity	1	1a
68.	dukug	cultic and cosmic place	270	
69.	e	house; temple; (temple) household; station (of the moon) (?); room; house lot; estate	13,124	
70.	ebgal	temple oval	40	
71.	edenlil	haunted desert	7	
72.	egal	palace; temple	1,848	
73.	egizid	priestess	18	
74.	emegar	magic	1	
75.	emegargar	witchcraft	1	
76.	emeš	priest	1	
77.	emezi	priest	1	
78.	en	priest	7,739	
79.	engiz	temple cook	8	
80.	engur	(cosmic) underground waters	45	
81.	enigkisig	funerary chapel	1	1a
82.	en	incantation, spell	1	1a
83.	enindakisig	funerary chapel	1	
84.	enkum	temple treasurer	10	

85.	ennam	an official	4	
86.	ennigi	priest	1	1a
87.	ennun	type of priest	33	
88.	ensi	dream interpreter	36	
89.	ensik	ruler, governor; quality designation	7,043	
90.	ensikgal	chief governor	7	
91.	enzid	priest	2	
92.	erešdiĝir	priestess	337	
93.	erubatum	festival	3	
94.	eš	shrine; an establishment	667	
95.	ešda	metal cultic vessel	9	
96.	ešeš	festival	209	
97.	ešgal	earth, land; underworld	1	1a
98.	ešgini	cultic place	1	1a
99.	esuhur	part of temple	4	
100.	ešusiga	temple room or building	1	1a
101.	e'urre	grave	1	1a
102.	ezem	festival	1,138	
103.	ezi	en priest of Ea	1	1a
104.	gabaria	an offering	4	
105.	gadala	priest	2	
106.	ĝagia	cloister	2	
107.	gala	lamentation singer	500	
108.	galamah	chief lament singer	98	
109.	galatura	cultic performer	135	
110.	galla	policeman; demon	107	
111.	ganda	cultic place	1	1a
112.	ganzer	earth, land; underworld, door to the underworld	3	
113.	ĝarza	rites; cultic or cosmic ordinance	132	
114.	gatil	vow; an offering	20	
115.	ĝeš tag	to make offerings	142	
116.	ĝešanaĝ	place of libation to the dead	12	
117.	ĝešbun	(cultic) meal	63	
118.	ĝešhe	firmament, vault of the sky	10	
119.	ĝeš tag	to make offerings	142	
120.	ĝeštaga	sacrifice	1	
121.	gidim	ghost	45	
122.	giguna	high sacred terrace	56	
123.	gina	regular offering, dues	1	
124.	ĝipar	cloister	156	
125.	giranum	wailing, wailing ceremony	57	
126.	ĝirsiga	an attendant	349	
127.	ĝiškim	omen; trust, aid	60	
128.	guda'abzu	priest	1	1a
129.	gudug	priest	829	
130.	gu'en	assembly room, throne room	1	

Appendix D

131.	gug	offering; cake	68	
132.	gune	place; cult center (?); oven (?)	10	
133.	hal	divide, deal out, distribute; to perform an extispicy; to open; secret; to pour away; to sieve; to slink, crawl away; qualification of grain	55	
134.	halib	Netherworld	1	
135.	hulĝal	evil	50	
136.	huwawa	figurine (of face) of ~; mythological monster	2	
137.	idu	cultic room	1	1a
138.	igid	divination (?)	16	
139.	igidua	priestess	3	
140.	ilu	god	2	
141.	Inannukurrim	priest of Inanna	1	
142.	inanna	divine entreaty	1	
143.	inimdug	peace, reconciliation with the gods	3	
144.	irhandi	sorcerer	1a	
145.	irigal	earth, land; underworld; grave	19	
146.	išib	sorcerer, magician; incantation priest, exorcist; (to be) pure; (to be) clear; purification priest; incantation, spell	146	
147.	itima	shrine, chapel	20	
148.	kaʾinima	incantation formula	1	1a
149.	kamuĝal	incantation priest	1	
150.	ki sub	to prostrate oneself	9	
151.	ki za	to bow down	1	1a
152.	kiʾana	cultic location	1	1a
153.	kiʾanaĝ	place of libations to the dead	1	1a
154.	kiʾešbar	place of (divine) decisions	1	1a
155.	kiʾezem	festival place	1	1a
156.	kiĝgia	a designation of an animal suitable for extispicy	2	
157.	kilugaldu	cultic place	18	
158.	kimah	grave; cultic place	21	
159.	kinamesira	side of the forehead, temples	1	
160.	kingal	grandee; crown authority over land, labor recruiter	23	
161.	kiri du	to pay homage to	1	
162.	kiri ki sub	to prostrate oneself	5	
163.	kiri šu ĝal	to pay homage to	48	
164.	kisalmah	main court of temple	9	
165.	kiši	the Netherworld	1	1a
166.	kišib	cylinder seal, sealed tablet	17,468	
167.	kisiga	funerary offerings	18	

168.	kišuk	cultic place	5	
169.	kišupeš	cultic place	6	
170.	kišur	grave; hole	1	
171.	kišutag	cultic place	4	
172.	kitila	deity	1	
173.	kitum	burial	7	
174.	ki'utu	cultic location; ritual	1	
175.	kizah	cultic place	6	
176.	kuĝĝal	holy	1	
177.	kur	underworld; land, country; mountain(s); east; easterner; east wind	2,494	
178.	kurĝara	cultic performer	12	
179.	kurku	purification priest	1	1a
180.	kušla	garment; functionary	5	
181.	lagar	priest	5	
182.	lahama	mythical being	9	
183.	lal	type of priest	1	
184.	lalešaga	priest or cultic functionary	1	
185.	lamahuš	garment; clothing	1	1a
186.	lamhu	netherworld	1	1a
187.	lammar	(female) tutelary deity; ~ figurine	220	
188.	lil	wind, breeze; ghost	92	
189.	lillaen	type of demon	1	
190.	lillilgi	demon	1	
191.	lillilgia	demon	1	
192.	lu'alede	an ecstatic	1	1a
193.	lu'ede	ecstatic	1	1a
194.	luĝešgisaĝkeš	type of cult performer	5	
195.	luguba	ecstatic	4	
196.	luhša	temple functionary	7	
197.	luka'inima	magical expert	1	1a
198.	lukur	priestess; (junior) wife of deified king	172	
199.	lumah	priest	98	
200.	lumumun	incantation priest	15	
201.	luniĝkisiga	funerary carer	1	1a
202.	lunindaba	cultic functionary	1	1a
203.	lunisub	an ecstatic	4	
204.	lusaĝDUa	divinely punished person	1	
205.	lusaĝlugal	royal officer	1	
206.	marmah	priest	1	1a
207.	maš	goat; extispicy; sacrificial animal for omens	10,699	
208.	mašĝik	(nocturnal) vision	1	1a
209.	maškim	an administrative position; demon	3,492	
210.	mašmaš	sorcerer, incantation priest	33	
211.	maššugidgid	diviner	26	

Appendix D

212.	maššugigi	diviner	1	1a
213.	me	being, divine properties enabling cosmic activity; office; (cultic) ordinance	750	
214.	men	type of crown	83	
215.	mete	image	1	1a
216.	mitum	divine weapon	46	
217.	mu	incantation, spell	18	
218.	mulan	heavenly star	33	
219.	mumunĝal	exorcist	2	
220.	munugu	festival	1	1a
221.	munusĝešgi	type of cult performer	1	
222.	muraš	female dream interpreter	1	
223.	murub	priest	3	
224.	muš	flat space; holy area	81	
225.	mušmah	mythical creature	4	
226.	muššatur	(mythical) snake; horned viper	15	
227.	muzug	ritually unclean, impure person	8	
228.	na deg	to make clear, explain; to consecrate, purify; to separate; to clear out, cut out	80	
229.	nabrium	an offering; festival	2	
230.	nadeg	incense	5	
231.	nam tar	to decree fate	357	
232.	nam	determined order; will, testament; fate, destiny	567	
233.	nambarag	royalty	4	
234.	namdiĝir	divinity	36	
235.	namegirzid	the office of egirzid priest	2	
236.	namen	the office of en priest; kingship	116	
237.	namenlil	cosmic sovereignty	8	
238.	namenlilbanda	cosmic status	1	
239.	namensik	office of ruler	4	
240.	namerešdiĝir	office of erešdiĝir priestess	2	
241.	namgala	the art of lamentation singing	19	
242.	namgudug	office of gudug priest	34	
243.	namguzala	office of throne bearer	1	
244.	namišib	office of išib priest	15	
245.	namlagar	office of lagar Priest	3	
246.	namlugal	kingship	300	
247.	namlukur	office of lukur priestess	2	
248.	namlumah	office of lumah	98	
249.	namlunindaba	cultic function	2	
250.	namniĝir	office of herald	2	
251.	namnugig	office of the nugig	83	
252.	namšakkanak	governorship	1	
253.	namsikil	purity	1	
254.	namšita	priest	7	

255.	namšita	prayer; entreaty	40	
256.	namšub	incantation	12	
257.	namtar	fate, destiny; demon	80	
258.	nenkum	temple official	8	
259.	nesaĝ	first fruit offering; storage place	977	
260.	niĝak	magic	16	
261.	niĝataka	ointment	1	
262.	niĝdimdima	magical procedures	8	
263.	niĝdirig	extra, additional things; type of offering	88	
264.	niĝdun	prostration	1	
265.	niĝgig	that which is bad, forbidden; evil	89	
266.	niĝhulu	evil	16	
267.	niĝhuluĝal	evil	1	1a
268.	niĝkizah	type of offering	1	1a
269.	niĝlam	garment; ceremonial garment	765	
270.	niĝna	incense (burner)	114	
271.	niĝnadega	incense (burner)	1	1a
272.	niĝNERU	evil	63	
273.	niĝsiškur	an offering	113	
274.	niĝušria	witchcraft	1	
275.	nindaba	(food) offering	62	
276.	nu'ešak	priest	1	1a
277.	nugig	priestess; divine epithet; profession for women	83	
278.	nunuzzi	priestess	2	
279.	nusaĝ	priest	16	
280.	pašeš	priest	7	
281.	peš	to anoint	1	
282.	šabra	chief administrator of temple or other household	2,031	
283.	sadug	regular temple offerings; unit of liquid capacity	2,949	
284.	saĝa	priest	12	
285.	saĝbur	priest	1	
286.	šageguru	type of offering	1	
287.	saĝĝa	an official, the chief administrator of temple household	1,862	
288.	šaggadala	priest	8	
289.	saĝĝamah	an official, the senior chief administrator of temple household	1	
290.	saĝki	rites	13	
291.	saĝmen	crown	10	
292.	šagtubala	priest	1	
293.	saĝursaĝ	cultic performer	12	
294.	sahir	incense (?)	1	
295.	šakkanak	general, governor general	332	

Appendix D

296.	sallagarbad	type of priestess	1	
297.	šarrabdu	an administrator; demon	221	
298.	šedu	spirit	3	
299.	še'ila	festival	1	1a
300.	šennu	priest	4	
301.	šeš	to anoint	14	
302.	sigbar	priest	16	
303.	SIGEN	type of goddess (?)	3	
304.	SIGHI	birth goddess (?)	3	
305.	šimmu	priest	2	
306.	šimmumah	high priest	1	1a
307.	sisig	ghost (?); storm; breeze, wind	14	
308.	siškur	prayer; blessing; offering, sacrifice, rites; to pour (libation), sacrifice; to intercede	1,192	
309.	šita	priest; ~ figurine	17	
310.	šita'aba	priest	1	1a
311.	šita'inana	funerary priest	1	1a
312.	šita	prayer	14	
313.	šu e	to bless; to go out (?); to terrify (?)	22	
314.	šu gid	to examine (extispicy)	1	1a
315.	šu mu	to pray	20	
316.	su	flesh; body; entrails (omen); body	495	
317.	šuagina	type of offering	23	
318.	šud ša	to pray	1	
319.	šud	prayer, dedication; blessing	115	
320.	sud	to purify	1	1a
321.	sudaĝ	precious metal; (to be) shiny (divine epithet)	6	
322.	sug	shrine, chapel	3	
323.	šugurgur	purification (ceremony)	1	
324.	suh	crown	52	
325.	suhurmaš	mythical fish	7	
326.	šu'ila	kind of prayer; subscript	1	1a
327.	šukin dab	to prostrate oneself	8	
328.	šukin	prostration	3	
329.	sukud	crown or headdress	1	1a
330.	suluhu	long haired sheep; ceremonial garment; fleece	11	
331.	surru	priest	3	
332.	šuš	priest	1	
333.	susbu	priest	7	
334.	šutur	garment	5	
335.	tam	(to be) bright; (to be) pure; to purify; (to be) clean	16	
336.	tiridanu	(to be) evil	2	
337.	tu	incantation, spell	20	
338.	tu	type of priest	1	

339.	tuduga	incantation	1	
340.	tuduga	incantation formula	1	
341.	tukulšunir	divine emblem	1	1a
342.	ubara	divine protection	1	
343.	ububul	an ecstatic	1	1a
344.	ud	storm; storm demon	266	1a
345.	udug	demon (of desert, mountain, sea, tomb); ~ figurine	41	
346.	ug	lion; mythical lion; large cat	23	
347.	ugul ĝar	to pray	19	
348.	ukurrim	priest of Inanna	1	
349.	ul	vault of heaven, firmament	1	1a
350.	ulhe	firmament, vault of the sky	1	
351.	ulmaše	priest	1	1a
352.	ulu	south wind; south; demon	83	
353.	unir	ziggurat	12	
354.	unu	banquet; dining hall; most sacred part of temple; seat, throne; dwelling, abode; temple	1,511	
355.	unugal	tomb	1	
356.	unugi	office; rites, (cultic) ordinance	1	
357.	unuRIbanda	sacred area	2	
358.	ur	to rub in, anoint	1	1a
359.	urinak	sanctuary	1	
360.	uruh	priest who performs funerary rites	1	
361.	urur	cultic person; jackal; caterpillar	35	
362.	ušga	(palace) attendant; youth	8	
363.	ussaĝ	(cosmic) bond	4	
364.	usuh	en priest of Enki	1	
365.	utah	heaven	7	
366.	uzga	cella, shrine; goods, treasure; treasury	480	
367.	uzga	type of priest	7	
368.	uzu	flesh; body; entrails; omen	274	
369.	uzu	diviner	1	1a
370.	uzuga	entrail omen	2	
371.	zagmuk	new year, beginning of cycle (?)	180	
372.	zig	town, center	1	1a
373.	zigara	the heavens	1	1a
374.	zikum	the heavens	1	1a
375.	zirru	priestess	7	

$\sum 101{,}538$

a ePSD did not provide the frequency. I have elected to count them as 1.

Dataset App D.5. ePSD: Dictionary: PL, Their Frequencies Categorized by Period, and EV.

No.	Sumerian	English	Frequency by Period	Freq. for Word	EV
1.	a'aš	wish, desire; curse	1a	1	
2.	ad ša	to resound, to lament	Old Bab 19	19	NE
3.	al dug	to desire	Lagash II 1 Ur III 3 Old Bab 63	67	
4.	anir	lament	Old Bab 138	138	NE
5.	asilala	joy; to rejoice; decorative fancy work	Old Bab 35	35	PE
6.	banda	sagacity	Old Akk 12 Ur III 9 Old Bab 2	23	
7.	bar tab	to be angry, to feel feverish	Old Bab 2	2	NE
8.	buluh	to fear, tremble, be afraid	Old Bab 3	3	NE
9.	dada	(to be) hostile; to be difficult	Old Akk 1 Ur III 13 Old Bab 1	15	NE
10.	daparu	defeat, annihilation; (to be) resistant, obstinate	1a	1	NE
11.	di kud	to judge	ED IIIb 1 Old Akk 2 Lagash II 3 Old Bab 46	52	
12.	dib	to burn; wrath	1a	1	NE
13.	dimma	thought, planning, instruction	Old Akk 2 Ur III 15 Old Bab 48	65	
14.	dinig	(to be) resistant, obstinate	1a	1	NE
15.	du	lament	Old Bab 6	6	NE
16.	e	trust	1a	1	
17.	ed	to go up or down; to demolish; to scratch; to rage, be rabid	ED IIIb 241 Old Akk 3 Lagash II 21 Ur III 44 Old Bab 137	446	NE
18.	ene	pleasure (?)	ED IIIb 18 Old Akk 10 Ur III 4 Old Bab 3	35	PE

19.	ensi	dream interpreter	ED IIIa 1 ED IIIb 6 Old Akk 3 Ur III 11 Old Bab 15	36	
20.	er	weeping, mourning, tears, to weep	ED IIIb 3 Old Akk 3 Lagash II 2 Ur III 42 Old Bab 146	196	NE
21.	er pad	to weep	Old Bab 22	22	NE
22.	ereš	wise	1a	1	
23.	erišti	wise	Old Bab 1	1	
24.	ešbar	decision	Ur III 3 Old Bab 41	44	
25.	ešbar kiĝ	decide	Old Bab 14	14	
26.	gabal du	to be hostile, to challenge	Old Bab 7	7	NE
27.	gabarahum	despair	Old Bab 2	2	NE
28.	galam	(to be) skillful, elaborate, clever; to make artfully	Lagash II 1 Ur III 2 Old Bab 65	68	
29.	galanzu	wise, knowing	ED IIIb 1 Old Akk 1 Ur III 2 Old Bab 167	171	
30.	ĝalga	(fore)thought, plan(ning), understanding, instruction, advice	Old Bab 37	37	
31.	gašam	(to be) knowing, wise, sending, mission, work, craftsman, specialist	ED IIIb 6 Old Akk 1 Ur III 75 Old Bab 13	95	
32.	ĝeshur	plan	ED IIIb 3 Ur III 4 Old Bab 116	123	
33.	ĝeštug	reason, plan, (to be) wise, wisdom, understanding, ear	ED IIIb 19 Old Akk 5 Lagash II 5 Ur III 13 Old Bab 220	262	
34.	ĝeštug deg	to ponder	Old Bab 10	10	
35.	ĝeštug ĝar	to pay attention, to listen	Old Bab 9	9	
36.	ĝeštug gub	to pay attention, to plan	Old Bab 29 ED IIIb 1 Lagash II 1	31	
37.	ĝeštug šum	to listen, to give	ED IIIb 9	23	

Appendix D 155

		wisdom	Old Akk 1 Lagash II 1 Old Bab 12		
38.	ĝeštug ulu	to forget	Old Bab 7	7	
39.	geštugnisaba	wisdom	Old Bab 1	1	
40.	gi	judgment	Old Bab 3	3	
41.	gilim	to lie across, to be entwined, to entwine, twist, to block, (to be) difficult to understand	Old Bab 25	25	NE
42.	gir	anger, rage	1ª	1	
43.	ĝiškim	sign, omen; trust, aid	ED IIIb 2 Old Bab 58	60	
44.	ĝiškim til	to trust	Old Bab 9	9	
45.	ĝiškimti	trust, aid	Old Bab 16	16	
46.	ĝizzal	wisdom, understanding, ear, hearing	ED IIIa 2 Old Bab 48	50	
47.	gu bar	to dislike, hate	1ª	1	NE
48.	gu du	to neglect	Old Bab 4	4	NE
49.	gug	enmity, hostility	1ª	1	NE
50.	halam	(to be) bad, evil; to forsake, forget; to destroy	ED IIIb 13 Lagash II 1 Old Bab 93	107	NE
51.	hili	sex appeal, (to be) luxuriant, to have pleasure	Old Bab 209	209	PE
52.	hili kar	to love, be fond of, attracted to	Old Bab 1	1	PE
53.	hili teĝ	to love, be fond of, attracted to	Old Bab 6	6	PE
54.	hul	joy, rejoicing, to rejoice	ED IIIb 7 Ur III 4 Old Bab 336	347	PE
55.	hulu gig	to hate	Ur III 1 Old Bab 56	57	NE
56.	huluh	(to be) frightened	Old Bab 41	41	NE
57.	huš	furious, angry; (to be) reddish, ruddy	ED IIIB 4 Lagash II 3 Ur III 214 Old Bab 214	435	NE
58.	ib	angry; to curse	Ur III 1 Old Bab 34	35	NE
59.	igi gid	to look with disfavor	Old Bab 100	100	NE
60.	igi suh	to be angry	1ª	1	NE
61.	igi tur gid	to look contemptuously at someone	Old Bab 2	2	NE

62.	*igiĝal*	wise	Old Akk 1 Ur III 16 Old Bab 36	53	
63.	*igiĝaltuku*	wise, clever	Old Bab 11	11	
64.	*ilu*	joyful song; lament	Old Bab 114	114	
65.	*inim sig*	to express an idea, desire	ED IIIb 3 Lagash II 2 Old Bab 16	21	
66.	*isiš*	to laugh, laughter, wailing, lamentation, sorrow, to whisper	Old Bab 27	27	
67.	*isiš ĝar*	to wail	Old Bab 8	8	NE
68.	*kaš*	decision	ED IIIb 6 Old Akk 3 Ur III 8 Old Bab 53	70	
69.	*kaš bar*	to make a decision	1a	1	
70.	*ki'ešbar*	place of (divine) decisions	1a	1	
71.	*kirizal*	joy, rejoicing	ED IIIb 1 Old Akk 1 Old Bab 153	155	PE
72.	*kugzu*	wise	Ur III 8 Old Bab 50	58	
73.	*kurku*	wish	Old Bab 24	24	
74.	*kušum*	height; to look down on, despise	1a	1	NE
75.	*lala*	plenty, happiness, lust	Old Bab 53	53	PE
76.	*lib*	(to be) rich, well off, high quality, (to be) happy	Old Bab 35	35	PE
77.	*lil*	secret knowledge	Old Bab 1	1	
78.	*lipiš*	inner body, heart, anger, rage	ED IIIb 1 Old Bab 39	40	NE
79.	*lipišbala*	anger	Old Bab 1	1	NE
80.	*lirum*	strength; force; (to be) strong, powerful, mighty, great; (to be) resistant, obstinate, combative, quarrelsome; a noble; (crook of the) arm; wrestler	Old Bab 35	35	NE
81.	*lu'ede*	ecstatic	1a	1	PE
82.	*luguba*	ecstatic	Old Bab 4	4	PE
83.	*lu'ura*	ecstatic	1a	1	PE
84.	*mamud*	dream	ED IIIB 1	45	

Appendix D

			Old Akk 2 Ur III 2 Old Bab 40		
85.	*me*	desire	Old Bab 3	3	
86.	*melim*	frightening splendor, fearsome radiance	ED IIIb 4 Lagash II 2 Ur III 4 Old Bab 149	159	NE
87.	*mir*	(to be) angry, anger, rage	Old Bab 25	25	NE
88.	*mud*	joy	Old Bab 1	1	PE
89.	*mud*	(to be) scared, terrified	Old Bab 3	3	NE
90.	*mudmeĝar*	joy	Old Bab 2	2	PE
91.	*murgu*	rage	Old Bab 2	2	NE
92.	*nam*	(fore)thought, plan(ning), understanding, instruction	Old Akk 1	1	
93.	*namgalanzu*	wisdom	Old Bab 1	1	
94.	*namkugzu*	wisdom	Old Bab 15	15	
95.	*namsag*	pleasure	Old Bab 2	2	PE
96.	*namsuna*	humility	Old Bab 3	3	
97.	*namte*	fear	Old Bab 2	2	NE
98.	*namzu*	wisdom	Old Akk 1 Old Bab 4	5	
99.	NERUdu	hostile	Old Bab 25	25	NE
100.	*ni*	fear, aura	ED IIIb 1 Lagash II 5 Ur III 2 Old Bab 318	326	NE
101.	*ni dub*	to relax	Old Bab 20	20	PE
102.	*ni gur*	to feel proud	Old Bab 1	1	PE
103.	*ni ri*	to inspire fear	1a	1	NE
104.	*ni sig*	to plot	1a	1	
105.	*ni teĝ*	to fear, to become afraid	Old Bab 90	90	NE
106.	*ni ur*	to be scared	Old Bab 4	4	NE
107.	*niĝĝiskimtil*	trust	Old Bab 1	1	
108.	*niĝhul*	joy	Old Bab 7	7	PE
109.	*niĝinimsige*	wish (?)	1a	1	
110.	*niĝkur*	hostility	Old Bab 8	8	NE
111.	*niĝmeĝar*	jubilation, prosperity	Old Bab 3	3	PE
112.	*niĝsun*	humility	Old Bab 1	1	
113.	*niĝtukum*	conjecture	Old Bab 1	1	
114.	*niĝul*	joy	Old Bab 4	4	PE
115.	*niĝumun*	knowledge	Old Bab 3	3	

116.	niĝzu	knowledge	Old Bab 4	4	
117.	nihuš	terrifying appearance	1ᵃ	1	NE
118.	nir	trust, sign	Ur III 12 Old Bab 43	55	
119.	nir ĝal	to trust	Old Bab 27	27	
120.	nituku	pious, attentive	Old Bab 19	19	
121.	sa	advice, counsel; resolution, intelligence	ED IIIb 13 Old Akk 2 Ur III 19 Old Bab 12	46	
122.	šag dab	think, conceive an idea	Ur III 12 Old Bab 22	34	
123.	šag dab	to feel hurt, to be angry, to be worried	1ᵃ	1	NE
124.	šag dar	heartbroken	Old Bab 4	4	NE
125.	šag de	decide	Old Bab 29	29	
126.	šag dug	cheerful	Old Bab 38 Ur III 3	41	PE
127.	saĝ gid	to be(come) angry	Ur III 19 Old Bab 6	25	NE
128.	šag gur	feel wonderful	Old Bab 8	8	PE
129.	šag huĝ	soothe	Old Bab 19	19	PE
130.	šag hul	be happy	Lagash II 1 Ur III 47 Old Bab 141	189	PE
131.	saĝ kešed	to take care, attend carefully to something	Ur III 1 Old Bab 30	31	
132.	šag kušu	soothe	ED IIIb 2 Old Bab 52	54	PE
133.	šag sag	afflicted	Old Bab 31	31	NE
134.	šag sag	feel better	Old Akk 1 Old Bab 3	4	PE
135.	šag šed	to soothe the heart	Old Bab 15	15	PE
136.	šag sig	to plot	Ur III 5 Old Bab 7	12	
137.	saĝki gid	to be(come) angry	Old Bab 20	20	NE
138.	šala	pity	Ur III 1 Old Bab 15	16	
139.	šazarah	concern	Old Bab 1	1	
140.	šeš	to weep	ED IIIb 10 Old Akk 6 Ur III 31 Old Bab 75	122	NE
141.	si	to remember	1ᵃ	1	
142.	širsaĝ	lament	Old Bab 2	2	NE

143.	šu bar	to release, to forget	Lagash II 1 Old Bab 4	5	
144.	su zig	to fear, to have goose bumps	Old Bab 46	46	NE
145.	šudum	reckoning	Old Bab 11	11	
146.	šugalanzu	wise	1a	1	
147.	suh	to confuse, confusion	Ur III 3 Old Bab 61	64	NE
148.	sulum	contempt	1a	1	NE
149.	sumug	darkness, calamity, fear	Old Bab 7	7	NE
150.	sumur	(to be) angry, furious	Old Bab 46	46	NE
151.	sun	to be haughty	Old Bab 16	16	
152.	sur	furious	ED IIIa 1 Ur III 11 Old Bab 3	15	NE
153.	šušru	(to be) distressed	Old Bab 1	1	NE
154.	tam	to trust, to believe	ED IIIb 14 Ur III 19 Old Bab 13	46	
155.	u	admiration	ED IIIb 11 Lagash II 2 Ur III 11 Old Bab 54	78	PE
156.	u dug	to admire, to regard, observe	Old Bab 92	92	PE
157.	udi	admiration, (astonished) gaze	Ur III 1 Old Bab 2	3	PE
158.	ug	(to be) furious, anger	Ur III 2	2	NE
159.	uh	(to be) forgotten	1a	1	
160.	ul	to swell, (to be) distended, to love, attractiveness, pleasure, rejoicing	Ur III 3 Old Bab 71	74	PE
161.	ulilla	lament	Old Bab 1	1	NE
162.	ululumama	lament	Old Bab 3	3	NE
163.	umun	knowledge, workshop	ED IIIa 1 ED IIIb 2 Old Bab 13	16	
164.	umuš	(fore)thought, plan-(ning), understand-ing, instruction, consideration, sagacity	ED IIIb 1 Ur III 1 Old Bab 50	52	
165.	ur	liver [often used in psychological terms]	Old Bab 39	39	

166.	ur sag	ameliorate	Old Bab 36	36	
167.	ur ug	to despair	1[a]	1	NE
168.	urun	(to be) clever	1[a]	1	
169.	ururu	lament	Ur III 2 Old Bab 3	5	NE
170.	usandu	wise, clever	Old Bab 1	1	
171.	zara	(excessive) concern	Old Bab 2	2	
172.	zarah	wailing, lamentation	Old Bab 8	8	NE
173.	zi ir	to feel troubled	Ur III 1	1	NE
174.	zir	to tear out; to break, destroy; to be troubled; to erase	ED IIIb 84 Old Akk 104 Lagash II 2 Ur III 161 Old Bab 101	452	NE

$\sum 7{,}001$

[a] ePSD did not provide the period or frequency. I have elected to count them as 1.

Dataset App D.6. ePSD Dictionary: Sums and Frequencies of PL Categorized by Period.

(1) ED IIIa
1, 2, 1, 1
$n\,(1) = 4,\ \sum (1)\ 5$
(2) ED IIIb
1, 241, 18, 6, 3, 1, 6, 3, 19, 1, 9, 2, 13, 7, 4, 3, 6, 1, 1, 1, 4, 1, 13, 2, 10, 14, 11, 2, 1, 84
$n\,(2) = 30,\ \sum (2)\ 488$
(3) Old Akkadian
12, 1, 2, 2, 3, 10, 3, 3, 1, 1, 5, 1, 1, 3, 1, 2, 1, 1, 2, 1, 6, 104
$n\,(3) = 22,\ \sum (3)\ 166$
(4) Lagash II
1, 3, 21, 2, 1, 5, 1, 1, 1, 3, 2, 2, 5, 1, 1, 2, 2
$n\,(4) = 17,\ \sum (4)\ 54$
(5) Ur III
3, 9, 13, 15, 44, 4, 11, 42, 3, 2, 2, 75, 4, 13, 4, 1, 214, 1, 16, 8, 8, 2, 4, 2, 12, 19, 12, 3, 19, 47, 1, 5, 1, 31, 3, 11, 19, 11, 1, 2, 3, 1, 2, 1, 161
$n\,(5) = 44,\ \sum (5)\ 865$

(6) Old Bab

19, 63, 138, 35, 2, 2, 3, 1, 46, 48, 6, 137, 3, 15, 146, 22, 1, 41, 14, 7, 2, 65, 167, 37, 13, 116, 220, 10, 9, 29, 12, 7, 1, 3, 25, 58, 9, 16, 48, 4, 93, 209, 1, 6, 336, 56, 41, 214, 34, 100, 2, 36, 11, 114, 16, 27, 8, 53, 153, 50, 24, 53, 35, 1, 39, 1, 35, 4, 40, 3, 149, 25, 1, 3, 2, 2, 1, 15, 2, 3, 2, 4, 25, 318, 20, 1, 90, 4, 1, 7, 8, 3, 1, 1, 4, 3, 4, 43, 27, 19, 12, 22, 4, 29, 38, 6, 8, 19, 141, 30, 52, 31, 3, 15, 7, 20, 15, 1, 75, 2, 4, 46, 11, 61, 7, 46, 16, 3, 1, 13, 54, 92, 2, 71, 1, 3, 13, 50, 39, 36, 3, 1, 2, 8, 101

$n\ (6) = 145,\ \sum\ (6)\ 5397$

(7) Not categorized into periods

$n\ (7) = 26,\ \sum\ (7)\ 26$

$n: (1) + (2) + (3) + (4) + (5) + (6) + (7) = 288$
Frequencies: $(1) + (2) + (3) + (4) + (5) + (6) + (7) = 7,001$

Dataset App D.7. ETCSL NAMES: Their Types and Their Frequency.

Type of Name	Number of Unique Names	Number of Names	%age of Number of Names	Freq. of Names	%age of Freq. of Names
Divine	287	607	66.19%	9,781	78.02%
Temple	129				
Royal	191				
Personal	108	310	33.81%	2,756	21.98%
Settlement	82				
Watercourse	41				
Other	27				
Geographical	44				
Month	6				
Ethnic	2				
Totals =	917	917	100%	12,537	100%

Dataset App D.8. HG Hittite Dictionary: RL.

No.	Hittite	English
1.	addus DINGIR^{MEŠ}	ancestors gods, Manes
2.	alpant-	enchanted, bewitched
3.	alwanzah-	to bewitch
4.	alwanzatar	magic
5.	alwanzessar	witchcraft, magic
6.	aniur	religious task
7.	ariya-	to study an oracle, ask an oracle
8.	ariyasessar	oracle
9.	arkuwāi-	to pray; to apologize
10.	arkuwar	prayer
11.	arkuwar essa-, iya-	to send a prayer

12.	aruwāi-	to prostrate oneself, worship
13.	astayarātar	sin
14.	DINGIR^LIM-is kikkis-	become a god = to die (for kings)
15.	DINGIR^LIM-is kis-	become a god = to die (for Hittite kings)
16.	É karim(n)i-	ritual building, temple
17.	É sinapsi-	a ritual building
18.	esha- = isha-	lord, master
19.	É tarnu(zan)-	house of ablutions
20.	EZEN kuzzi-	a feast
21.	EZEN purulli-	an important festival
22.	ⁱdammara-	a servant of worship
23.	ᴳᴵˢhalmasuitt-	throne
24.	ᴳᴵˢlahhura-	a piece of furniture used for offerings
25.	hāliya-	to kneel
26.	handandatar	miracle
27.	harsanallāi-	to crown
28.	harsanalli-	crown
29.	hassu-	king
30.	hassuiznāi-	to govern as king
31.	hassusara-	queen
32.	hassuwāi-	to govern as king
33.	huek-	to swear, talk under oath
34.	hukmāi-	conjuration, incantation, raising
35.	(ᵈ)hurnissiya	name of a Hurrian god (?)
36.	hurt- = huwart-	to curse
37.	hurtāi-	curse
38.	huwap-	to do evil
39.	huwappa-	evil
40.	hūwartā-	to swear, curse
41.	(ᴺᴬ₄)huwasi-	grindstone; ritual monument, ritual stone
42.	idālawah-	to make evil, to act badly
43.	idālawatar	evil, nastiness
44.	ishā-	master, lord
45.	istanana-	a kind of altar
46.	iya-	to do; to realize; to father; to celebrate (a feast); to heal (with a ritual)
47.	kaniniya-	to prostrate, bow down
48.	kattan h.	to prostrate
49.	kuptar	offering remainder
50.	kusduwātar	evilness, wickedness
51.	lahharnuzzi-	kind of sacrifice altar
52.	lahhurnuzzi-	sacrificial altar
53.	ᴸᵁhaliyatalla-	guard of a temple
54.	ᴸᵁkīta-	a kind of priest (?)
55.	ᴸᵁpatili-	(a kind of priest).
56.	ᴸᵁsālasha-	palace servant
57.	ᴸᵁzilipuriyatalla-	a priest (?)
58.	mald-	to vow, swear

59.	*maltessar*	vow
60.	*marsastarri-*	a religious breach
61.	*marsessa-*	to become evil, rebel; to get spoiled
62.	MUNUS^MEŠ *azzennas (Pl.)*	female server for religious service (?)
63.	^MUŠEN*surassura-*	an oracle bird
64.	*paprāi-*	to commit an impurity
65.	*paprātar*	impurity, stain
66.	*papres-*	to be(come) impure
67.	*parā handanda-*	to do a miracle
68.	*parkues-*	to become pure; prove oneself innocent
69.	*parkui-*	pure, free from
70.	*parkunu-*	to cleanse; to excuse
71.	*parkus-*	to become pure
72.	*parkuyatar*	purification, atonement
73.	(^GU4)*puhugari-*	substitute ox, expiatory sacrifice of a bull or ox
74.	ŠA MUŠEN u.	oracle of bird
75.	*salli É-ir*	big house" = palace
76.	*salli pēdan*	throne
77.	*sankunni-*	priest
78.	*sankunniyant-*	priest
79.	*ses-*	to rest, sleep (also for sexual intercourse), go to bed; to stay; to enjoy rest, calmness; to establish the oracle of a dream
80.	*sihill(iy)as wātar*	pure water, holy water
81.	*siu-*	god
82.	*siuna-*	god
83.	*siunan antuhsa-*	man of god, oracle
84.	*siuniyah-*	to be smitten with illness by god
85.	*siusmis*	"my god"
86.	*sius-smis*	"their god"
87.	*siussummin*	their god
88.	*suppiyah-*	to cleanse; to expiate.
89.	*tarpalli-*	picture, figure of substitution (used in worship as a replacement for man)
90.	*tuppi- (n.)*	tablet, document
91.	*wasku-*	violation
92.	*wasta-*	to sin
93.	*wastāi-*	sin
94.	*wastanu-*	to make sin
95.	*wastul*	sin, sacrilege, crime
96.	*wastulas*	sinner, impious ("he of the sin")
97.	*zankilātar*	punishment, sentence; expiatory offering, penance, atonement
98.	*zāu-*	a ritual object
99.	*zila-*	information from an oracle

Dataset App D.9. HG Hittite Dictionary: PL and EV.

No.	Hittite	English	EV
1.	anda au(s)-	to look; to pay attention	
2.	appan sanh	to worry	NE
3.	arsanatalla-	envious, jealous	NE
4.	arsaniya-	to envy	NE
5.	assul-	salvation, happiness, prosperity	PE
6.	dusgarauwant-	joyful, happy, glad	PE
7.	dusk-	to rejoice, be happy	PE
8.	duskarati-	happiness	PE
9.	genzu-	fondness, love; genitals	PE
10.	genzuwāi-	to be lenient, have pity	PE
11.	genzuwala-	friendly, kind	PE
12.	hand-	sincere, honest	PE
13.	hanna-	to judge, decide	
14.	harpanalla	hostile	NE
15.	harpu-	hostile	NE
16.	hattatar	wisdom	
17.	hurkēl	atrocity, disgust	NE
18.	idālu-	bad, nasty; ill disposed	NE
19.	ilaliya-	to desire, envy	NE
20.	ishahruwa-	to cry	NE
21.	ishizziya-	to get angry	NE
22.	istanza(na)-	soul, will, mind	
23.	kappilalli-	hateful	NE
24.	kappilazza-	to lose one's temper, get angry	NE
25.	kardiyas	desire, wish ("it of the heart")	
26.	karpi-	rage, fury, anger, wrath	NE
27.	karpiwala-	angry, furious	NE
28.	karpiya-	to become angry	NE
29.	kartimmiya-	to be angry	NE
30.	kartimmiyatt-	anger	NE
31.	kartimmiyawant-	angry	NE
32.	kikki-	to lie down, keep calm	PE
33.	kup-	to intend, plan	
34.	kūrur	hostile	NE
35.	kururant-	enmity	NE
36.	kururiyah-	to be hostile, make war	NE
37.	lahlahhima-	grief, affliction	NE
38.	lahlahhiya-	to worry, be anxious; to mill	NE
39.	markiya-	to disagree	NE
40.	marlant-	stupid, foolish	
41.	memiya(n)-	word, speech; chattering; business; story; reason, motive; relation, opinion	
42.	mimma-	to refuse; reject, refuse to know anything	
43.	nah-	to fear, afraid; respectful; cautious	NE
44.	nahhan-	fear; respect	NE

45.	*nahhant-*	anxious, cautious	NE
46.	*nahsaratt-*	fear; respect	NE
47.	*nahsariya-*	to fear, be afraid; to show respect	NE
48.	*parā handātar*	wisdom; care	
49.	*puntarriyalli-*	stubborn, obstinate, headstrong	
50.	*sāi-*	to be angry	NE
51.	*sak-*	to know; to recognize	
52.	*sakinu-*	to understand (?)	
53.	*sānt-*	furious (part. of sāi-)	NE
54.	*sarkaliya-*	to be arrogant, feel superior	
55.	*sausiyar*	anger, rage	NE
56.	*sāuwar*	resentment, anger	NE
57.	*sekkant-*	known; conscious	
58.	*sullātar*	argument, quarrel; arrogance	NE
59.	*tesha-*	sleep, dream	
60.	*teshanesk-*	to appear in a dream	
61.	*teshaniya-*	to sleep, dream	
62.	*tuwadd-*	to have mercy, pity	PE
63.	*uttar*	word, speech; chattering; business; story; reason, motive; legal matter	
64.	*uwai-*	worry	NE
65.	*waggariya-*	to be indignant, rebel; make rebel	NE
66.	*walla-*	to glorify, praise; to pride oneself	
67.	*wars-, warsiya-*	to calm down (intrans.)	PE
68.	*warsanu-*	to calm down, pacify (trans.)	PE
69.	*wek-*	to wish, ask, demand, claim	
70.	*weritema-*	fear	NE
71.	*werites-*	to worry	NE
72.	*zashāi-*	dream	
73.	*zashi-*	dream	
74.	*zazhāi-*	dream	
75.	*zazhi-*	dream	

Dataset App D.10. LRC-UTA Hittite Dictionary: RL.

No.	Hittite	English
1.	*BAL*	make sacrifice
2.	*BE-LÍ-*	lord
3.	*BĒLU*	lord, master
4.	$^D IM$	Stormgod
5.	$^D INANNA$	Inanna (goddess)
6.	*DINGIR*	god
7.	*DINGIR.MAH*	presiding deity, Mother Goddess
8.	*DINGIR^{MEŠ}.ARAD*	servant of the god
9.	$^D IŠKUR$	Stormgod
10.	$^D U$	Stormgod
11.	*DUMU.É.GAL*	son of the palace
12.	*DUMU.LUGAL*	king's son, prince

13.	ᴰU-tassa	Tarhuntassas
14.	ᴰUTUˢᴵ	my majesty
15.	EN	lord
16.	EN.SISKUR	lord of the ritual
17.	EZEN	festival
18.	EZEN₄	festival, feast
19.	ᴳᴵˢDAG	throne
20.	GU.ZA	throne
21.	halientū-	palace complex
22.	hassuwezziya-	become king
23.	hekur	rock sanctuary
24.	Halmasuitt-	deified throne dais
25.	HUL	evil, harm
26.	idālu	evil, harm
27.	idālu-	evil, harm
28.	istanāna-	altar table
29.	IŠTAR	Ishtar (goddess)
30.	kattan haliya-	bow down, prostrate
31.	-LIM	deity
32.	LUGAL	king
33.	-LUM	deity
34.	ᴸᵁkīta-	a cult functionary, reciter (?)
35.	ᴸᵙSANGA	priest
36.	mēma-, mēmiya-	say, speak
37.	nēpis	heaven
38.	NÍ.TE	soul
39.	paprātar	impurity
40.	parā handandātar	divine might, power
41.	parā handantēss-	show divine guidance
42.	parkunu-	clean, purify
43.	sankunni-	priest
44.	sankunniya-	serve as priest
45.	sarnikzil	restitution
46.	sarnink-	make restitution
47.	sarra-	break, transgress
48.	sipānt-	make a libation, sacrifice
49.	Siusummin	our god, our Sius
50.	tuppi-	tablet
51.	TUPPI	tablet
52.	TUPPU	tablet
53.	UTU	Sungod
54.	wasta-	sin, err
55.	wastul	sin, fault, blame
56.	ZA.LAM.GAR	ceremonial tent

Dataset App D.11. LRC-UTA Hittite Dictionary: PL and EV.

No.	Sumerian	English	EV
1.	hanna-	decide judicially	
2.	isduwa-	be known	
3.	kappilāi-	become angry	NE
4.	lahlahhiya-	agitation, worry	NE
5.	nahh-	fear, revere	NE
6.	nahsariya-	fear, become afraid	NE
7.	SÀ	heart, innards	
8.	ŠÀ	heart, innards	
9.	Ù	dream	

Dataset App D.12. Dickson: Middle Egyptian Dictionary of PL.

No.	Egyptian	English	EV
1.	Abi	desire, wish for	
2.	Ad	be savage, be aggressive, be angry, attack, anger	NE
3.	aD	perceive	
4.	am	swallow, breathe in, absorb, know	
5.	arq	know, perceive, gain full knowledge of, be wise, skilled	
6.	biAi	wonder, marvel	
7.	d ib r	set one's heart on	
8.	Dar	search out, investigate, seek, probe, palpate (wound), plan (work), take thought (for)	
9.	Dd	say, speak, speak of, utter, recite (spell), tell, expect	
10.	Dnd	be angry	NE
11.	DnDn	be angry	NE
12.	Dw	bad, evil, sad (of heart)	NE
13.	Dwt	evil, sadness (of heart), dirt (encumbering ruin)	NE
14.	Haaw	rejoice	PE
15.	Haawt	joy	PE
16.	HAgAg	rejoice (over)	PE
17.	Hai	joyful, rejoice	PE
18.	HAty	heart, central chest, thought	
19.	Hawt	joy	PE
20.	hb ib	far-ranging of desire (?)	
21.	Hkn	be joyful, acclaim	PE
22.	hrp	sink, be immersed, suppress (one's desires), downhearted	
23.	Hryt ib	terror	NE
24.	Hryt	terror, dread, respect	NE
25.	Htp	be pleased, be happy, be gracious, pardon (someone), be at peace, peaceful, become calm	PE
26.	Hwa ib	apprehensive	NE
27.	Hwrw ib	poor of understanding	
28.	ib	heart, mind, understanding, intelligence, will, desire, mood, wish	

29.	imyw Xt	thoughts	
30.	ip	exact, detail, claim, examine, recognize, take heed of	
31.	ir ihhy	rejoice	PE
32.	is ib	light-minded	
33.	iwxm	(passive participle) know not, be ignorant of	
34.	kAt	thought, plan, device, plot	
35.	m HHy n ib	with ingenious mind	
36.	m hims	humbly	
37.	mh ib	the heart is forgetful	
38.	mHi	be concerned (for), take thought (for), ponder (on)	
39.	mht ib	negligence (of poor heart action)	
40.	mht	forgetfulness, negligence	
41.	mhy	be forgetful, neglectful	
42.	mnx ib	pleasing to the heart	PE
43.	mnx	be joyful (?)	PE
44.	mnxt	willingness (of heart)	
45.	mri	love, want, wish, desire	
46.	mrwt	love, will, desire	
47.	mrwty	the well-beloved	
48.	mXA	incline (one's heart to)	
49.	nDm ib	joyful	PE
50.	nDm	well, hale, comfortable, joy	PE
51.	nfr	necessary, good/fair (character), happy/well/good (condition), well-supplied, lawful	PE
52.	nHA ib	sad man	NE
53.	nHAt ib	sadness, a sad matter	NE
54.	nhm	dance for joy (?)	PE
55.	nHn	rejoice	PE
56.	nri	fear (someone), overawe	NE
57.	nrw	fear, dread, disturbance (?)	NE
58.	nsr	anger (?)	NE
59.	pgA Hr	honest	
60.	pgA ib	open hearted	
61.	pxA ib	clean of heart	
62.	qbb	cool, cold, cooling (of remedy), calm, quiet, be purified, take one's ease	PE
63.	qnd	be angry, furious	NE
64.	qni	powerful (of speech), stout (of heart), active, conquer, amount (to), be profuse	
65.	rdi m ib	determine, place in one's heart, prompt	
66.	rnn	rejoice (over), extol	PE
67.	rnnwt	joy, exultation	PE
68.	rS	joyful	PE
69.	rSrS	rejoice, joy	PE
70.	rswt	awakening, dream	
71.	rSwt	joy	PE
72.	rx xt	wisdom	

Appendix D

73.	rx	know, be aware of, inquire, learn, opinion	
74.	rxt	knowledge, amount, number	
75.	SA	ordain, order, predestine, assign, settle, decide	
76.	sAA	wisdom	
77.	sAi	be wise, prudent	
78.	sAq ib r	set one's heart on	
79.	sAr	be wise	
80.	sArt	wisdom, understanding	
81.	sAt	prudence, wisdom	
82.	sDdm	make envious	NE
83.	sDm	hear (voice etc), hear of (something), listen (to), obey, understand, judge, satisfy	
84.	sh	terrorize	NE
85.	siA	perception, knowledge	
86.	siA	recognize, perceive, know, be aware of	
87.	sk Xt	pour out one's heart	
88.	skm ns	wise	
89.	smx	forget, ignore	
90.	snaa ib	soothe, calm	PE
91.	snD	fear, respect	NE
92.	snDm	ease (suffering), please, give pleasure	PE
93.	snDm	make happy, make pleasant, ease (suffering), make content, please, give pleasure	PE
94.	snDt	fear	NE
95.	snDw	timid, frightened man	
96.	snm	be sad	NE
97.	SnT ib	be angry	NE
98.	Spt ib	anger	NE
99.	Spt	be discontented, angry	NE
100.	Spt	discontent, anger	NE
101.	sqbb	make cool, calm (disturbed land), refresh (oneself)	
102.	sr	foretell, make known	
103.	srf	warm, warmth, temperature, inflammation, fever, mood	
104.	SsA	be wise, be conversant (with), be skilled (in), know	
105.	SsA	know, be wise, skill	
106.	ssAi	satisfy, make wise	
107.	sSsA	make wise	
108.	st ib	favorite, favorite place, wish, affection	
109.	swAwA	ponder	
110.	swbA ib	open the heart (to wisdom)	
111.	swDA	make healthy, keep safe, calm (fear)	
112.	swmt	make thick, make stout (the heart)	
113.	sxi	remember, call to mind, think about, mention	
114.	sxm ib	stout-hearted, violent, violence	
115.	sxm	forget	
116.	sxmx ib	distract the heart (of someone), take recreation, enjoyment	

117.	sxr Xt	thought	
118.	THw	joy	PE
119.	THw	rejoice	PE
120.	Tnf	enjoyment	PE
121.	Tsi	be angry (with), bear a grudge	NE
122.	wAD	fortunate, happy	PE
123.	wAD	green, pale, fresh, raw, hale, sturdy, fortunate, happy, make green, make to flourish	PE
124.	wAH ib	be kindly, patient, clemency, benevolence	
125.	wAH	live long, endure, be patient	
126.	wbA	drill (stone), open, expose, reveal, determined	
127.	wdi	stir up (strife), instill (terror), extend (protection)	
128.	wmt ib	stout-hearted	
129.	wnf	be joyful	PE
130.	wpy	decision	
131.	wxd	be painful, suffer, endure, be patient with, forbearance	
132.	xAx ib	impatient	NE
133.	xm	know not, be ignorant of, be unconscious of, ignorance	
134.	xmt	intend, plan, take thought (for), expect, anticipate	
135.	xnti ib	be glad of heart, outstanding of mind	PE
136.	xntS	have enjoyment (of), be glad, make glad	PE
137.	xrt ib	wish, desire, favor	
138.	xsf	reprove (words), drive (cattle), divert (water), avoid (anger), prevent	

Dataset App D.13. Mycenaean/Linear B Dictionary: RL.

No.	Mycenaean	English
1.	ko-r-te	governor
2.	wa-na-ka	king
3.	wa-naka-te-ro	king's palace
4.	te-ra-ta	master of ceremonies
5.	te-o-i	gods
6.	mu-jo-me-no	those initiated
7.	te-me-no	temple
8.	na-wi-jo	(from the) temple
9.	Da-da-re-o-de	temple (name)
10.	Da-pu-ri-to-jo	temple (name)
11.	Pi-pi-tu-na	Goddess
12.	Po-ti-ni-a	Goddess
13.	Ko-ma-we-te-jo	Goddess
14.	E-re-u-ti-ja	Goddess (of parturition)
15.	E-ra	Goddess
16.	Di-we	Zeus

Dataset App D.14. Mycenaean/Linear B Dictionary: PL.

No.	Mycenaean	English
1.	*e-u-ke-to*	wishes

Appendix E

Statistical Analyses for Chapter 4 and 5

App Calculation 4.1. Correlations between Periods and Types of Words.

Four Hypothesis & Variables	Correlation (r)	Coefficient of Determination (r^2)	P-value	df = 2, One-tailed. Critical Value	Null Hypothesis, $p < 0.05$
(1) 4 Periods and Supernatural Words (Totals from Table 4.1)	−0.8800	0.7744	0.1199	0.9000	Accepted
(2) 4 Periods and Supernatural Words (Totals from Table 4.2)	−0.8859	0.7848	0.1140	0.9000	Accepted
(3) 4 Periods and MWs (Totals)	−0.9860	0.9722	0.0134	0.9000	Rejected
(4) MWs and Supernatural (Totals from Tables 4.1 + 4.2 averaged)	−0.9425	0.8883	0.0574	0.9000	Rejected

App Calculation 4.2. Supernatural Words: Totals from Table 4.1. Chi-Sq G of F (percentages changed to whole numbers).

Period	Observed	Expected	Diff	Diff Sq	Diff Sq/Exp Fr
1st	140	101.5	38.50	1482.25	14.60
2nd	167	101.5	65.50	4290.25	42.27
3rd	83	101.5	−18.50	342.25	3.37
4th	16	101.5	−85.50	7310.25	72.02

P-Value	Significant at	df	χ^2	Critical Value
< 0.001	$p \leq 0.05$	3	132.266	7.82

H_0:	$P_1 = P_2 = P_3 = P_4$
H_1:	$P_1 \neq P_2 \neq P_3 \neq P_4$

Appendix E

App Calculation 4.3. Supernatural Words: Totals from Table 4.2. Chi-Sq G of F (percentages changed to whole numbers).

Period	Observed	Expected	Diff	Diff Sq	Diff Sq/Exp Fr
1st	108	74.5	33.50	1122.25	15.06
2nd	128	74.5	53.50	2862.25	38.42
3rd	48	74.5	-26.50	702.25	9.43
4th	14	74.5	-60.50	3660.25	49.13

P-Value	Significant at	df	χ^2	Critical Value
< 0.001	$p \leq 0.05$	3	112.040	7.82

H_0:	$P_1 = P_2 = P_3 = P_4$
H_1:	$P_1 \neq P_2 \neq P_3 \neq P_4$

App Calculation 4.4. MWs. Chi-Sq G of F (percentages changed to whole numbers).

Period	Observed	Expected	Diff	Diff Sq	Diff Sq/Exp Fr
1st	44	135.25	-91.25	8326.56	61.56
2nd	80	135.25	-55.25	3052.56	22.57
3rd	179	135.25	43.75	1914.06	14.15
4th	238	135.25	102.75	10557.56	78.06

P-Value	Significant at	df	χ^2	Critical Value
< 0.001	$p \leq 0.05$	3	176.346	7.82

H_0:	$P_1 = P_2 = P_3 = P_4$
H_1:	$P_1 \neq P_2 \neq P_3 \neq P_4$

App Calculation 4.5. NE Outnumber PE Words in *Shuowen Jiezi*. Chi-Sq G of F (percentages changed to whole numbers).

Word Type	Observed	Expected	Diff	Diff Sq	Diff Sq/Exp Fr
PE Words	101	500	-399.00	159201.00	318.40
NE Words	899	500	399.00	159201.00	318.40

P-Value	Significant at	df	χ^2	Critical Value	ES
< 0.001	$p \leq 0.05$	1	636.804	3.84	0.7980

H_0:	PE = NE
H_1:	PE $\neq$ NE

App Calculation 4.6. Logographs with Heart Signific Representing NE Words Outnumber PE Words

	No. of NEs (%)	No. of PEs (%)
No. of Heart Significs with EV = 127 (100%)	98 (77.17%)	29 (22.83%)
Ratio	3.38:1	

App Calculation 4.7. Logographs with Heart Signific Representing NE Words Outnumber PE Words. Chi-Sq G of F.

Word Type	Observed	Expected	Diff	Diff Sq	Diff Sq/Exp Fr
NE Words	98	63.5	34.50	1190.25	18.74
PE Words	29	63.5	-34.50	1190.25	18.74

P-Value	Significant at	df	χ^2	Critical Value	ES
< 0.001	p ≤ 0.05	1	37.488	3.84	0.7683

H_0:	PE = NE
H_1:	PE ≠ NE

App Calculation 5.1. Differences among No. of MWs Are Salient. Chi-Sq G of F.

	Observed	Expected	Diff	Diff Sq	Diff Sq/Exp Fr
HEART	168	106	62.00	3844.00	36.26
NO HEART	84	106	-22.00	484.00	4.57
EXTERNAL	66	106	-40.00	1600.00	15.09

P-Value	Significant at	df	χ^2	Critical Value
< 0.001	p ≤ 0.05	2	55.925	5.99

H_0:	HEART = NO HEART = EXTERNAL
H_1:	HEART ≠ NO HEART ≠ EXTERNAL

App Calculation 5.2. Differences among MWs Compounds/Idioms Are Salient. Chi-Sq G of F.

	Observed	Expected	Diff	Diff Sq	Diff Sq/Exp Fr
HEART	1863	0.33	781.26	610367.19	564.25
NO HEART	836	0.33	-245.74	60388.15	55.83
EXTERNAL	579	0.33	-502.74	252747.51	233.65

P-Value	Significant at	df	χ^2	Critical Value
< 0.001	p ≤ 0.05	2	853.72	5.99

H_0:	HEART = NO HEART = EXTERNAL
H_1:	HEART ≠ NO HEART ≠ EXTERNAL

Appendix E

App Calculation 5.3. Observed Distribution of Terms across INTERNAL and EXTERNAL Categories Are Salient.

	Observed	Expected	Diff	Diff Sq	Diff Sq/Exp Fr
INTERNAL	252	159	93.00	8649.00	54.40
EXTERNAL	66	159	−93.00	8649.00	54.40

P-Value	Significant at	df	χ^2	Critical Value	ES
< 0.001	$p \leq 0.05$	1	108.792	3.84	0.584

H_0:	INTERNAL = EXTERNAL
H_1:	INTERNAL ≠ EXTERNAL

App Calculation 5.4. Observed Distribution of Compounds across INTERNAL and EXTERNAL Categories Are Salient.

	Observed	Expected	Diff	Diff Sq	Diff Sq/Exp Fr
INTERNAL	2699	1639	1060.00	1123600.00	685.54
EXTERNAL	579	1639	−1060.00	1123600.00	685.54

P-Value	Significant at	df	χ^2	Critical Value	ES
< 0.001	$p \leq 0.05$	1	1371.080	3.84	0.646

H_0:	INTERNAL = EXTERNAL
H_1:	INTERNAL ≠ EXTERNAL

Appendix F

Datasets for Chapters 4 and 5

Dataset App F.1. Spiritual Entities: hun3, ling2, po4, shen2.

Mandarin (Pinyin)	Logograph	Literal Meaning	English
diu1hun2	丟魂	lost + soul	distracted
dong4po4	動魄	move + mortal soul	shocking; shattering
hun2bu4fu4ti3li	魂不附體	soul + not + attach + body	body & soul separated (idiom), scared out of one's wits, beside oneself
hun2ling2	魂靈	soul + spirit	soul, mind, idea
hun2qian1meng4rao4	魂牽夢繞	soul + involve/pull + dream + circle	captivated, wonder, enchanting
hun2qian1meng4ying2	魂牽夢縈	soul + involve/pull + dream + entangle	miss, yearn day & night
ji1ling2	機靈	machine + clever	clever, quick-witted
ling2gan3	靈感	spirit + feel	inspiration/ insight
ling2min3	靈敏	spirit + sensitive	smart, clever, sensitive, keen, quick, sharp
po4li4	魄力	mortal soul + strength	courage; daring; boldness; resolution; drive
qi4po4	氣魄	cosmic energy + mortal soul	spirit, boldness, positive outlook, imposing attitude
ru4shen2	入神	enter + god/spirit	enthralled, entranced
shen2hun2	神魂	spirit + soul	state of mind, mind
shen2jing1	神經	spirit + channel	nerves
shen2se4	神色	spirit + color	facial expression
shen2tai4	神態	spirit + appearance	facial expression, appearance, manner, bearing, deportment, look, expression

Appendix F

Dataset App F.2. Emotional Valence of Characters with Heart Signific.

	Mandarin (Pinyin)	Logograph	English	Emotional Valence
1.	ai4	愛	love, affection	PE
2.	ao4	懊	regretful, remorseful, annoyed, vexed	NE
3.	bei1	悲	sad, sorrowful, mournful, woeful, lament, mourn, pity, sympathize	NE
4.	bei4	悖	contrary to, perverse, erroneous	NE
5.	bei4	憊	exhausted, fatigued	NE
6.	bi4	愎	willful, self-willed	NE
7.	bian4	忭	glad, happy	PE
8.	bie1	憋	suppress, hold back (words, breath), suffocate, oppressed	NE
9.	bu4	怖	fear, afraid	NE
10.	can2	慚	feel ashamed	NE
11.	can3	慘	miserable, pitiful, cruel, savage, disastrously	NE
12.	ce4	惻	sad, sorrowful	NE
13.	chan4	懺	regret, confess one's sins	NE
14.	chang4	悵	disappointed, sorry	NE
15.	chen2	忱	sincere feeling, true sentiment	PE
16.	chi3	恥	shame, disgrace, humiliation, feel ashamed	NE
17.	chong1	憧	irresolute, indecisive, yearn for, aspire	
18.	chong1	忡	pleasant	PE
19.	chou2	惆	stressed, regretful, sad	NE
20.	chou2	愁	worry, anxious	NE
21.	chu4	憷	fear, apprehensive	NE
22.	chu4	怵	fear, shrink from	NE
23.	chuang4	愴	sorrowful	NE
24.	ci2	慈	kind, loving, mother	PE
25.	cong1	怱	alarm, agitation	NE
26.	cui4	悴	haggard, worn-out, tired out, worried, sad	NE
27.	cun3	忖	turn over in one's mind	
28.	dai4	怠	idle, remiss, slack	NE
29.	dan4	憚	fear, dread	NE
30.	dao4	悼	mourn	NE
31.	dian4	惦	remember with concern, miss	NE
32.	dong3	懂	understand, know	
33.	dong4	恫	fear	NE
34.	dui4	懟	rancor, resentment	NE

35.	duo4	惰	lazy, indolent	NE
36.	e4	愕	startled, astonished, amazed	
37.	e4	惡	bad, evil, wicked, vice, wickedness, fierce, ferocious	NE
38.	en1	恩	kindness, favor, grace	PE
39.	fei3	悱	be at a loss of words for	NE
40.	fen4	忿	anger, indignation, fury, complaining, hatred, a grudge	NE
41.	fen4	憤	indignation, anger, resentment	NE
42.	gan3	感	feel, sense, move, touch, effect, be grateful, obliged, be affected (medical)	
43.	gong1	恭	respectful, reverent, deferential	PE
44.	guai4	怪	strange, odd, queer	
45.	guan4	慣	be used to, in the habit of	
46.	han1	憨	foolish, straightforward, naive, ingenuous	NE
47.	han4	憾	regret	NE
48.	han4	悍	brave, bold, fierce, ferocious	
49.	hen4	恨	hate	NE
50.	heng2	恆	permanent, eternal, everlasting	
51.	hu1	惚	in a trance, absentmindedly, dimly	NE
52.	hu1	忽	neglect, overlook	NE
53.	hu4	怙	rely on, father (formal)	
54.	huai2	懷	bosom, keep in mind	
55.	huan4	患	trouble, peril, anxiety, worry, contract, suffer from	NE
56.	huang1	慌	flurried, flushed, confused	NE
57.	huang2	惶	afraid, fearful, apprehensive, anxious, uneasy, flurried, hurried	NE
58.	huang3	恍	suddenly, be in a trance	
59.	hui1	恢	extensive, vast	
60.	hui3	悔	regret, repent	NE
61.	hui4	慧	intelligent, bright	PE
62.	huo4	惑	puzzled, bewildered, delude, mislead	NE
63.	ji2	急	impatient, anxious, worry, irritated, fast, urgent,	NE
64.	ji4	忌	jealous, fear, prohibit, taboo, death anniversaries of one's parents or grandparents	NE
65.	ji4	悸	throb with terror, palpitate	NE

Appendix F

66.	jing1	惊	surprised, frightened	NE
67.	jing3	憬	realize, come to understand, awake	
68.	jing4	憼	respect	PE
69.	ju4	懼	fear, dread	NE
70.	kai3	恺	indignant	NE
71.	kai4	慨	indignant, deeply touched, generous, regret	NE
72.	kang1	慷	ardent, impassioned, generous, unselfish	PE
73.	ke4	恪	scrupulously and respectfully	PE
74.	ken3	懇	earnest	PE
75.	kong3	恐	fear, dread	NE
76.	kuai4	快	fast, hurry, quick-witted, sharp (knife), forthright, pleased, happy	PE
77.	kui1	悝	sad	NE
78.	kui4	憒	muddleheaded	NE
79.	kui4	愧	ashamed, remorseful, conscience	NE
80.	lan3	懒	lazy, indolent	NE
81.	leng4	愣	dumbfounded, distracted, stupefied	NE
82.	lian2	憐	sympathize with, pity	
83.	lian4	戀	love (of other sex), be in love, feel persistent attachment (for a thing)	PE
84.	lin3	懍	filled with awe, awe-struck, inspiring awe, awful	PE
85.	mao4	懋	diligent, luxuriant	PE
86.	men1	悶	suffocating, stuffy (weather, rooms), muffled, shut oneself indoors	NE
87.	men4	懣	melancholy	NE
88.	men4	悶	melancholy, depressed, bored, in low spirits	NE
89.	meng3	懵	muddled, ignorant	NE
90.	min3	憫	commiserate, pity, sorrow	NE
91.	mu4	慕	to yearn for, long for, adore, admire	
92.	nao3	惱	angry, irritated, annoyed	NE
93.	ni2	怩	shy, timid, bashful, look ashamed	NE
94.	nian4	念	think of, thought, idea, read aloud, study, attend school	
95.	niu3	忸	accustomed, blush, shy	
96.	nu4	怒	anger, rage, fury	NE

97.	nuo4	懦	cowardly, weak	NE
98.	nü4	恧	ashamed	NE
99.	ou4	慪	irritate, annoyed	NE
100.	pa4	怕	fear	NE
101.	peng1	怦	impulsive	NE
102.	ping2	憑	lean against, rely on, on the basis of, proof	
103.	qi1	慽	mournful, woeful, ashamed	NE
104.	qi1	悽	grieved, sorrowful, afflicted, tragic, pathetic, pitiful	NE
105.	qian1	慳	stingy, miserly	NE
106.	qiao3	愀	change countenance, worry	NE
107.	qiao3	悄	quiet, sad	NE
108.	qie4	怯	timid, cowardly, lacking in courage, cowardly, nervous, timid, afraid	NE
109.	qie4	愜	satisfied	PE
110.	qing2	情	feeling, affection, sentiment, love, passion, favor, kindness	PE
111.	qing4	慶	festivity, blessing, felicity, joy, celebrate, congratulate, rejoice	PE
112.	quan1	悛	repent, make amends	NE
113.	re3	惹	invite or ask, offend, provoke, attract, cause	
114.	ren3	忍	bear, endure, tolerate, be hardheaded	
115.	shen4	慎	careful, cautious	
116.	shi4	恃	rely on, depend on (one's abilities)	
117.	shu4	恕	forgive, pardon, excuse, forbearance	PE
118.	si1	思	contemplate, consider, memory, remember, think of, mourn, grieve, pine for	
119.	song3	悚	terrified, horrified	NE
120.	song3	慫	instigate, incite	
121.	su4	愫	sincere feeling, sincerity	PE
122.	tai4	態	form, appearance, condition, state, voice (linguistics)	
123.	tan3	忐	mentally disturbed, nervous	NE
124.	tang1	恫	pain	NE
125.	te4	慝	do evil in secret, evil, vice	NE
126.	ti4	悌	love and respect for one's elder brother	PE
127.	ti4	惕	cautious, watchful	
128.	tian2	恬	quiet, tranquil, calm	
129.	tong4	慟	deep sorrow, grief	NE

130.	wan3	惋	sigh in regret or pity	NE
131.	wang3	惘	feel frustrated, disappointed	NE
132.	wang4	忘	forget, omit, neglect, overlook	NE
133.	wei2	惟	think, meditate, only, alone, but, however	
134.	wei4	慰	console, comfort, be relieved	PE
135.	wu1	惡	how, where, abhor, loathe	NE
136.	wu3	忤	disobedient, uncongenial	NE
137.	wu4	惡	hate, detest, dislike, abhor, loathe	NE
138.	wu4	悟	become aware of, realize, awake to, comprehend	
139.	xi2	惜	pity, sympathize, feel sorry, value highly, high opinion of (something), show love for, grudge	NE
140.	xi3	憙	like, love, enjoy, joyful	PE
141.	xiang3	想	think, suppose, want, remember with longing	
142.	xie4	懈	slack, lax, negligent	NE
143.	xing1	惺	clever, intelligent, wise, wavering, indecisive	
144.	xing3	惺	become aware of, awake from ignorance	
145.	xing4	悻	angry, resentful	NE
146.	xu4	恤	pity, sympathize	
147.	xuan2	懸	hang, suspend, unresolved, anxious, solicitous, imagine, conjecture, dangerous	
148.	yang4	怏	disgruntled, disheartened	NE
149.	yang4	恙	disease, worry	NE
150.	yi2	怡	happy, joyful	PE
151.	yi4	憶	recall, recollect	
152.	yi4	意	thought, idea, sentiments, intention, inclination, meaning, hint, suggestion	
153.	yong1	慵	weary, lethargic	NE
154.	yong3	慂	urge, incite	
155.	you1	悠	long drawn out, remote in time and space, leisurely	
156.	yu2	愉	pleased, happy, cheerful	PE
157.	yu2	愚	foolish, stupid, make a fool of, my humble opinion	
158.	yu4	慾	desire, appetite, passion, lust, greed	
159.	yuan4	怨	resentment, enmity, blame	NE
160.	yuan4	願	hope, wish, desire, be willing,	

			ready, vow, honest and cautious	
161.	yue4	悦	happy, pleased	PE
162.	yun4	愠	angry, irritated	NE
163.	zeng1	憎	hate, detest, abhor	NE
164.	zhe2	慴	fearful, awe-struck	NE
165.	zheng1	怔	seized with terror, panic stricken	NE
166.	zhi4	忎	jealously	NE
167.	zhong1	忠	faithful, loyal, sincere, sincerity, devoted, honest	PE
168.	zhuang4	戇	blunt and tactless, simple and honest	
169.	zhui4	惴	anxious and fearful	NE
170.	zi4	恣	throw off restraint, do as one pleases, carefree, unbridled, extremely conceited	PE
				∑ NE = 98
				∑ PE = 29

Dataset App F.3. Compounds with xin1 (Heart).

	Mandarin (Pinyin)	Logographs	Literal Meaning	English
1.	ai4xin1	愛心	love + heart	compassion
2.	an1xin1	安心	peace + heart	peace of mind
3.	bian4xin1	變心	change + heart	cease to be faithful
4.	cao1xin1	操心	operate + heart	worry about
5.	chen1xin1	稱心	fit/match + heart	find something satisfactory, gratified
6.	cheng2xin1	誠心	sincere + heart	sincere desire, wholeheartedness
7.	cheng2xin1	誠心	sincere + heart	intentionally, on purpose
8.	chi1xin1	癡心	craving + heart	infatuation, absorbed
9.	chi4xin1	赤心	bare/red + heart	loyal heart, loyalty
10.	chunxin1	春心	spring + heart	thoughts/stirrings of love
11.	cu1xin1	粗心	coarse/thick + heart	careless, thoughtless
12.	cu4xin1	醋心	vinegar + heart	cherish certain intentions, intentionally
13.	cun4xin1	寸心	inch + heart	feelings
14.	dan1xin1	擔心	undertake + heart	worry, feel anxious
15.	dang1xin1	當心	manage + heart	take care, careful
16.	ding4xin1	定心	decide/fix +	at ease, relaxed

Appendix F

				heart
17.	dong4xin1	動心	move + heart	perturbed, arouse one's interest
18.	duo1xin1	多心	more + heart	oversensitive, suspicious
19.	e3xin1	噁心	nauseated/sickening + heart	feel like vomiting, nauseated
20.	er4xin1	二心	double/two + heart	disloyalty, half-heartedness
21.	fang4xin1	放心	put/settle + heart	set one's mind at ease
22.	fang1xin1	芳心	fragrant + heart	heart of a young woman
23.	fei4xin1	費心	cost/spend + heart	take much care
24.	fen1xin1	分心	separate + heart	divert one's attention
25.	fu4xin1	腹心	belly + heart	true thoughts and feelings
26.	gan1xin1	甘心	sweet/willing + heart	willingly, readily resign oneself to
27.	guan1xin1	關心	concern + heart	concerned with
28.	gui3mi2 xin1qiao4	鬼迷心竅	ghost + bewilder + heart + aperture	be possessed by, obsessed
29.	han2xin1	寒心	cold + heart	bitterly disappointed
30.	hao3xin1	好心	good + heart	good intention
31.	hei1xix1	黑心	black + heart	evil mind
32.	heng2xin1	恆心	lasting/permanent + heart	perseverance
33.	heng2xin1	橫心	horizontal + heart	determined (to do something); bent on
34.	huai4xin1yanr3	壞心眼兒	bad + heart + eye + [nominal suffix]	evil intention, ill will
35.	huan1xin1	歡心	merry + heart	favor, liking, love
36.	hui1xin1	灰心	grey + heart	lose heart, discouraged
37.	hui4xin1	會心	able/meet + heart	understanding, knowing, wisdom
38.	jiang4xin1	匠心	artisan/craftsman + heart	ingenuity, craftsmanship
39.	jiao1xin1	焦心	charred + heart	feel terribly worried
40.	jiao1xin1	交心	deliver/turn over + heart	lay one's heart bare
41.	jie4xin1	戒心	guard against + heart	vigilance, wariness
42.	jin4xin1	盡心	exhaust + heart	with all one's heart
43.	jing1xin1	經心	pass through +	careful, mindful,

			heart	conscientious
44.	jing1xin1	精心	perfect/excellent + heart	meticulously, painstakingly, elaborately
45.	jing1xin1 dong4po4	驚心動魄	surprise + heart + move + soul/spirit	profoundly affecting
46.	jiu1xin1	揪心	clutch + heart	anxious, worried, heartrending
47.	ju1xin1	居心	reside/occupy + heart	harbor (evil) intentions
48.	jue2xin1	決心	determine + heart	determination, resolution
49.	jun1xin1	軍心	soldier + heart	soldiers' morale
50.	kai1xin1	開心	open + heart	feel happy, rejoice, amuse oneself at somebody's expense
51.	ke4gu3 ming2xin1	刻骨銘心	chisel + bone + inscription + heart	be engraved on one's bones and heart, remember with gratitude to the end of one's life
52.	ke3xin1	可心	can/may + heart	satisfying, to the liking of
53.	kong4xin1	空心	empty + heart	on an empty stomach
54.	kou3shi4 xin1fei1	口是心非	mouth + yes + heart + no	say yes and mean no, say one thing but mean another
55.	kou4ren2 xin1xian2	扣人心弦	buckle + person + heart + string	exciting, thrilling
56.	ku3xin1	苦心	bitter + heart	trouble, take pains
57.	kui1xin1	虧心	deficient + heart	have a guilty conscience
58.	lang2xin1 gou3fei4	狼心狗肺	wolf + heart + dog + lung	rapacious as a wolf and savage as a cur, cruel and unscrupulous
59.	lao2xin1	勞心	work/labor + heart	work with one's mind or brains
60.	li2xin1	離心	leave + heart	at odds with community or leadership
61.	li2xin1 li2de2	離心離德	leave + heart + leave + morals/virtue	dissension and discord, disunity
62.	li3kui1 xin1xu1	理虧心虛	reason + deficient + heart + empty	feel apprehensive because one is not on solid ground
63.	li4bu4 cong2xin1	力不從心	strength + not + from + heart	ability falling short of one's wishes

64.	li4yu4 xun1xin1	利慾熏心	benefit/profit + lust/desire + smoke/burn + heart	blinded by greed
65.	liang2xin1	良心	good/virtuous + heart	conscience
66.	liang3tiao2xin1	兩條心	two + bar/stripe + heart	in fundamental disagreement, not of one's mind
67.	liu2xin1	留心	retain + heart	careful, take care
68.	man3xin1	滿心	full + heart	have one's heart filled
69.	man4bu4 jing1xin1	漫不經心	overflow + no + pass through + heart	careless, casual, negligent
70.	men2xin1 zi4wen4	捫心自問	stroke/touch + heart + self + ask	examine one's conscience
71.	min2xin1	民心	public/people + heart	popular feelings
72.	nai4xin1	耐心	endure + heart	patient
73.	nei4xin1	內心	inner + heart	one's innermost being
74.	ou3xin1	嘔心	vomit/throw up + heart	exert one's utmost effort
75.	ou3xin1 li4xue4	嘔心瀝血	vomit/throw up + heart + trickle + blood	shed one's heart's blood, take infinite pains
76.	pian1xin1	偏心	partial/biased + heart	partiality, bias
77.	ping2xin1 er2lun4	平心而論	calm + heart + and + discuss	in all fairness, give somebody his due
78.	ping2xin1 ing4qi4	平心硬氣	peace + heart + harden + cosmic energy	calmly, dispassionately
79.	qi2xin1	齊心	neat/similar + heart	be of one mind (heart)
80.	qian2xin1	潛心	hidden/latent + heart	with great concentration
81.	qin4ren1 xin1pi2	沁人心脾	soak + person + heart + spleen	gladdening the heart and refreshing the mind, mentally refreshing
82.	qing1xin1	傾心	incline + heart	admire, fall in love, cordial
83.	quan2xin1 quan2yi4	全心全意	whole + heart + whole + meaning	wholeheartedly, heart and soul
84.	re4xin1	熱心	hot + heart	enthusiastic, ardent, earnest

85.	re4xin1chang2	熱心腸	hot + heart + intestines	warmheartedness
86.	ren2xin1	人心	people + heart	popular feeling, will of the people
87.	ren3xin1	忍心	tolerate/endure + heart	have the heart to, be hardhearted enough
88.	san1xin1	散心	scatter + heart	drive away one's cares, relieve boredom
89.	sang4 xin1 bing4kuang2	喪心病狂	lose + heart + sick + crazy	frenzied, unscrupulous, perverse
90.	sha4fei4 ku3xin1	煞費苦心	fierce god + spend/cost + bitter + heart	cudgel one's brains, take great pains
91.	shan4xin1	善心	good/virtuous + heart	mercy, benevolence
92.	shang1xin1	傷心	wound + heart	sad, grieving, brokenhearted
93.	shang1xin1 can3mu4	傷心慘目	wound + heart + miserable + eye	too ghastly to look at; tragic (scene)
94.	shang3xin1 yue4mu4	賞心悅目	admire + heart + pleased + eye	find the scenery pleasing to both eye and mind
95.	xiao3xin1	小心	little/small + heart	to be careful, take care
96.	shen1xin1	身心	body + heart	body and mind
97.	shi2xin1yanr3	實心眼兒	solid + heart + eye + [nominal suffix]	one track mind
98.	si3xin1	死心	die + heart	drop the idea forever
99.	shou1xin1	收心	receive/collect + heart	get into the frame of mind for work, have a change of heart
100.	shua3xin1yan3r	耍心眼兒	play + heart + eye + [nominal suffix]	exercise one's wits for personal gain
101.	shun4xin1	順心	obey/follow + heart	satisfactory
102.	si1xin1	私心	selfish + heart	selfish motives
103.	si3xin1ta1di4	死心塌地	die + heart + cave in + land	be dead set
104.	si3xin1yanr3	死心眼兒	die + heart + eye + [nominal suffix]	stubborn, person with one track mind
105.	sui2xin1 suo3yu4	隨心所欲	adapt to + heart + place/that + desire/want	follow one's inclination, have one's own way
106.	sui4xin1	遂心	satisfy/succeed + heart	to one's liking

107.	tan1xin1	貪心	greedy + heart	greed, avarice, rapacity
108.	tan2xin1	談心	talk + heart	heart-to-heart talk
109.	ta1xin1	塌心	fall down + heart	set one's mind at ease
110.	tie1xin1	貼心	glue + heart	intimate, close
111.	tie3shi2 xin1chang2	鐵石心腸	iron + rock + heart + intestines	iron-hearted, hardhearted
112.	tong2li3xin1	同理心	similar + reason + heart	empathy
113.	tong2xin1	童心	child + heart	(old man) childlike innocence, (young man) childlike innocence, playfulness
114.	tong2xin1	同心	similar + heart	work as one heart
115.	tong2xin1 tong2de2	同心同德	similar + heart + similar + morals/virtue	be of one heart and one mind
116.	tong4xin1	痛心	hurt + heart	pained, distressed, grieved
117.	tong4xin1 ji2shou3	痛心疾首	hurt + heart + disease + head/first	with bitter hatred
118.	tui1xin1 zhi4fu4	推心置腹	pull + heart + place/install + belly	put full confidence in somebody
119.	wa1kong1 xin1si1	挖空心思	dig + empty + consider/ponder + heart	rack one's brains
120.	wai4xin1	外心	external/outside + heart	unfaithful intentions (husband or wife)
121.	wei2xin1	違心	against/violate + heart	against one's will, contrary to one's convictions
122.	wei2xin1 shu3yi4	唯心主義	only + heart + main + meaning	idealism
123.	wen4xin1 wu2kui4	問心無愧	ask + heart + no + shame	have a clear conscience
124.	wen4xin1 you3kui4	問心有愧	ask + heart + has + shame	feel a twinge of conscience
125.	won4zhing4 yi4xin1	萬眾一心	ten thousand + public + one + heart	millions of people all one mind
126.	wu2xin1	無心	no + heart	not be in the mood for, not intentionally
127.	xi1xin1	悉心	all/entirely + heart	devote all one's attention, take the utmost care

128.	xi1xin1	悉心	all/entirely + heart	careful, attentive
129.	xi3xin1 ge2mian4	洗心革面	wash + heart + leather/remove + face	turn over a new leaf, thoroughly reform oneself
130.	xian2xin1	閑心	idle + heart	leisurely mood
131.	xiao3xin1	小心	little/small + heart	take care, be careful, cautious
132.	xie2xin1	邪心	evil + heart	evil thought
133.	xin1ai4	心愛	heart + love	love, treasure
134.	xin1an1 li3de2	心安理得	heart + peace + reason + acquire	feel at ease and justified, easy conscience
135.	xin1bing4	心病	heart + disease	worry, anxiety, secret trouble
136.	xin1bu2 zai4yan1	心不在焉	heart + no + be + where/how	absent-minded, inattentive
137.	xin1cai2	心裁	heart + trim	idea, conception
138.	xin1chang2	心腸	heart + intestines	heart, intention, state of mind, mood
139.	xin1chao2	心潮	heart + trend	surging thoughts, emotions
140.	xin1ci2 shou3ruan3	心慈手软	heart + kind + hand + soft	softhearted
141.	xin1dan3	心膽	heart + gallbladder	will and courage
142.	xin1de2	心得	heart + acquire	what one has learned from study
143.	xin1di4	心地	heart + land	person's mind, character, moral nature
144.	xin1fan2	心煩	heart + irritated	perturbed
145.	xin1fu2	心服	heart + convinced	genuinely convinced, acknowledge one's mistake/defeat
146.	xin1fu2	心浮	heart + float	flighty and impatient
147.	xin1gan1	心肝	heart + liver	conscience
148.	xin1gan1 qing2yuan4	心甘情願	heart + pleasant/sweet + emotion + desire/hope	most willing to, happy to
149.	xin1han2	心寒	heart + cold	bitterly disappointed
150.	xin1hen3	心狠	heart + ruthless	cruel, merciless
151.	xin1hua1 nu4fang4	心花怒放	heart + flower + anger/fury + expand	burst with joy, elated
152.	xin1huai2	心懷	heart + bosom/mind	entertain, cherish, intention, purpose, mood, state of mind

153.	xin1huan2 ru2ma2	心慌如麻	heart + anxiety/fear + like/as + hemp	utterly confused and disconcerted
154.	xin1huang1	心慌	heart + panicking	flushed, nervous
155.	xin1hui1 yi4lan3	心灰意冷	heart + grey/frustrated + meaning + cold	feel disheartened
156.	xin1huo3	心火	heart + fire	internal heat, mental uneasiness, thirst, rapid pulse; (2) hidden anger, pent-up fury
157.	xin1ji1	心機	heart + machinery	thinking, scheming
158.	xin1ji1	心跡	heart + trace/mark	true state of mind, true feelings
159.	xin1ji2	心急	heart + rush/hurry	impatient
160.	xin1jiao1	心焦	heart + anxious/burned	anxious, worried
161.	xin1jing1 dan3zhan4	心驚膽戰	heart + surprised + gut + battle/fight	tremble with fear
162.	xin1jing1 rou4tiao4	心驚肉跳	heart + surprise + meat + jump	palpitate with anxiety and fear
163.	xin1jing4	心境	heart + condition/condition	state or frame of mind, mood
164.	xin1jing4	心靜	heart + quiet/calm	calm
165.	xin1kan3	心坎	heart + threshold/pit	bottom of one's heart
166.	xin1kou3 ru2yi1	心口如一	heart + mouth + like/as + one	frank and unreserved
167.	xin1kuang4 shen2yi2	心曠神怡	heart + spacious + god/spirit + harmony/joyful	relaxed and happy
168.	xin1li3	心裡	heart + inside/internal	in the heart, in the mind
169.	xin1li3	心理	heart + reasoning	psychology
170.	xin1li4	心力	heart + power/effort	mental and physical efforts
171.	xin1li3hua4	心裡話	heart + inside/internal + words	one's innermost thoughts and feelings
172.	xin1ling2	心靈	heart + soul	clever, intelligent, spirit, heart
173.	xin1ling3	心領神會	heart + receive +	understand tacitly

	shen2hui4		god/spirit + can/gather	
174.	xin1luan4 ru2ma2	心亂如麻	heart + messy + like/as + hemp	utterly confused and disconcerted
175.	xin1man3 yi4zu2	心滿意足	heart + full + meaning + enough	perfectly content
176.	xin1ming2 yan3liang4	心明眼亮	heart + clear + eye + bright	see and think clearly
177.	xin1mu4	心目	heart + eye	mood, frame of mind, memory, mental view
178.	xin1ping2 qi4he2	心平氣和	heart + calm + cosmic energy + peaceful	even-tempered and good humored
179.	xin1qiao4	心竅	heart + aperture	capacity for clear thinking
180.	xin1qing2	心情	heart + emotion	frame of mind, mood
181.	xin1qu3	心曲	heart + melody	innermost being, mind
182.	xin1ru2 dao1ge1	心如刀割	heart + like/as + knife + cut	feel as if a knife were piercing one's heart
183.	xin1ruan3	心軟	heart + soft	softhearted, tenderhearted
184.	xin1shen	心身	heart + body	mind and body
185.	xin1shen2	心神	heart + god/spirit	mind, state of mind
186.	xin1sheng	心生	heart + birth	in high spirits, enthusiastic
187.	xin1sheng1	心聲	heart + voice	heartfelt wishes, aspirations
188.	xin1shi4	心事	heart + matter/thing	something weighing on one's mind, worry
189.	xin1shu4	心術	heart + art/method	intention, design
190.	xin1si3	心死	heart + die	see the futility of one's attempt
191.	xin1si	心思	heart + consider/ponder	thought, idea, thinking, state of mind, mood
192.	xin1suan1	心酸	heart + sour	grieved, feel sad
193.	xin1suan4	心算	heart + calculate	doing sums in one's head, mental arithmetic
194.	xin1teng2	心疼	heart + ache	love dearly, feel sorry
195.	xin1teng2	心疼	heart + pain/sore	love dearly, feel sorry
196.	xin1tian2	心田	heart + farm	heart, intention
197.	xin1tou2	心頭	heart + head	mind, heart

198.	xin1xi4	心細	heart + think/slender	careful, scrupulous
199.	xin1xian2	心弦	heart + string	heartstrings
200.	xin4xin1	信心	trust + heart	confidence, faith
201.	xin1xing4	心性	heart + nature/quality	one's nature, temperament
202.	xin1xiong1	心胸	heart + chest	breadth of mind
203.	xin1xu1	心虛	heart + void/vain	(1) afraid of being outed, guilty conscience, (2) lacking self-confidence, diffident
204.	xin1xu4	心緒	heart + mood/mental state	state of mind, mood
205.	xin1xue4	心血	heart + blood	painstaking care
206.	xin1xue4 lai2chao2	心血來潮	heart + blood + come + trend	prompted by sudden impulse, seized by a whim
207.	xin1yanr3	心眼兒	heart + eye + [nominal suffix]	heart, mind, intention, intelligence
208.	xin1yi4	心意	heart + meaning	regard, kindly feelings, intention, purpose
209.	xin1yin1	心音	heart + sound	cardiac sounds
210.	xin1ying4	心硬	heart + harden	hard-hearted, callous, unfeeling
211.	xin1you3 yu2ji4	心有餘悸	heart + has + remainder + palpitate	one's heart still fluttering with fear
212.	xin1yuan2 yi4ma3	心猿意馬	heart + ape + meaning + horse	restless and whimsical, capricious
213.	xin1yuan4	心願	heart + hope/wish	cherished desire, aspiration, wish, dream
214.	xin1yue4 cheng2fu2	心悅誠服	heart + happy/pleased + honest/sincere + convinced	feel heartfelt admiration, completely convinced
215.	xin1zhan4	心戰	heart + war	psychological warfare
216.	xin1zhao4bu4 xuan1	心照不宣	heart + illuminate + no + declare	understand without being told
217.	xin1zhi2 kou3kuai4	心直口快	heart + direct + mouth + fast	frank and outspoken
218.	xin1zhong1 you3shu4	心中有數	heart + inside/internal + has + number/idea	have a pretty good idea of
219	xin1zui4	心醉	heart + drunk	charmed, be

				enchanted, be fascinated
220.	xin4xin1	信心	trust + heart	confidence, faith
221.	xinji4	心計	heart + calculate/plan	calculation, scheming, planning
222.	xiong2xin1	雄心	grand/powerful + heart	great ambition, lofty aspiration
223.	xin1wu2 er4yong4	心無二用	heart + no + two + use	cannot keep one's mind on two things at once
224.	xuan2xin1	懸心	hanging + heart	filled with anxiety, fearful
225.	yan2wei2 xin1sheng1	言為心聲	words + for/as + heart + voice	words are the voice of the mind, what the heart thinks the tongue speaks
226.	ye3xin1	野心	wild + heart	wild ambition, careerism
227.	yi2ge xin1yanr3	一個心眼兒	one + [measure word] + heart + eye + [nominal suffix]	be of one mind (heart set on something)
228.	yi1tiao1xin1	一條心	one + [measure word] + heart	to be of one mind, to think or act alike
229.	yi4xin1 yi4de2	一心一德	one + heart + one + morals/virtue	be of one heart and one mind
230.	yi4xin1	一心	one + heart	wholeheartedly
231.	yi4xin1 yi2yi4	一心一意	one + heart + one + meaning	heart and soul
232.	yi2xin1	疑心	suspicious + heart	suspicion
233.	yi2xin1bing4	疑心病	suspicious + heart + disease	suspicious frame of mind
234.	yi4xin1	一心	one + heart	infidelity, disloyalty
235.	yong4xin1	用心	use + heart	diligently, attentively, motive, intention, purpose
236.	you1xin1	憂心	concerned + heart	concerned, worried, disturbed, anxious
237.	you3xin1	有心	has + heart	have a mind to, intentionally, deliberately
238.	you3xin1ren2	有心人	has + heart + person	person who sets his mind on doing something useful, observant and conscientious person
239.	yu3zhong4 xin1chang2	語重心長	language/speech + heart +	sincere words and earnest wishes

				long	
240.	zai4xin1	在心		exist/at + heart	feel concerned, mind, be attentive
241.	zao1xin1	糟心		distillers' grain + heart	vexed, annoyed, dejected
242.	zhen1xin1	真心		real/true + heart	wholeheartedly, heartfelt, sincere
243.	zhen1xin1 shi2yi4	真心實意		real/true + heart + authentic + meaning	genuinely and sincerely, truly and wholeheartedly
244.	zhi2xin1	執心		grasp/hold + heart	open, frank, straightforward
245.	zhong1xin1	衷心		inner feelings + heart	heartfelt, wholehearted, cordial
246.	zhu1xin1 zhi1lun4	誅心之論		kill + heart + of + theory	penetrating criticism, exposing somebody's ulterior criticism
247.	zhuan1xin1	專心		focus + heart	concentrate one's attention, absorbed
248.	zui4xin1	醉心		drunken + heart	enthralled, fascinated
249.	zuo4zei2 xin1xu1	作賊心虛		act + thief + heart + empty/void	have a guilty conscience

Dataset App F.4. Bodily Parts.

Mandarin (Pinyin)	Logographs	Literal Meaning	English
da4dan3	大膽	big + gallbladder	bold, daring
dan3	膽	gallbladder	courage, guts, bravery
dan3da4	膽大	gallbladder + big	bold, audacious
dan3han2	膽寒	gallbladder + cold	terrified, struck with terror
dan3liang4	膽量	gallbladder + quantity	courage, pluck
dan3lüe4	膽略	gallbladder + plan	courage and resourcefulness
dan3qie4	膽怯	gallbladder + timid	timid, cowardly
dan3shi4	膽識	gallbladder + knowledge	courage and insight
dan3xiao3	膽小	gallbladder + small	timid, cowardly
dan3zhan4 xin1jing1	膽戰心驚	gallbladder + shiver + heart + frightened	tremble with fear
dan3zi	膽子	gallbladder + [plus nominal suffix]	courage, nerve

fei4fu3	肺腑	lungs + internal organs	bottom of one's heart
fu2ying1	服膺	convince + breast	bear in mind, feel deeply convinced
fu4gao3	腹稿	belly + draft	draft worked out in one's head, mental notes
hui2mou2	回眸	turn around + eye	look back, recollect
hui2shou3	回首	turn around + head	look back, recollect
ku3nao3	苦惱	bitter + brain	vexed, worried
nao3dai4	腦袋	brain + bag	brains, mental capability
nao3hai3	腦海	brain + sea	brain, mind
nao3jin1	腦筋	brain + muscle	brain, mind, way of thinking, ideas
nao3zi	腦子	brain + [nominal suffix]	brain, mind, head
qu3qi4	骨氣	bones + cosmic energy	vital energy, strength of character, moral integrity, back bone
qu3zili3	骨子裡	bones + [nominal suffix] + inside	in one's heart of hearts
tou2jiao3	頭角	head + horn	brilliance (of a young person)
tou2nao3	頭腦	head + brain	brains, mind
xiong1huai2	胸懷	chest + bosom	mind, heart
xiong1jin1	胸襟	chest + front of a garment	mind, breadth of mind
xiong1yi4	胸臆	chest + breast	inner feelings
xiong1you3 cheng2zhu2	胸有成竹	chest + are/has + complete + bamboo	have a well thought-out plan, stratagem
xiong1zhong1 you3shu4	胸中有數	chest + inside + are/has + count	have a good idea of how things stand
xue4qi4	血氣	blood + cosmic energy	courage and uprightness (also, animal spirits)
xue4xing4	血性	blood + raw meat	courage, uprightness
zi4	自	nose	personal, private, in person, or personally

Dataset App F.5. Psychological Terms and Their Compounds Listed in Alphabetical Order.

ai1	jing1 (essence)	nian4	xiang3
ai4	jing1(surprise)	nu4	xing4
an1	ji4	qi4	yan4
bei1	jiao1	qing2	yi4
cai1	jue2	re4	you1
chi1	kong3	ren4	yu4
chu4	ku3	shi2	zhi1
dong4 (cave)	le4	si1	zhi4
dong4 (move)	liao3	wang4 (forget)	zi4
fa1	man3	wang4 (hope)	
fan2	mu4	xi1	
gan3	nan4	xi3	

ai1

Mandarin (Pinyin)	Logograph	Literal Meaning	English
ai1dao4	哀悼	sad + mourn	mourn
ai1shang1	哀傷	sad + wound	grief, distress, bereavement

ai4

Mandarin (Pinyin)	Logograph	Literal Meaning	English
ai4hu4	愛護	love + protect	cherish, treasure
ai4lian2	愛憐	love + pity	show affection for
ai4mian4zi3	愛面子	love + face + [nominal suffix]	sensitive about one's reputation
ai4mu4	愛慕	love + admire	adore, admire
ai4xi1	愛惜	love + cherish	cherish, treasure, use sparingly
jing4ai4	敬愛	honor + love	respect and love

an1

Mandarin (Pinyin)	Logograph	Literal Meaning	English
an1ning2	安寧	peace + quiet	peaceful, tranquil, calm
an1wei4	安慰	peace + console	comfort, console
an1xiang2	安詳	peace + detailed, thorough	serene, composed
an1xiang2	安祥	peace + auspicious/lucky	serene, composed, unruffled
an1yu2	安於	peace + in/at	feel contented with

bei1

Mandarin (Pinyin)	Logograph	Literal Meaning	English
bei1ai1	悲哀	sad + mourn	grieved, sorrowful
bei1can3	悲慘	sad + misery	miserable, tragic
bei1chou2	悲愁	sad + grieve	melancholy, grieved
bei1fen4	悲憤	sad + indignant	grieved and indignant
bei1guan1	悲觀	sad + vision/ sight	pessimistic
bei1shang1	悲傷	sad + distressed	sad, sorrowful
bei1tong4	悲慟	sad + deep sorrow	grieved, sorrowful
bei1tong4	悲痛	sad + hurt	grieved, sorrowful
bei1qi4	悲泣	sad + weep	weep with grief
ci2bei1	慈悲	kind + sad	mercy, compassion
guo4bei1	過悲	excessive + sad	extremely sad
shang1bei1	傷悲	wound + sad	sorrowful

cai1

Mandarin (Pinyin)	Logograph	Literal Meaning	English
cai1ce4	猜測	guess + measure	guess, conjecture, surmise
cai1duo4	猜度	guess + degree	surmise, conjecture
cai1ji4	猜忌	guess + jealous	suspicious and jealous
cai1meir2	猜謎	guess + riddle	guess a riddle

chi1

Mandarin (Pinyin)	Logograph	Literal Meaning	English
chi1cu4	吃醋	eat + vinegar	jealous
chi1dexiao1	吃得消	eat + get + consume	able to stand, (exertion, fatigue)
chi1jin3	吃緊	eat + tighten/urgent	entail much effort
chi1jing1	吃驚	eat + surprise	startled, shocked
chi1ku3	吃苦	eat + bitter	bear hardships
chi1ku3tou2	吃苦頭	eat + bitter + head	suffer
chi1kui1	吃虧	eat + lose	suffer losses, come to grief
chi1li4	吃力	eat + strength	entail strenuous effort
chi1ruan3 bu4chi1ying4	吃軟不吃硬	eat + soft + not + eat + hard	be open to persuasion but not coercion
chi1tou4	吃透	eat + head	have a thorough grasp
chi1zhong4	吃重	eat + heavy	arduous, strenuous

chu4

Mandarin (Pinyin)	Logograph	Literal Meaning	English
chu4dong4	觸動	touch + move	touch; to stir up (trouble or emotions); to move (somebody's emotions)
chu4fan4	觸犯	touch + offend	offend
chu4ji2	觸及	touch + reach	touch (physically, one's feelings); to touch on (a topic)

dong4 (cave)

Mandarin (Pinyin)	Logograph	Literal Meaning	English
dong4che4	洞徹	cave + penetrating	understand clearly
dong4da2	洞達	cave + reach	understand clearly
dong4xi1	洞悉	cave + know/entire	understand clearly
dong4xiao3	洞曉	cave + understand/dawn	have clear knowledge of

dong4 (move)

Mandarin (Pinyin)	Logograph	Literal Meaning	English
dong4ren2	動人	move + person	touching, moving
dong4yao2	動搖	move + shake	shake, waver, be indecisive
ji1dong4	激動	arouse + move	excite, agitate
rao3dong4	擾動	disturb (PS: hand) + move	disturb, harass, agitate

fa1

Mandarin (Pinyin)	Logograph	Literal Meaning	English
fa1chou2	發愁	send + worry	worry, be anxious
fa1chu4	發怵	send + fear	feel timid
fa1feng1	發瘋	send + crazy	out of one's mind
fa1hen3	發狠	send + cruel	make a determined effort, be angry
fa1huang1	發慌	send + panicky	feel nervous, flustered
fa1hun1	發昏	send + dizzy	feel giddy, lose one's head,
fa1huo3	發火	send + fire	get angry
fa1ji2	發急	send + hurry	become impatient
fa1kuang2	發狂	send + crazy/wild	go mad
fa1lan3	發懶	send + lazy	feel lazy

Mandarin (Pinyin)	Logograph	Literal Meaning	English
fa1mao2	發毛	send + fur	scared, get gooseflesh, lose one's temper
fa1meng1	發悶	send + stuffy	get confused
fa1pi2qi	發脾氣	send + spleen + cosmic energy	lose one's temper

fan2

Mandarin (Pinyin)	Logograph	Literal Meaning	English
fan2luan4	煩亂	vexed + confusion (CG: kneeling person with hands untangling twisted string)	anxious, agitated
fan2men1	煩悶	vexed + gloomy	unhappy
fan2nao3	煩惱	vexed + tense, excited, irritable (PS: foot)	jittery, agitated
nai4fan2	耐煩	endure, resist + vex (CG: head burning with fire)	patient

gan3

Mandarin (Pinyin)	Logograph	Literal Meaning	English
fang3gan3	反感	in reverse + feel	disgusted
gan2qing2 yong4shi4	感情用事	feel + emotion + use + matter	act impetuously
gan3chu4	感觸	feel + touch	thoughts and feelings
gan3dong4	感動	feel + move	move, touch
gan3en1	感恩	feel + grace	feel grateful
gan3fen4	感憤	feel + anger	indignant
gan3ji1	感激	feel + arouse/incite	express thanks, grateful
gan3jue2	感覺	feel + sense	sense, perception, sensation, feel, perceive
gan3kai3	感慨	feel + sigh emotionally	lament, sigh with emotion
gan3nian4	感念	feel + miss	recall with gratitude
gan3qing2	感情	feel + emotion	emotion, feeling, affection, attachment
gan3shang1	感傷	feel + distressed	sad, sorrowful, sentimental
gan3shou4	感受	feel + take	affected by, experience
gan3tan4	感嘆	feel + sigh	sigh with feeling
gan3xiang3	感想	feel + think	impressions, reflections, thoughts
gan3xie4	感謝	feel + thank	be grateful
gan3xing4	感性	feel + sex	perceptual

gan3zhao4	感召	feel + summon	move and inspire, impel
tong2gan3	同感	same + feel	similar feeling/ sympathy/consensus

jing1 (essence)

Mandarin (Pinyin)	Logograph	Literal Meaning	English
jing1ming2 qian2gan4	精明強幹	essence + clear + strong + trunk	intelligent and capable
jing1ming2	精明	essence + clear	astute, shrewd, sagacious
jing1shen2	精神	essence + god/spirit	spirit, mind, consciousness (also, means vigor, vitality, drive, life force)
jing1shen2bing4	精神病	essence + god/spirit + disease	mental disease
jing1tong1	精通	essence + flow	proficient in

jing1 (surprise)

Mandarin (Pinyin)	Logograph	Literal Meaning	English
da4jing1	大驚	big + surprise	with great alarm
jing1dong4	驚動	surprise + move	startle, alarm, alert, disturb
jing1huang1	驚慌	surprise + panic	frightened, scared
jing1qi2	驚奇	surprise + strange	amazed
jing1ren2	驚人	surprise + person	astonishing
jing1tan4	驚歎	surprise + acclaim/sigh	exclaim in surprise
jing1tan4	驚嘆	surprise + sigh	exclaim in surprise
jing3ti4	警惕	warning + watchful	vigilant, alert, on guard
jing1ya4	驚訝	surprise + surprised	amazed, astonished, surprised, amazing
jing1yi4	驚異	surprise + different/strange	amazed, astonished
zhen4jing1	震驚	shock + surprise	shock, astonish

ji4

Mandarin (Pinyin)	Logograph	Literal Meaning	English
dian4ji4	惦記	miss + remember	think of, keep thinking about, concerned about
ji4de	記得	remember + acquire	remember
ji4yi4	記憶	remember + recall	remember, recall, memory

jiao1

Mandarin (Pinyin)	Logograph	Literal Meaning	English
jiao1ji2	焦急	burned, scorched + hurry	anxious
jiao1lü4	焦慮	burned, scorched + be concerned	anxious, worried, apprehensive

jue2

Mandarin (Pinyin)	Logograph	Literal Meaning	English
bu4jue2	不覺	not + feel	unconsciously
cha2jue2	察覺	examine/investigate + feel	sense, perceive, come to realize, aware
jue2de hao3xiang4	覺得好像	feel + acquire + good + alike	feel as if
jue2de2	覺得	feel + acquire	feel, think
jue2wu4	覺悟	feel + realize	consciousness, awareness, understanding, come to understand, Buddhist enlightenment
jue2xing3	覺醒	feel + awaken	awaken, come to realize, awakened to the truth, become aware
shi1qu4 zhi1jue2	失去知覺	lose + leave + know + feel	lose consciousness
zhi2jue2	直覺	direct +feel	consciousness
zi4jue2	自覺	self + feel	conscious, aware

kong3

Mandarin (Pinyin)	Logograph	Literal Meaning	English
huang2kong3	惶恐	anxiety + horrify	terrified
kong3bu4	恐怖	horrify + fear	terrible, frightful, frightening
kong3dong4	恐動	horrify + move	disturb, harass, agitate
kong3huang1	恐慌	horrify + panic	panic, panicky, panic-stricken
kong3jing1	驚恐	surprise + horrify	alarm, dismay, appall
kong3ju4	恐懼	horrify + dread	fear, dread, phobia
kong3pa4	恐怕	horrify + scare	fear, dread
wei2kong3	唯恐	only + horrify	for fear that

ku3

Mandarin (Pinyin)	Logograph	Literal Meaning	English
ku3du2	苦毒	bitter; hardship, suffering + poison	pain, suffering, hate
ku3e4	苦厄	bitter; hardship, suffering + adversity, difficulty, distress	suffering
ku3nan4	苦難	bitter; hardship, suffering + difficult	suffering
ku3nao3	苦惱	bitter; hardship, suffering + angered	annoyed, distressed, vexed
kun4ku3	困苦	surround + bitter; hardship, suffering	distressed, miserable

le4

Mandarin (Pinyin)	Logograph	Literal Meaning	English
an1le4	安樂	peace + happy	peace and happiness
huan1le4	歡樂	pleased + happy	happy, joyous, gay
ji2le4	極樂	extreme + happy	bliss
kuai4le4	快樂	fast + happy	happy
le4guan1	樂觀	happy + vision	optimistic, hopeful
le4he1he1	樂呵呵	happy + breathe out + breathe out	buyout, happy
le4qu4	樂趣	happy + fun	delight, pleasure, joy
le4yu2	樂於	happy + at/in	be happy, take delight in
le4zi1zi	樂滋滋	happy + grow + grow	contented, pleased
xin1le4	訢樂	glad/happy + happy	happy, joyous, gay

liao3

Mandarin (Pinyin)	Logograph	Literal Meaning	English
liao3jie3	瞭解	understand + solve	know, understand
liao3liao3	了了	understand + understand	know clearly
liao3ran2	瞭然	understand + so	understand, be clear
liao3ru2 zhi3zhang3	瞭如指掌	understand + as + finger + palm	know something like the palm of one's hand

man3

Mandarin (Pinyin)	Logograph	Literal Meaning	English
bu4man3	不滿	not + full/satisfy	be resentful, be

			discontented, be dissatisfied
man3qiang1	滿腔	full + chest cavity	one's heart filled with, full of
mei3man3	美滿	beauty + full	happy, blissful

mu4

Mandarin (Pinyin)	Logograph	Literal Meaning	English
jing4mu4	敬慕	honor + long for (PS: heart)	respect, venerate, admire
xian4mu4	羨慕	envy, praise (PS: ram, spittle) + long for (PS: heart)	envy, admire
xiang4mu4	向慕	toward, direction, trend + long for (PS: heart)	adore

nan4

Mandarin (Pinyin)	Logograph	Literal Meaning	English
nan4guo4	難過	difficult + pass	feel sorry, be grieved
nan4kan1	難堪	difficult + adequately capable of	embarrassing
mo2nan4	磨難	grind, polish + difficult	a torment, a trial, a hardship

nian4

Mandarin (Pinyin)	Logograph	Literal Meaning	English
dong4nian4	動念	move + miss	be disturbed
gua4nian4	掛念	hang + miss	concerned, to miss
hui2nian4	懷念	bosom + miss	think back, recollect, recall
xin4nian4	信念	belief + miss	faith, belief, conviction
yi4nian4	憶念	recall + miss	long for, to miss

nu4

Mandarin (Pinyin)	Logograph	Literal Meaning	English
chen1nu4	嗔怒	angry + rage	become angry
dong4nu4	動怒	move + rage	become angry
fen4nu4	忿怒	anger + rage	angry, indignant, wrath, ire
hui4nu4	恚怒	anger + rage	hate, be in a rage
hui4nu4	憓怒	anger + rage	hate, in a rage

Appendix F

Mandarin (Pinyin)	Logograph	Literal Meaning	English
ji1nu4	激怒	irritate + angry	infuriate, enrage, exasperate
nu4hou3	怒吼	rage + yell	bellow, rave, to snarl
nu4huo3	怒火	rage + fire	rage, fury, hot anger
nu4qi4	怒氣	rage + cosmic energy	anger
qian1nu4	遷怒	move + rage	take one's anger out on somebody
shi3nu4	使怒	employ + rage	exasperate

qi4

Mandarin (Pinyin)	Logograph	Literal Meaning	English
chu1qi4	出氣	depart + vital energy	give vent to anger
fa1pi2qi4	發脾氣	deliver + spleen + vital energy	get angry
fengaqi4	風氣	wind + vital energy	general mood, atmosphere, common practice
fu2qi4	服氣	convince + vital energy	convinced
jiao1qi4	嬌氣	fragile/lovely + vital energy	delicate, squeamish, finicky
pi2qi4	脾氣	spleen + vital energy	temperament, disposition, temper
qi4fen1	氣氛	vital energy + atmosphere	atmosphere, mood
qi4fen4	氣憤	vital energy + anger	indignant, furious
qi4gai4	氣概	vital energy + deportment	lofty quality
qi4hu1hu1	氣呼呼	vital energy + exhale	panting with rage
qi4ji2bai4huai4	氣急敗壞	vital energy + rush + defeat + bad	flustered and exasperated
qi4jie2	氣節	vital energy + node	integrity, moral courage
qi4li4	氣力	vital energy + strength	effort, energy, strength
qi4liang4	氣量	vital energy + quantity	tolerance
qi4nao3	氣惱	vital energy + angry	get angry, take offence
qi4tou2shang	氣頭上	vital energy + head + above	in a fit of anger
qi4xing4	氣性	vital energy + nature	temperament
qi4yan4	氣焰	vital energy + flame	arrogance, bluster
qi4zhi2	氣質	vital energy + characteristic	temperament

Mandarin (Pinyin)	Logograph	Literal Meaning	English
qi4zhi2	氣質	vital energy + character	temperament, disposition, qualities, making
sang4qi4	喪氣	lose + cosmic energy	disheartened
sheng1qi4	生氣	give birth + vital energy	get angry, take offence (also, life, vitality)
su2qi4	俗氣	vulgar + vital energy	tacky, inelegant, in poor taste, vulgar, banal
xe4qi4	洩氣	look out + vital energy	feel discouraged

qing2

Mandarin (Pinyin)	Logograph	Literal Meaning	English
biao3qing2	表情	expression + emotion	facial expression, express one's feelings
en1qing2	恩情	grace + emotion	deep affection, loving-kindness
fan2qing2	凡情	ordinary + emotion	ordinary feelings and desires
feng1qing2	風情	wind + emotion	feelings, amorous feelings
ji1qing2	激情	excite + emotion	strong emotion, passion, fervor
qing2gan3	情感	emotion + feel	feeling, emotion
qing2gan3	情感	emotion + feel	to move (emotionally)
qing2huai2	情懷	emotion + bosom	feelings, mood
qing2qu4	情趣	emotion + fun	emotional appeal
qing2xu4	情緒	emotion + clue	feeling, sentiment
qing2yi4	情意	emotion + meaning	affection
qing2yu4	情欲	emotion + lust/desire	lust, desire
re4qing2	熱情	hot + emotion	cordial, enthusiastic
shen1qing2	深情	deep + emotion	deep emotion
tong2qing2	同情	same + emotion	sympathize
wu2qing2	無情	no/lacking + emotion	pitiless, ruthless, merciless, heartless
xing4qing2	性情	nature + emotion/affection	disposition

re4

Mandarin (Pinyin)	Logograph	Literal Meaning	English
huo3re4	火熱	fire + hot, fever	fervent, ardent, passionate
qin1re4	親熱	relatives, parents; intimate + hot, fever	affectionate, intimate, warm-hearted

Appendix F 205

Mandarin (Pinyin)	Logograph	Literal Meaning	English
re4ai4	熱愛	hot; heat; fever + love	love ardently, adore
re4qie4	熱切	hot; heat; fever + cut	fervent
re4zhong1	熱衷	hot; heat; fever + from bottom of one's heart	crave

ren4

Mandarin (Pinyin)	Logograph	Literal Meaning	English
bian4ren4	辨認	differentiate + recognize	recognize, identify
cheng2ren4	承認	bear/hold + recognize	admit, concede, recognize, recognition
ren4cuo4	認錯	recognize/admit + mistake	acknowledge a mistake
ren4de	認得	recognize + get	know, recognize
ren4ding4	認定	recognize + settle	firmly believe, set one's mind to
ren4qing1	認清	recognize + clear	see clearly, recognize
ren4shi	認識	recognize + know	know, understand, recognize,
ren4wei2	認為	recognize + become	think, consider, hold, deem,
ren4zhen1	認真	recognize + authentic	conscientious, earnest serious, to take seriously, take to heart

shi2

Mandarin (Pinyin)	Logograph	Literal Meaning	English
chang2shi2	常識	common + knowledge	common sense, general knowledge
jian4shi	見識	see + knowledge	knowledge and experience, increase one's knowledge
shi4bie2	識別	know + distinguish	distinguish
shi4 huo4	識貨	know + product	know what's what
shi4 jian4	識見	know + see	knowledge and experience
shi2li4	實力	solid/true + strength	discernment, ability to judge
shi4 po4	識破	know + break	see through, penetrate
shi4qu4	識趣	know + fun	know how to behave in a difficult situation
shi4 xiang4	識相	know + appearance	sensible, tactful

si1

Mandarin (Pinyin)	Logograph	Literal Meaning	English
ku3si1	苦思	bitter + think	think hard
si1chao2	思潮	think + tide	trend of thought, thoughts
si1cun3	思忖	think + ponder/consider	ponder, consider
si1kao3	思考	think + test	think deeply, ponder
si1lian4	思戀	think + love	miss, long for
si1liang	思量	think + estimate/measure	consider, turn over on one's mind
si1lu4	思路	think + road	train of thought
si1lü4	思慮	think + consider	consider carefully, deliberate
si1mu4	思慕	think + admire	think of sb. with respect, admire
si1nian4	思念	think + miss	think of, long for, miss
si1suo3	思索	think + rope	think deeply, ponder
si1wei2	思維	think + search	thought, thinking
si1xiang3	思想	think + think	thought, thinking, idea, ideology
si1xu4	思緒	think + clue	train of thought, feeling

wang4 (forget)

Mandarin (Pinyin)	Logograph	Literal Meaning	English
jian4wang4	健忘	health + forget	absent-minded
nan2wang4	難忘	difficult + forget	unforgettable
shan4wang4	善忘	be apt to + forget	forgetful, amnesia
wang4huai2	忘懷	forget + bosom	forget
wang4ji4	忘記	forget + remember	forget, overlook
wang4qing2	忘情	forget + emotion	unmoved, indifferent, unruffled by sentiment
wang4que4	忘卻	forget + off/out/away	forget (esp. in writing)
wang4wo3	忘我	forget + I	selflessness, altruism

wang4 (hope)

Mandarin (Pinyin)	Logograph	Literal Meaning	English
jue2wang4	絕望	terminate + hope	desperate, forlorn, hopeless
ke3wang4	渴望	thirsty + hope	wish, desire
pan4wang4	盼望	hope/look for + hope	hope for, look forward to

Mandarin (Pinyin)	Logograph	Literal Meaning	English
she1wang4	奢望	wasteful + hope	extravagant hope, excessive expectations
shi1wang4	失望	lose + hope	disappointed, lose hope, despair
xi1wang4	希望	rare + hope	wish for, desire hope
yu4wang4	慾望	desire + hope	desire, longing, appetite, craving
yuan4wang4	願望	wish + hope	desire, wish
zhi3wang4	指望	finger + hope	hope for, count on

xi1

Mandarin (Pinyin)	Logograph	Literal Meaning	English
xi1ji4	希冀	hope + look forward to	hope for, wish for, aspire after
xi1qiu2	希求	hope + beg	hope and request
xi1tu2	希圖	hope + picture	harbor the intention to
xi1wang4	希望	hope + look	wish for, desire, hope

xi3

Mandarin (Pinyin)	Logograph	Literal Meaning	English
huan1xi3	歡喜	joyous + happy	joyful
jing1xi3	驚喜	surprise + happy	pleasantly surprised
jing1xi3	驚喜	surprise + happy	pleasant surprise
ke3xi3	可喜	able + happy	gratifying, heartening
xi3ai4	喜愛	happy + love	like, love
xi3huan	喜歡	happy + happy	like, love, be fond of, happy, elated, fill with joy
xi3le4	喜樂	happy + joy	joy
xi3qing4	喜慶	happy + celebrate	joyful, jubilant
xi3yue4	喜悅	happy + pleased	happy, joyous
xin1xi3	欣喜	glad/happy + happy	happy

xiang3

Mandarin (Pinyin)	Logograph	Literal Meaning	English
xiang3	響	sound	sound
cai1xiang3	猜想	guess + think	suppose, guess, estimate
gan3xiang3	感想	feel + think	impressions, reflections, thoughts
huan4xiang3	幻想	illusion + think	illusion, fantasy
hui2xiang3	回想	return + think	think back, recollect,

Mandarin (Pinyin)	Logograph	Literal Meaning	English
			recall
kong1xiang3	空想	empty + think	idle dream, fantasy
liao4xiang3	料想	materialexpect + think	expect, think, presume
meng4xiang3	夢想	dream + think	dream of, vainly hope, earnest wish
ming2xiang3	冥想	dark + think	deep thought, mediation
she4xiang3	設想	set up + think	imagine, envisage, conceive, tentative plan
shi4xiang3	試想	try, test + think	just think
wang4xiang3	妄想	vain, hope + think	wishful thinking
xiang3	想	think	think
xiang3bukai1	想不開	think + not + open	take things too hard
xiang3chu1	想出	think + depart	figure out
xiang3dao4	想到	think + arrive	think of, call to mind
xiang3de	想得	think + acquire	think of
xiang3dedao4	想得到	think + acquire + arrive	think, imagine, expect
xiang3dekai1	想得開	think + acquire + open	not take to heart, look at the bright side
xiang3fa3	想法	think + way	idea, opinion
xiang3jianna4	想見	think + see	infer, gather
xiang3nian4	想念	think + miss	remember with longing
xiang3qi3	想起	think + rise	remember, recall, think of, call to mind
xiang3qi3	想起	think + rise	think of, remember
xiang3ru4 fei1fei1	想入非非	think + into + wrong + wrong	indulge in fantasy
xiang3tong1	想通	think + through	become convinced, come round
xiang3tou2	想頭	think + head	hope
xiang3wang4	想望	think + hope	wish, desire
xiang3xiang4	想像	think + appear/ picture	imagine, fancy, visualize, imagination
xiang3yao4	想要	think + want	want
xiang4wang3	嚮往	guide/direct + toward	desire, long for
xiu1xiang3	休想	stop, cease + think	don't imagine that it's possible

xing4

Mandarin (Pinyin)	Logograph	Literal Meaning	English
gao1xing4	高興	high + thrive	glad, happy, cheerful
sao3xing4	掃興	sweep + thrive	have one's spirits dampened, feel disappointed

xing4chong1chong1	興沖沖	thrive + pour + flush	to do something with joy, excitedly
xing4fen4	興奮	thrive + act vigorously	excited
xing4gao1 cai3lie4	興高采烈	thrive + high + bright color + intense	in high spirits, great delight
xing4hui4	興會	thrive + be able to/meet	sudden flash of inspiration
xing4qu4	興趣	thrive + fun	interest
xing4tou2	興頭	thrive + head	enthusiasm, keen interest
xing4wei4	興味	thrive + taste	interest
xing4zhi4	興致	thrive + deliver	interest, mood to enjoy

yan4

Mandarin (Pinyin)	Logograph	Literal Meaning	English
bu2yan4	不厭	not + disgust	not mind doing something, not tire of, not object to
sheng1yan4	生厭	life, birth + disgust	disgust, fed up, tedious, cloying, boring, irritating
tao3yan4	討厭	discuss + disgust	dislike, loathe, disagreeable, troublesome, annoying
xiang3yan4	想厭	want + disgust	loathe
yan4hen4	厭恨	disgust + hate	hate, detest
yan4juan4	厭倦	disgust + tire	weary of, fed up with, tedious
yan4qi4	厭棄	disgust + abandon	spurn, reject
yan4shi4	厭世	disgust + world	world-weary, pessimistic
yan4wu4	厭惡	dislike + evil/wicked	loathe, hate, disgusted with something

yi4

Mandarin (Pinyin)	Logograph	Literal Meaning	English
ben3yi4	本意	original + meaning	original idea, real intention
bu3guo4yi4	不過意	not + cross + meaning/intention	feel sorry
bu4hao3yi4si	不好意思	not + good + meaning + [final particle to	be embarrassed (for inconveniencing

			sound off an expression]	somebody)
bu4yi4	不意		not + meaning/ intention	unexpectedly, unaware, unprepared
cheng2yi4	誠意		sincere + meaning	good faith, sincerity
chun1yi4	春意		spring + meaning	beginning of spring; thoughts of love
da2yi4	達意		reach + meaning	express one's wishes
da4yi4	大意		big + meaning	general idea
da4yi4	大意		big + meaning	careless, negligent, inattentive
de2yi4	得意		acquire + meaning	proud of oneself
de2yi4	敵意		enemy + meaning	enmity, hostility
di2yi4	敵意		enemy + meaning	hostility, enmity, animosity
e4yi4	惡意		vicious + meaning	evil intentions, malice
gong1yi4	公意		public + meaning/ will	public will
gou4yi4si	夠意思		enough + meaning + [final particle to sound off an expression]	generous
gu4yi4	故意		old/ancient/cause + meaning	intentionally, willfully, deliberately
guo4yi4 bu2qu4	過意不去		pass + meaning+ not + to/go	feel apologetic, feel sorry
hao3yi4	好意		good + meaning	good intention
hao3yi4si	好意思		good + meaning + [final particle to sound off an expression]	have the nerve
he2yi4	合意		combine + meaning	suit, be to one's taste
hui4yi4	會意		able + meaning	understanding, knowing
jia1yi4	加意		add + meaning	with special care, with close attention
jia3yi4	假意		fake + meaning	insincerity, pretend, put on
jie4yi4	介意		introduce + meaning	take offence, to mind
jing1yi4	經意		scriptures + meaning/intention	careful, mindful
jing4yi4	敬意		respect + meaning/intention	respect, tribute
jiu3yi4	酒意		wine/alcohol + meaning	tipsy feeling
jue2yi4	決意		determined + meaning/intention	have one's mind made up, determined
ke3yi4	可意		approve + meaning/	gratifying,

		intention	satisfactory
ke4yi4	刻意	carve + meaning	painstakingly, sedulously
kuai4yi4	快意	rapid + meaning/ intention	pleased, satisfied, comfortable
lai2yi4	來意	come + meaning/ intention	one's purpose in coming
le4yi4	樂意	cheerful + meaning/ intention	willing to, ready to
le4yi4	樂意	joy + meaning/ intention	pleased (willing), willing, satisfied
li4yi4	立意	stand + meaning/ intention	determined (conception, approach)
liu2yi4	留意	stay/remain + meaning	careful, look out
man3yi4	滿意	full + meaning	satisfied, pleased
min2yi4	民意	people + intention/ will	will of the people
na2zhu3yi4	拿主意	take + host + meaning	make a decision, make up one's mind
nao4yi4jian4	鬧意見	disturb + meaning/ intention + vision	on bad terms, due to difference of opinion
nao4yi4qi4	鬧意氣	disturb + meaning + air	feel resentful because something is not to one's liking, sulk
qian4yi4	歉意	insufficient + meaning	apology, regret
qie4yi4	愜意	cheerful + meaning	pleased
qing2yi4	情意	emotion + meaning	tender regards, affection
qu1yi4 feng2ying2	曲意逢迎	bend + meaning/ intention + meet + greet	go out of one's way to curry favor
ru2yi4	如意	as + intention	as one wishes
ru2yi4 suan4pan	如意算盤	as + meaning + count + check/tray	wishful thinking
shan4yi4	善意	good/kind + meaning	good will, good intentions
sheng4yi4	盛意	flourishing/prosperous/intention	great kindness, generosity
shi1yi4	失意	lost + meaning	have one's aspirations, plans, thwarted, frustrated, disappointed
shi4yi4	適意	suit + meaning	agreeable, enjoyable, comfortable
sho4yi4	授意	hand over + intention	get sb. to do something, inspire

si4yi4	肆意	reckless + intention	wantonly, recklessly, willfully
sui2yi4	隨意	follow + intention	at will, as one pleases
tian1yi4	天意	sky + intention	will of Heaven, God's will
tong2yi4	同意	same + intention	agree, consent
wu2yi4	無意	no + meaning	have no intention of, inadvertently
wu2yi4shi2	無意識	no + meaning + recognition	unconscious
xie3yi4	寫意	write + meaning	comfortable, enjoyable
xie4yi4	謝意	thank + meaning	gratitude
xu4yi4	蓄意	breed + meaning	premeditated, deliberate
ya3yi4	雅意	elegant + intention	your kindness, you kind offer
yi2yi4 gu1xing2	一意孤行	one + meaning + alone + walk	cling obstinately to one's course, act willfully
yi4le4	意樂	meaning + joy	joy, happiness
yi4nian4	意念	meaning + miss	idea, thought
yi4qi4	義氣	righteousness + cosmic energy	will and spirit
yi4qu4	意趣	meaning + fun	interest and charm
yi4shi4	意識	meaning + recognition	consciousness, realize, awake to
yi4si	意思	meaning + [final particle to sound off an expression]	meaning, idea, opinion, wish, desire, appreciation, gratitude
yi4tu2	意圖	meaning + picture	intention
yi4wai4	意外	meaning + outside	unexpected, accident, unforeseen, mishap
yi4xiang4	意向	meaning + to face	intention, purpose,
yi4xiang4	意象	meaning + elephant	image, imagery
yi4xing4	意興	meaning + thrive	interest, enthusiasm
yi4yu4	意欲	meaning + desire	wishing to, intending to
yi4yuan4	意願	meaning + ambition	wish, desire, aspiration
yi4zhi3	意旨	meaning + aim/purpose	intention, wish, will
yi4zhi4	意志	meaning + will	will
you3yi4	有意	have + meaning	have a mind to, intentionally, deliberately
you3yi4shi4	有意識	have + meaning +	consciously

		recognition	
you3yi4si	有意思	have + meaning + [final particle to sound off an expression]	interesting, enjoyable
yuan2yi4	原意	original + meaning	meaning, original intention
yuan4yi4	願意	hope + meaning	willing, ready, wish, like, want
zai4yi4	在意	in + meaning	take notice of, care about, mind, take to heart
zhi2yi4	執意	insist + meaning	insist on, determined
zhi4yi4	致意	deliver + meaning	give one's regards, present one's compliments
zhon1yi4	鍾意	concentrate + meaning	to one's liking, catch the fancy of
zhu3yi4	主意	host + meaning	idea, plan, decision
zhu4yi4	注意	infuse + meaning	pay attention to, take note of
zhuo2yi4	著意	bear/take + meaning	act with care and effort, take pains
zui4yi4	醉意	drunk + meaning	signs or feelings of getting drunk

you1

Mandarin (Pinyin)	Logograph	Literal Meaning	English
dan1you1	擔憂	shoulder + worry	worry, concerned
fen1you1	分憂	distribute + worry	share tribulations, help somebody with worries, difficulties
yin3you1	隱憂	concealed + worry	secret concern, private worry
you1bei1	憂悲	worry + sad	be worried and sad
you1chou2	憂愁	worry + anxious	be worried
you1huan4	憂患	worry + suffer/trouble	suffering, misery, hardship
you1ku3	憂苦	worry + bitter	be worried and suffering
you1lü4	憂慮	worry + concern	worry, anxiety
you1shang1	憂傷	worry + sorrow	distressed, laden with grief
you1si1	憂思	worry + think	anxious and worried, agitated, pensive
you1yi4	憂悒	worry + recall	unhappy
you1yu4	憂鬱	worry + gloomy	sullen, depressed,

			melancholy, dejected

yu4

Mandarin (Pinyin)	Logograph	Literal Meaning	English
shi4yu4	嗜慾	like + desire/lust	lust
yu4huo3	慾火	desire/lust + fire	lust
yu4wang4	慾望	desire/lust + wish	desire, longing, appetite, craving

zhi1

Mandarin (Pinyin)	Logograph	Literal Meaning	English
zhi1dao4	知道	know + path	know, realize, be aware of
zhi1jue2	知覺	know + feel	consciousness
zhi1qing2	知情	know + emotion	know the facts or details of a case, in the know
zhi1shi	知識	know + recognition	knowledge, pertaining to learning, intellectual
zhi1xi1	知悉	know + know/learn	know, learn, be informed
zhi1xiao3	知曉	know + know/dawn	know, be aware of, understand

zhi4

Mandarin (Pinyin)	Logograph	Literal Meaning	English
li4zhi4	立志	stand + will	determined, resolved
you3zhi4	有志	have + will	ambitious, devoted
zhi4yuan4	志願	will + wish	aspiration, wish, ideal

zi4

Mandarin (Pinyin)	Logograph	Literal Meaning	English
zi4bei1	自卑	self + inferior	feeling inferior
zi4hao2	自豪	self + proud	proud
zi4man3	自滿	self + full	complacent, self-satisfied
zi4xin4	自信	self + belief	confident
zi4zai	自在	self + exist	comfortable, at ease

Dataset App F.6. Mind-Words Based on Perception.

Mandarin (Pinyin)	Logograph	Literal Meaning	English
an4dan4	暗淡	dim/gloomy + thin, light/dull	sad
ao4shi4	傲視	haughty + look at	turn up one's nose
bi3shi4	鄙視	scorn + look at	despise, disdain
duan3jian4	短視	short + view	shortsighted view
er3ru2 mu4ran3	耳濡目染	ear + immerse + eye + dye	be imperceptibly influenced by what one constantly sees and hears
guan1dian3	觀點	view + point	viewpoint, standpoint
guan1jian4	關鍵	close + key	my humble opinion
guan1nian4	觀念	view + think of	sense, idea, concept
hu1shi4	忽視	overlook + look at	ignore, overlook, neglect
jian4jie3	見解	see + interpret/understand	view, opinion, understanding
jian4shi4	見識	see + recognize	widen one's knowledge, experience, knowledge, sensibleness
kan4bian3	看扁	see + flat	underestimate (a person)
kan4cheng2	看成	see + become	look upon, regard as
kan4chu1	看出	see + go out	make out, see
kan4chuan1	看穿	see + pull on	see through
kan4dai	看待	see + treat	look upon, regard, treat
kan4deqi3	看得起	see + obtain + rise/get up	not look down
kan4di1	看低	see + low	look down, belittle
kan4fa3	看法	see + law/way	way of looking at a thing
kan4po4	看破	see + broken	see through
kan4qing1	看輕	see + light	underestimate, look down upon
kan4shang4	看上	see + upward	take a fancy to, settle on
kan4tou4	看透	see + thorough	understand thoroughly, see through
kan4zhong4	看重	see + heavy	regard as important, value
kan4zhong4	看中	see + hit	take a fancy to, settle on
kan4zuo4	看作	see + as/make	look upon as, regard

le4guan1	樂觀	happy + view	optimistic, hopeful
ming2bai	明白	bright + white	understand, realize, know also, clear obvious
pian1jian4	偏見	tilted + view	prejudiced, biased opinion
qian3jian4	淺見	shallow + view	superficial view, my humble opinion
mie4shi4	蔑視	disdain, disregard slight + see	loathe, despise
qing1shi4	輕視	light + look at	belittle, look down on, underrate
yan3ba1ba1	眼巴巴	eye + cling to + cling to	(expecting) eagerly, anxiously, helplessly (watching sth. unpleasant happen)
yan3re4	眼熱	eye + hot	covet, be envious
zheng4shi4	正視	straight + look at	face squarely, deal with seriously and carefully
zhen1shi4	珍視	precious + look at	value, prize cherish
zhong4shi4	重視	heavy + look at	attach importance to, pay attention to, think highly of
zhu3guan1	主觀	host + view	subjective
zhuo1jian4	卓見	tall/erect + view	excellent opinion

Dataset App F.7. Other Mind-Words and Compounds.

	Mandarin (Pinyin)	Logo-graph	Literal Translation/ Other Meanings	English
1.	an2yang2	昂揚	rise, raise + scatter, spread	elated, high-spirited
2.	bei4	狽	legendary animal	distressed, wretched
3.	bi3	鄙	mean, low (CG: rural place)	despise
4.	bo3chang2	飽嘗	eat heartily + taste	enjoy fully, experience to the full
5.	bu4sheng4	不勝	not + victory	cannot bear or stand, be unequal to
6.	bu4zai4hu	不在乎	not + exist + interrogative or exclamatory final particle	not to care
7.	cang1cu4	倉促	granary + urge (PS: person)	hurried
8.	cha4	詫	brag, exaggerate	surprised
9.	cha4yi4	詫異	brag + different	surprised
10.	chang4	暢	smoothly, freely,	joyful, happy,

				unrestrained	smooth, fluent
11.	chen1	嗔		(PS: mouth)	be angry
12.	chen2tong4	沉痛		sink + pain	grieved
13.	chi1mi2	痴迷		foolish (PS: sickness) + bewitch (PS: walk)	be infatuated, be obsessed
14.	chou2	仇		enemy	hatred, animosity, enmity, rival, enemy, feud
15.	diao4	弔		person armed with bow guarding body from scavengers	lament
16.	du4	妒		(PS: women)	envy, be jealous
17.	e4	厄		adversity, difficulty, distress	distress
18.	fen4yong	奮勇		strive (CG: bird spreading its wings over field) + brave (PS: strength)	dauntlessly, courageously
19.	fu2zao4	浮躁		float + tense	over-active, impetuous, impulsive, restless
20.	gan1ga4	尷尬		(PS: weak) + limp	embarrassed, ill at ease
21.	gan3yu2	敢於		dare (CG: hand holding stick attacking wild animal) + in	dare, have the courage to
22.	gan4jin4	幹勁		trunk, main part, manage + strong	enthusiasm
23.	gu1	孤		orphan	lonely
24.	gu1dan1	孤單		orphan, fatherless + single	lonely
25.	gu1du2	孤獨		orphan, fatherless +	lonely, solitary
26.	gu3tou	骨頭		bone + head	strong character, courage
27.	gu3wu3	鼓舞		drum + dance	heartening
28.	gu4lian4	顧戀		look back + love	miss
29.	gu4lü4	顧慮		look back + be concerned	anxiety, misgivings, apprehensions
30.	gua4	挂		hang (PS: hand, fortune telling)	be anxious
31.	guan1qie4	關切		frontier pass + cut, mince, slice, carve	concerned
32.	guan1zhao4	關照		frontier pass + shine	concern, care
33.	guo4yin3	過癮		pass + rash; addiction, craving, habit	gratify, satisfy
34.	hai4xiu1	害羞		injure + disgrace (PS: hand presenting mutton)	shy, ashamed

35.	he4	赫	bright, radiant	awe-inspiring
36.	hen3	狠	vicious (PS: dog)	fierce, ruthless
37.	hu2yi2	狐疑	fox + doubt, suspicious (CG: old man with hand on cane asking for directions)	be suspicious, doubt
38.	huan1xin1	歡訢	happy, pleased + (PS: speech)	elated, overjoyed
39.	huan1yue4	歡悅	happy, pleased + pleased	happiness, joy
40.	hui1	灰	ashes; dust; lime, mortar	discouraged, dejected
41.	ji1ang2	激昂	arouse + rise, raise	aroused to indignation
42.	ji2	疾	illness, disease, sickness	hate, envy
43.	ji2	嫉	(PS: woman)	envy, be jealous
44.	ji2du4	嫉妒	(PS: woman) + (PS: woman)	envy, be jealous
45.	ji2shou3	疾首	illness, disease, sickness + head	extremely angry, infuriated, enraged
46.	ji4	寂	still, silent, quiet, desolate	lonesome, tranquil
47.	ji4mo4	寂寞	still, silent + silent, still	lonely
48.	jian1ao2	煎熬	fry in oil or fat + boil	ordeal, suffering, a torture, a torment
49.	jie2	結	knot, tie; join, connect	pent-up
50.	jie2yuan4	結怨	knot, tie; join, connect + hatred	arouse dislike, incur hatred
51.	jin3	緊	tense, tight, firm, secure	nervous, strict, tight
52.	jing1	兢	(PS: double "man with helmet" meaning cautious)	be fearful, be apprehensive
53.	jing4fu2	憼服	honor + clothes, wear, dress	esteem, admire
54.	jiong3	窘	(PS: tent opening, to break in)	distressed, embarrassed
55.	juan4	眷	take interest in (PS: eye)	care about
56.	juan4lian4	眷戀	take interest in (PS: eye) + (PS: heart)	miss, long for, remember with longing, yearn
57.	kai1lang3	開朗	open, begin + clear, bright	optimistic, cheerful, carefree
58.	kai1shi4	開示	open, begin + manifest	inspire, enlighten

59.	kao3	考	take an exam + (PS: old man leaning on cane)	reflect on, ponder over
60.	kao3lü4	考慮	take an exam (PS: old man leaning on cane) + be concerned	think over, consider, consideration
61.	ku4	酷	strong (as of wine)	ruthless
62.	kuan1	寬	broad, wide, spacious, vast	relieve, relax
63.	kuang2	狂	violent, wild (PS: dog)	unrestrained, mad, conceited
64.	kuang2luan4	狂亂	violent, wild (PS: dog) + (CG: kneeling person with hands untangling twisted string)	hysterical
65.	kun4	困	surround	be in distress
66.	kun4huo4	困惑	surround + confuse (PS: heart)	bewildered, perplexed, confused
67.	lao2	勞	labor, toil, do manual work	be worried
68.	leng3dan4	冷淡	cold, cool + weak, watery	cold, indifferent, slack
69.	liang4jie3	諒解	excuse, forgive (PS: speech) + untie	understand
70.	liao2	寥	few, scarce; empty, deserted	lonesome
71.	lin3ran2	凜然	shiver with cold or fear + yes, certainly; pledge, promise	awe-inspiring
72.	ma2mu4	麻木	hemp + tree	numb, insensitive, apathetic
73.	mian3li4	勉勵	make effort + strive (PS: whetstone, power)	encourage
74.	ming2	鳴	cry of bird or animal	astonish
75.	mo4	寞	silent, still	lonely, desolate
76.	na4men4	納悶	admit, receive + gloomy (PS: heart)	puzzled, bewildered
77.	qi1	期	period of time, date	hope
78.	qi1pan4	期盼	period of time, date + look, gaze	anticipate, look forward, await expectantly
79.	qie4shi2	切實	cut + real, true	feasible, earnest, conscientious, realistic, practical
80.	qin1	欽	(PS: metal)	admire
81.	qing1dao3	傾倒	pour out, overflow +	admire

				fall over
82.	sa3tuo1	灑脫	sprinkle, splash; scatter + take off, peel	free and easy, unaffected
83.	shan4	善	good, virtuous	happy
84.	shan4liang2	善良	good, virtuous + good, virtuous	kind-hearted
85.	shen1	深	deep	intimate, close
86.	sheng1wei4	生畏	life, birth + fear (pictographic; man with scary head)	feel intimidated
87.	shi4yuan4	誓願	pledge (PS: speech) + desire, want (PS: leaf)	unyielding will
88.	shou4zui4	受罪	receive + hardship	endure, suffer
89.	shu1chang4	舒暢	open up, unfold + smoothly, freely	happy, entirely free from worry
90.	tao2	陶	pottery (PS: place)	be pleased
91.	tao2zui4	陶醉	infatuated with, drunk with	enchanted with
92.	wan2	頑	obstinate (PS: leaf)	mischievous, obstinate, stubborn, naughty
93.	wan2gu4	頑固	obstinate (PS: leaf) + become solid	stubborn, obstinate
94.	wan2qiang2	頑強	obstinate (PS: leaf) + strength	tenacious, indomitable
95.	wo1nang2	窩囊	nest, cave, den + bag, purse	feel vexed
96.	xia4	嚇	(PS: mouth)	frighten, scare, intimidate, threaten
97.	xian2	嫌	(PS: woman)	dislike, suspect
98.	xiang4	向	toward, direction, trend	like
99.	xiang4wang3	嚮往	guide, direct + depart	yearn for, look forward to
100.	xin1	訢	(PS: speech)	happy
101.	xin1shang3	欣賞	(PS: lack) + reward, grant	appreciate, enjoy, admire
102.	xin1wei4	欣慰	(PS: lack) + comfort (PS: heart)	be gratified
103.	xin4ren4	信任	trust, believe (CG: person's word) + rely on	trust, have confidence in
104.	xing4	幸	good fortune, luck(ily), favor (pictographic handcuffs)	hope, trust
105.	xing4fu4	幸福	good fortune, luck(ily), favor (pictographic handcuffs) +	happiness, well-being

			blessing	
106.	xiu1	羞	disgrace, shame (PS: hand presenting mutton)	be shy, be ashamed
107.	xuan1	暄	warm (PS: sun)	genial and warm
108.	xuan4	眩	dizzy, dazed (PS: eye)	dizzy, dazzled
109.	xuan4	炫	shine, glitter	brave
110.	ya4	訝	(PS: speech)	be astounded
111.	yan2	嚴	strict, rigorous, rigid	bitter, cruel
112.	yao4	要	important, ask for, going to (future auxiliary), must (used in a comparison) must be, probably, if (CG: woman with hands on her waist)	want, will
113.	yi4	臆	chest, bosom	feelings, opinion, thoughts
114.	yi4li4	毅力	resolute, decisive, firm + strength	perseverance, willpower
115.	you2yu4	猶豫	similar to + relaxed (PS: (elephant))	hesitant
116.	yu4	鬱	luxuriant; dense, thick	melancholy
117.	zai4hu	在乎	exist + interrogative or exclamatory final particle	care about, mind
118.	zao4	躁	tense (PS: foot)	hot-tempered, impatient
119.	zhao2ji2	著急	manifest + hurry	worry, anxious
120.	zhen4fen4	振奮	raise, excite, arouse action + strive (CG: bird spreading its wings)	inspire
121.	zhong1	衷	bottom of one's heart (PS: clothes)	inner feelings
122.	zhu4yuan4	祝願	pray for blessings + desire, want (PS: leaf)	wish

Dataset App F.8. Summary of Data about Mind-Words.

	Mandarin (Pinyin)	Logo-graph	No. of Compounds/ Idioms	Category/Subcategory
1.	ai1	哀	24	EXT-Bodily
2.	ai4	愛	33	HEART SIG
3.	an1	安	5	EXT-Bodily
4.	ang2	昂	10	NO HEART-Bodily
5.	ao2	熬	3	EXT-Bodily

6.	ao4	懊	5	HEART SIG
7.	ba1	巴	4	EXT-Bodily
8.	bei1	悲	22	HEART SIG
9.	bei4	悖	3	HEART SIG
10.	bei4	憊	1	HEART SIG
11.	bei4	狽	1	EXT-Bodily
12.	bi3	鄙	4	EXT-Bodily
13.	bi4	愎	1	HEART SIG
14.	bian4	忭	2	HEART SIG
15.	bie1	憋	2	HEART SIG
16.	bo3	飽	3	NO HEART-Bodily
17.	bu4	怖	1	HEART SIG
18.	cai1	猜	4	EXT-Bodily
19.	can2	慚	14	HEART SIG
20.	can3	慘	8	HEART SIG
21.	ce4	惻	9	HEART SIG
22.	cha4	詫	1	NO HEART-Bodily
23.	chan4	懺	1	HEART SIG
24.	chang2	嘗	2	NO HEART-Percep
25.	chang4	悵	4	HEART SIG
26.	chang4	暢	7	NO HEART-Bodily
27.	chen1	嗔	9	NO HEART-Bodily
28.	chen2	沈	14	NO HEART-Percep
29.	chen2	忱	4	HEART SIG
30.	chi1	吃	12	NO HEART-Bodily
31.	chi1	痴	18	EXT-Bodily
32.	chi3	恥	9	HEART SIG
33.	chong1	憧	1	HEART SIG
34.	chong1	忡	1	HEART SIG
35.	chou2	惆	3	HEART SIG
36.	chou2	愁	10	HEART SIG
37.	chou2	仇	12	EXT-Bodily
38.	chu4	觸	4	NO HEART-Percep
39.	chu4	憷	2	HEART SIG
40.	chu4	怵	5	HEART SIG
41.	chuang4	愴	3	HEART SIG
42.	ci2	慈	7	HEART SIG
43.	cong1	恩	1	HEART SIG
44.	cu4	促	11	NO HEART-Bodily
45.	cui4	悴	1	HEART SIG
46.	cun3	忖	5	HEART SIG
47.	dai4	怠	7	HEART SIG
48.	dan3	膽	10	NO HEART-Organs
49.	dan4	憚	2	HEART SIG
50.	dan4	淡	8	NO HEART-Percep
51.	dao3	倒	5	EXT-Bodily

52.	dao4	悼	6	HEART SIG
53.	dian4	惦	1	HEART SIG
54.	diao4	弔	4	EXT-Bodily
55.	dong3	懂	22	HEART SIG
56.	dong4	恫	1	HEART SIG
57.	dong4 (cave)	洞	4	EXT-Bodily
58.	dong4 (move)	動	4	NO HEART-Percep
59.	du4	妒	2	EXT-Bodily
60.	dui4	憝	1	HEART SIG
61.	duo4	惰	6	HEART SIG
62.	e4	愕	3	HEART SIG
63.	e4	厄	1	EXT-Bodily
64.	e4 (e3, wu4)	惡	6	HEART SIG
65.	en1	恩	4	HEART SIG
66.	er3	耳	1	NO HEART-Organs
67.	fa1	發	13	EXT-Bodily
68.	fan2	煩	5	EXT-Bodily
69.	fei3	悱	1	HEART SIG
70.	fei4	肺	1	NO HEART-Organs
71.	fen4	忿	4	HEART SIG
72.	fen4	奮	14	NO HEART-Bodily
73.	fen4	憤	27	HEART SIG
74.	fu3	腑	1	NO HEART-Organs
75.	gan1	尷	1	EXT-Bodily
76.	gan3	感	21	HEART SIG
77.	gan3	敢	8	NO HEART-Bodily
78.	gan4	幹	10	EXT-Bodily
79.	gong1	恭	3	HEART SIG
80.	gu1	孤	12	EXT-Bodily
81.	gu3	骨	4	EXT-Bodily
82.	gu3	鼓	8	EXT-Bodily
83.	gu4	顧	12	NO HEART-Bodily
84.	gu4	固	6	NO HEART-Percep
85.	gua4	挂	8	EXT-Bodily
86.	guai4	怪	4	HEART SIG
87.	guan1	觀	5	NO HEART-Percep
88.	guan1	關	4	EXT-Bodily
89.	guan4	慣	1	HEART SIG
90.	hai4	害	3	NO HEART-Percep
91.	han1	憨	4	HEART SIG
92.	han4	憾	4	HEART SIG
93.	han4	悍	6	HEART SIG
94.	he4	赫	1	NO HEART-Percep
95.	hen3	狠	9	EXT-Bodily
96.	hen4	恨	43	HEART SIG

97.	heng2	恒	2	HEART SIG
98.	hu1	惚	3	HEART SIG
99.	hu4	怙	1	HEART SIG
100.	huai2	懷	40	HEART SIG
101.	huan1	歡	26.	EXT-Bodily
102.	huan4	患	4	HEART SIG
103.	huang1	慌	14	HEART SIG
104.	huang2	惶	8	HEART SIG
105.	huang3	恍	8	HEART SIG
106.	hui1	恢	2	HEART SIG
107.	hui1	灰	6	EXT-Bodily
108.	hui3	悔	25	HEART SIG
109.	hui4	慧	5	HEART SIG
110.	hun2	魂	20	INTER-Immortal
111.	huo4	惑	15	HEART SIG
112.	ji1	激	12	NO HEART-Percep
113.	ji2	急	23	HEART SIG
114.	ji2	疾	3	NO HEART-Percep
115.	ji2	嫉	4	EXT-Bodily
116.	ji4	記	3	NO HEART-Bodily
117.	ji4	忌	12	HEART SIG
118.	ji4	悸	4	HEART SIG
119.	ji4	寂	4	EXT-Bodily
120.	jian1	煎	3	EXT-Bodily
121.	jian4	見	7	NO HEART-Percep
122.	jiao1	焦	5	NO HEART-Percep
123.	jie2	結	4	EXT-Bodily
124.	jie3	解	8	NO HEART-Bodily
125.	jin3	緊	2	EXT-Bodily
126.	jin4	勁	21	EXT-Bodily
127.	jing1	惊	79	HEART SIG
128.	jing1	兢	4	EXT-Bodily
129.	jing1 (essence)	精	5	EXT-Bodily
130.	jing1 (surprise)	驚	11	EXT-Bodily
131.	jing3	憬	2	HEART SIG
132.	jing4	憼	1	HEART SIG
133.	jiong3	窘	4	EXT-Bodily
134.	ju4	懼	17	HEART SIG
135.	juan4	眷	7	NO HEART-Organs
136.	jue2	覺	30	NO HEART-Percep
137.	kai3	愾	1	HEART SIG
138.	kai4	慨	9	HEART SIG
139.	kan4	看	15	NO HEART-Percep
140.	kang1	慷	5	HEART SIG

141.	kao3	考		5	EXT-Bodily
142.	ke4	恪		2	HEART SIG
143.	ken3	懇		6	HEART SIG
144.	kong3	恐		8	HEART SIG
145.	ku3	苦		5	NO HEART-Percep
146.	ku4	酷		8	EXT-Bodily
147.	kuai4	快		15	HEART SIG
148.	kuan1	寬		34	NO HEART-Percep
149.	kuang2	狂		25	EXT-Bodily
150.	kui1	悝		1	HEART SIG
151.	kui4	憒		1	HEART SIG
152.	kui4	愧		28	HEART SIG
153.	kun4	困		6	NO HEART-Organs
154.	lan3	懶		17	HEART SIG
155.	lang3	朗		2	NO HEART-Percep
156.	lao2	勞		6	NO HEART-Bodily
157.	le4	樂		15	EXT-Bodily
158.	leng3	冷		8	NO HEART-Percep
159.	leng4	愣		9	HEART SIG
160.	li4	勵		5	NO HEART-Bodily
161.	li4	力		25	NO HEART-Percep
162.	lian2	憐		10	HEART SIG
163.	lian4	戀		25	HEART SIG
164.	liang4	諒		3	NO HEART-Bodily
165.	liao2	寥		1	EXT-Bodily
166.	liao4	料		8	EXT-Bodily
167.	lin3	懍		1	HEART SIG
168.	ling2	靈		4	EXT-Spirit-Soul
169.	lü4	慮		22	NO HEART-Percep
170.	luan4	亂		9	NO HEART-Percep
171.	ma2	麻		5	EXT-Bodily
172.	man3	滿		3	NO HEART-Percep
173.	mao4	懋		1	HEART SIG
174.	men1/4	悶		21	HEART SIG
175.	men4	懣		3	HEART SIG
176.	meng3	懵		2	HEART SIG
177.	mi2	迷		30	NO HEART-Percep
178.	mian3	勉		9	NO HEART-Bodily
179.	min3	憫		4	HEART SIG
180.	ming2	明		7	NO HEART-Percep
181.	ming2	鳴		3	EXT-Bodily
182.	mo4	寞		2	EXT-Bodily
183.	mou2	眸		1	NO HEART-Organs
184.	mu4	慕		3	HEART SIG
185.	nan4	難		3	NO HEART-Percep
186.	nao3	腦		20	NO HEART-Organs

187.	nao3	惱		12	HEART SIG
188.	ni2	怩		3	HEART SIG
189.	nian4	念		32	HEART SIG
190.	niu3	忸		3	HEART SIG
191.	nu4	怒		12	HEART SIG
192.	nü4	恧		1	HEART SIG
193.	nuo4	懦		4	HEART SIG
194.	ou4	慪		1	HEART SIG
195.	pa4	怕		26	HEART SIG
196.	peng1	怦		4	HEART SIG
197.	ping2	憑		1	HEART SIG
198.	po4	魄		9	INTER-Mortal
199.	qi1	慼		2	HEART SIG
200.	qi1	悽		3	HEART SIG
201.	qi1	期		5	EXT-Bodily
202.	qi4	氣		24	INTER-Cosmic
203.	qian1	慳		2	HEART SIG
204.	qiao3	愀		1	HEART SIG
205.	qiao3	悄		1	HEART SIG
206.	qie4	怯		15	HEART SIG
207.	qie4	愜		1	HEART SIG
208.	qie4	切		6	NO HEART-Bodily
209.	qin1	欽		5	EXT-Bodily
210.	qing1	傾		16	EXT-Bodily
211.	qing2	情		17	HEART SIG
212.	qing4	慶		1	HEART SIG
213.	qu3	骨		3	NO HEART-Organs
214.	quan1	悛		1	HEART SIG
215.	re3	惹		3	HEART SIG
216.	re4	熱		5	NO HEART-Percep
217.	ren3	忍		33	HEART SIG
218.	ren4	認		35	NO HEART-Bodily
219.	shan4	善		6	NO HEART-Bodily
220.	shang3	賞		10	NO HEART-Bodily
221.	she4 (zhe2)	慴		3	HEART SIG
222.	shen1	深		12	EXT-Bodily
223.	shen2	神		9	EXT-Spirit-God
224.	shen4	慎		2	HEART SIG
225.	shi2	識		68	NO HEART-Bodily
226.	shi4	視		9	NO HEART-Percep
227.	shi4	恃		2	HEART SIG
228.	shou3	首		1	NO HEART-Organs
229.	shou4	受		12	NO HEART-Bodily
230.	shu4	恕		5	HEART SIG
231.	si1	思		66	HEART SIG
232.	song3	悚		4	HEART SIG

Appendix F

233.	song3	慫	1	HEART SIG
234.	su4	愫	1	HEART SIG
235.	tai4	態	11	HEART SIG
236.	tan3	忐	2	HEART SIG
237.	tang1	恫	1	HEART SIG
238.	tao2	陶	1	EXT-Bodily
239.	te4	慝	1	HEART SIG
240.	ti4	悌	3	HEART SIG
241.	ti4	惕	4	HEART SIG
242.	tian2	恬	18	HEART SIG
243.	tong4	慟	2	HEART SIG
244.	tong4	痛	20	NO HEART-Percep
245.	tou2	頭	6	NO HEART-Organs
246.	wan2	頑	12.	EXT-Bodily
247.	wan3	惋	3	HEART SIG
248.	wang3	惘	2	HEART SIG
249.	wang4	望	12	HEART SIG
250.	wang4	忘	45	EXT-Bodily
251.	wei2	惟	1	HEART SIG
252.	wei4	慰	17	HEART SIG
253.	wei4	畏	15	NO HEART-Percep
254.	wu3	忤	3	HEART SIG
255.	wu4	悟	20	HEART SIG
256.	xi1	希	4	EXT-Bodily
257.	xi2	惜	15	HEART SIG
258.	xi3	憙	20	HEART SIG
259.	xia4	嚇	14	NO HEART-Organs
260.	xian2	嫌	20	EXT-Bodily
261.	xiang3	想	80	HEART SIG
262.	xiang4	向	4	EXT-Bodily
263.	xie4	懈	8	HEART SIG
264.	xin1	心	268	HEART/"Heart"
265.	xin1	欣	4	NO HEART-Percep
266.	xin1	訢	1	NO HEART-Bodily
267.	xin4	信	18	EXT-Bodily
268.	xing1	惺	3	HEART SIG
269.	xing4	興	29	EXT-Bodily
270.	xing4	悻	2	HEART SIG
271.	xiong1	胸	15	NO HEART-Organs
272.	xiu1	羞	21	NO HEART-Organs
273.	xu4	恤	6	HEART SIG
274.	xuan1	諠	1	EXT-Bodily
275.	xuan2	懸	1	HEART SIG
276.	xuan4	眩	2	NO HEART-Organs
277.	xue4	血	2	NO HEART-Organs
278.	ya4	訝	3	NO HEART-Organs

279.	yan3	眼	21	NO HEART-Organs
280.	yan4	厭	16	EXT-Bodily
281.	yang2	揚	3	NO HEART-Bodily
282.	yang4	怏	1	HEART SIG
283.	yang4	恙	5	HEART SIG
284.	yao4	要	2	EXT-Bodily
285.	yi2	怡	4	HEART SIG
286.	yi2	疑	14	EXT-Bodily
287.	yi4	意	143	HEART SIG
288.	yi4	憶	5	HEART SIG
289.	yi4	毅	4	NO HEART-Percep
290.	yi4	臆	7	NO HEART-Organs
291.	ying1	膺	2	NO HEART-Organs
292.	yong1	慵	1	HEART SIG
293.	yong1	勇	18	NO HEART-Percep
294.	yong3	恿	1	HEART SIG
295.	you1	憂	19	HEART SIG
296.	you1	悠	2	HEART SIG
297.	yu2	愉	5	HEART SIG
298.	yu2	愚	27	HEART SIG
299.	yu4	慾	10	HEART SIG
300.	yu4	鬱	15	EXT-Bodily
301.	yuan4	怨	18	HEART SIG
302.	yuan4	願	27	HEART SIG
303.	yue4	悅	14	HEART SIG
304.	yun4	愠	1	HEART SIG
305.	zao4	躁	11	NO HEART-Organs
306.	zeng1	憎	5	HEART SIG
307.	zhao5	照	5	NO HEART-Percep
308.	zhen4	振	7	EXT-Bodily
309.	zheng1	怔	6	HEART SIG
310.	zhi1	知	6	HEART SIG
311.	zhi4	志	3	HEART SIG
312.	zhong1	忠	13	HEART SIG
313.	zhong1	衷	9	EXT-Bodily
314.	zhuang4	戆	1	HEART SIG
315.	zhui4	惴	1	HEART SIG
316.	zi4	自	12	NO HEART-Organs
317.	zi4	恣	7	HEART SIG
318.	zui4	醉	7	NO HEART-Percep

Appendix G

Abnormal Hallucinations

Among medical and mental health practitioners, hallucinations have been deeply associated with psychopathology of one sort or another, such as Parkinson's disease. Barnes and David (2001) report 8% to 40% of those with Parkinson's disease experience visual hallucinations (N = 44) (see also Barnes et al. [2010]). Barnes et al. (2011) investigated the linkages among personality, stress, sleep, and hallucinations in a normal student population (N = 127). They found significant associations between stress and sleep, with stress being a significant predictor of hallucinations. Also a predictive relationship between hallucinations and schizotypal personality traits was found (age did not seem to play a noticeable role). Nettle (2006) sees a linkage between schizotypy and mental illness amongst poets, visual artists, and mathematicians (N = 501).

But hallucinations have been particularly linked to schizophrenia and dissociative disorders.[1] For example, Morrison and Haddock (1997) asked schizophrenics experiencing auditory hallucinations, schizophrenics not experiencing them, and normal controls to complete the private self-consciousness subscale of the Self Consciousness Scale. It was found that hallucinators exhibited significantly higher levels of self-focus than non-hallucinators. The latter did not differ from normal subjects. The level of self-focus predicted whether or not subjects experienced hallucinations (N = 30). Johns and Van Os (2001) explore the continuity of psychotic experiences in the general population. They contend that schizophrenia is not a discrete illness and that the distribution of psychosis, with symptoms of hallucinations and delusions, would not be represented by a normal curve nor a bimodal or dichotomous curve, but rather a continuous but only half-normal distribution. They see a need for a "psychosis continuum" (which might have implications for improved therapy).

Ross, Joshi, and Currie (1990) administered the 28-item Dissociative Experiences Scale respondents (N = 1055) in Winnipeg and found that 26% of the general population experienced dissociative experiences. Using factor analysis, they found that three factors accounted for 47.1% of the combined variance of the score: (1) absorption-imaginative involvement (benign: ignoring pain, missing part of a conversation, etc.); (2) dissociated states; and (3) depersonalization-derealization (not recognizing friends or family members, not recognizing one's reflection in a mirror, etc.). "Hearing voices in one's head" (prevalence of 26%) was included in the third factor.

Hallucinations may not be directly caused by or related to psychopathology, but studies typically find what are taken to be significant correlations. Barrett and Etheridge (1994) selected hallucinators (N = 18) and non-hallucinators (N = 24) among normals using the Verbal Hallucination Questionnaire and had them take the Millon's Clinical Multiaxial Inventory (MCMI; measures dysfunctional personality correlates). They found that hallucinators experience heightened negative affect, feelings of rejection, and incompetence in social situations. In their analysis of the links between hallucinations and imagery in a normal population (N = 24), Jakes and Hemsley (1987) found that psychoticism (Eysenck Personality Questionnaire) was significantly related to reports of hallucinatory experiences and a measure of hallucinatory predisposition was significantly associated with strong hypnogogic/hypnopompic imagery. Launay and Slade (1981), in a study of male and female prisoners (N = 297), used Eysenck's psychoticism (P) scale to discern a link between aggressive-paranoid tendencies and hallucinatory predisposition. Using the Sleep-EVAL system, Ohayon and Schatzberg (2002) analyzed the general population (N = 18,980) in the UK, Germany, Italy, Spain, and Portugal. They found that 12.5% of those with depressive episodes had psychotic features (either delusions or hallucinations). Feelings of worthlessness or guilt were also associated with high rates of hallucinations (9.7%).

Young et al. (1987) investigated the relation between suggestibility and the elicitation of auditory and visual hallucinations in normal and psychiatric subjects. One experiment, using the LSHS-A, assessed if normal subjects were predisposed to hallucinate. The second experiment assessed hallucinating psychiatric and non-hallucinating psychiatric patients. High LSHS-A scorers and hallucinating psychiatric patients were significantly more likely to hear suggested sounds and see suggested objects than were their respective controls (but this finding was not replicated in the psychiatric patients). No significant differences on measures of suggestibility were found between the groups, although for the psychiatric group the Barber Test Suggestion and Subjective Involvement scores correlated positively with LSHS-A scores (N = 203).

Using the South African Stress and Health Study, Temmingh et al. (2011) utilized the Composite International Diagnostic Interview (CIDI) in a survey of the general population of South African adults (N = 4,250). They found a prevalence rate of 12.7% of people reporting hallucinations, which is comparable to reports in other parts of the world. They also found correlations between reported auditory or visual hallucinations and role impairment, service utilization, and suicidality. In an investigation of a non-psychiatric population of Caribbean descent residing in the US, Izquierdo (2000) found that culture shapes the way reality is interpreted and that hallucinations are to be taken as a weak symptom of mental instability (at least among those of Caribbean descent).

Basing their methodology upon that used by Feelgood and Rantzen (1994), Pearson et al. (2001) exposed child participants (aged 9–11 years old) to ambiguous stimuli which then generated hallucinations. Their findings indicated a "developmental continuum" of hallucinatory experiences between children and adults. Pearson et al. (2008) propose a two-axis model: (1) child/adolescent versus adult; and (2) non-clinical versus pathological continua. This developmental model, based on adults (N = 496), links child abuse to pathological hallucinations and possible later mental illness. Pearson et al. (2008), in their study of AVHs among adolescents and adults, see the need for early intervention for psychosis.

Several studies have examined the connection between emotions and hallucinations, but again, the underlying premise seems to be that hallucinations are inherently abnormal. Freeman and Garety (2003), in the context of neurosis and psychosis, investigated the influence of emotion on delusions and hallucinations. Laroi, van der Linden, and Marczewski (2004) looked at how emotionality and meta-cognitive beliefs impacted monitoring tasks in hallucination-prone subjects. Davies, Griffin, and Vice (2001) looked at reactions to auditory hallucinations in psychotic, evangelical, and control groups: 27% of the control group (non-psychotic, non-evangelical) heard voices, while 59% of evangelical Christians and 100% of the psychotic group did, respectively (N = 102). Not surprisingly, the experiences of the evangelical group were more positive than those of the control group (which were significantly more positive than those of the psychotic group). Delespaul, deVries, and van Os (2002) found anxiety to be the most prominent emotion and the strongest predictor of hallucinations intensity, though an array of contextual influences play a role for schizophrenics.

Death is of course an emotionally stressful event. Osis and Haraldsson (1977) researched deathbed observations by physicians and nurses in the US and India of mostly terminally ill patients (N = 877). The most frequently reported phenomena were hallucinations of human figures (471 cases; 53.7%). Four-fifths of the hallucinations were of deceased persons and religious figures.

According to Kumari et al. (2008), previous small-sample studies have shown altered frontotemporal activity in schizophrenia patients with auditory hallucinations. Utilizing fMRI, Kumari et al. (2008) attempted to study monitoring of self- and externally generated speech in two samples: among schizophrenics (N = 63) and a group of healthy controls (N = 20). Participants were asked to perform a self-monitoring task while undergoing fMRI using verbal feedback: (1) their own voice (self-undistorted); (2) their own voice lowered in pitch by 4 semitones (self-distorted); (3) voice of another person matched on a participant's sex (other-undistorted); and (4) another person's voice with the pitch lowered by 4 semitones (other-distorted). Participants indicated the origin of voices by pressing buttons marked "self" for their own voices, "other" for "other" voice, and "unsure." Kumari et al. (2008) did not scan during AVHs, so their findings are indirect evidence of the neurological correlations of hallucinations. Moreover, given that the focus of my review is to discern the level of right-sided neural activation, the use of subjects' own voice, whether distorted or not, may introduce an unnecessary confounding variable.

Kumari et al. (2008) detected activation of the thalamus (medial geniculate nucleus, MGN) and frontotemporal regions. Among poorly performing patients (one standard deviation below controls' mean; N = 36), less activation of the thalamus (MGN, pulvinar) and superior-middle temporal and inferior frontal gyri was evident (relative to the combined group of controls and well-performing patients). They found greater deactivation of the ventral striatum and hypothalamus occurred when hearing one's own voice among schizophrenics. This was combined with nonsignificant activation of the same regions to the voice of others and was associated with negative symptoms, e.g. blunted affect, emotional withdrawal, poor rapport, passive social avoidance, regardless of performance. They also found that heightened activation of the right superior-middle temporal gyrus during undistorted feedback (their own voice or the voice of another) was associated with both positive symptoms (hallucinations, persecution) and poor performance.[2] For all participants, increased brain activity associated with individual task conditions were reported 34 times, 20 of which were on the right side (52.94%). Decrease in activity associated with individual task conditions were reported 24 times, 12 of which were on the right side (50.00%). Tables Appendix G.1, Appendix G.2, and Appendix G.3 summarize these results.

Table Appendix G.1. Increases and Decreases of Neural Activation in Association with Individual Tasks Conditions.[a]

Side of Brain	Decrease	Increase
Left	50.00%	43.75%
Right	50.00%	56.25%

[a] From Kumari et al. (2008: 745); abbreviated.

Table Appendix G.2. Increases in Association with Individual Task Conditions.[a]

Verbal Feedback	Brain Region	Brodmann Area	Side
Self-undistorted	Superior temporal gyrus	22	R
		22	L
		22	R
	Lingual gyrus/cuneus	18	R
		18	L
		18	L
Self-distorted	Superior temporal gyrus	22	R
		22	R
	Postcentral gyrus	40	R
	Heschl's gyrus	41	L
	Superior temporal gyrus	22	L
	Thalamus	n/a	R
	Cuneus	19	L
		18	L
	Middle occipital gyrus	19	R
		19	R
		19	R
Other-undistorted	Superior temporal gyrus	22	R
		22	R
		22	R
		22	L
		44	L
		22	L
	Brain stem	n/a	L
	Thalamus	n/a	R
	Thalamus	n/a	L
Other-distorted	Superior temporal gyrus	22	L
		22	R
		22	R
	Thalamus	n/a	R
	Superior temporal gyrus	22	L
		22	R
		22	R
	Precentral gyrus	6	R
		$\Sigma = 34$, L = 14, R = 20	

[a] From Kumari et al. (2008: 745); abbreviated.

Table Appendix G.3. Decreases in Association with Individual Task Conditions.[a]

Verbal Feedback	Brain Region	Brodmann Area	Side
Self-undistorted	Posterior cingulate gyrus	30	L
		30	R
	Parahippocampal gyrus	n/a	R
	Medial frontal gyrus	32	R
	Anterior cingulate gyrus	24	R
	Caudate nucleus	n/a	R
Self-distorted	Parahippocampal gyrus	n/a	L
	Calcarine sulcus	n/a	L
	Parahippocampal gyrus	n/a	R
	Caudate nucleus	n/a	L
	Anterior cingulate gyrus	24	L
		24	R
Other-undistorted	Parahippocampal gyrus	n/a	L
	Angular gyrus	39	L
	Posterior cingulate gyrus	30	R
	Anterior cingulate gyrus	24/32	L
		32	R
		32	R
Other-distorted	Posterior cingulate gyrus	30	R
		23	L
	Angular gyrus	39	R
	Anterior cingulate gyrus	24	L
	Medial frontal gyrus	10	L
		10/32	L
		$\sum = 24$, L = 12, R = 12	

[a] From Kumari et al. (2008: 746); abbreviated.

Kumari et al. (2008) found that if brain areas showing activation changes for "source" and "distortion effects" are measured (for all participants), 5 out of 7 (71.4%) instances were on the right side. If neural activity, differentiated by "good" and "poor performers," is measured (regardless of diagnosis), 21 out of 42 (50%) instances were on the right side. If neural activity, differentiated by healthy participants and schizophrenic patients, is measured (regardless of performance), 8 out of 17 (47.1%) instances were on the right side.

In conclusion, Kumari et al. (2008) surmise that hypoactivation of a neural network, consisting of the thalamus and frontotemporal regions, is involved in the impaired speech monitoring in schizophrenia. They also believe that a common activation abnormality is shared by positive symptoms and poor monitoring in the right superior temporal gyrus during processing of degraded speech.

In a review of relevant studies,[3] Diederen, van Lutterveld, and Sommer (2012) found that in non-psychotic individuals AVHs were associated with increased sensitivity of auditory areas to auditory stimulation as well as aberrant connectivity for frontal and temporo-parietal language regions, and of language production and perception, particularly in the anterior cingulate regions (Brodmann's areas 24, 32, and 33). Hallucinators appear to possess an attention bias to auditory stimuli that may be related to aberrant activation of the anterior cingulate regions.[4] Diederen, van Lutterveld, and Sommer (2012) also discovered that decreased cerebral dominance for language as well as dopamine dysfunction (commonly associated with schizophrenia) are probably not in themselves related to AVHs (these abnormalities were not apparent in non-psychotic voice hearers). Finally, specific aspects of AVHs, such as voluntary control, may be related to the timing of the supplementary motor area and language areas.

Sommer et al. (2010) studied 103 non-clinical individuals with AVHs. These were compared to a control group of 60 individuals matched for sex, age, and education. They did find that, after a battery of tests (including the Schizotypal Personality Questionnaire [SPQ] and the Peters Delusion Inventory), the hallucinating individuals had a lower level of global functioning and a "general increased schizotypal and delusional tendency." Evidence of childhood trauma among those who experienced hallucinations was also apparent. They concluded that AVHs in otherwise healthy individuals are not an "isolated phenomenon" but rather part of a "general vulnerability for schizophrenia."

Endnotes

[1] Numerous studies investigate such matters. For a general treatment, see Slade (1973) and Slade and Bentall (1988).
[2] Thalamic abnormality characterized schizophrenics regardless of performance and symptoms.
[3] Barkus et al. (2007); Diederen et al. (2010); de Weijers et al. (2011); Howes et al. (2013); Linden et al. (2011); Lewis-Hanna et al. (2011); Szechtman et al. (1998); van Lutterveld et al. (2010).
[4] Not specifically related to AVHs are decreased cerebral dominance for language and dopamine dysfunction (typically evident in schizophrenia). Such abnormalities were absent in non-clinical voice hearers. Also, voluntary control may be related to the timing of the supplementary motor area and language areas in AVHs.

Bibliography

Al-Issa, I. (1995). The illusion of reality or the reality of illusion: Hallucinations and culture. *British Journal of Clinical Psychology*, 166, 368–373.

Allen, P., Laroi, F., McGuire, P. K., and Aleman, A. (2008). The hallucinating brain: a review of structural and functional neuroimaging studies of hallucinations. *Neuroscience Review*, 32, 175–191.

American Psychiatric Association (2013). *Diagnostic and Statistical Manual of Mental Disorders* (5th ed.). Washington, D.C.: American Psychiatric Association.

Andrew, E. M., Gray, N. S., and Snowden, R. J. (2008). The relationship between trauma and beliefs about hearing voices: A study of psychiatric and non-psychiatric voice-hearers. *Psychological Medicine*, 38, 1409–1417.

Barclay, Michael W. (1997). The metaphoric foundation of literal language: Towards a theory of the reification and meaning of psychological constructs. *Theory & Psychology*, 7(3), 355–72.

Barkus, E. J., Sterling, J., Hopkins, R., McKie, S., and Lewis, S. (2007). Cognitive and neural processes in non-clinical auditory hallucinations. *British Journal of Psychiatry*, 51, 76–81.

Barnes, J. and David, A. S. (2001). Visual hallucinations in Parkinson's disease: a review and phenomenological survey. *Journal of Neurology, Neurosurgery, & Psychiatry*, 70, 727–733.

Barnes, J., Connelly, V., Wiggs, L., Boubert, L., and Maravic, K. (2010). Sleep patterns in Parkinson's disease patients with visual hallucinations. *International Journal of Neuroscience*, 120, 564–569.

Barnes, J., Koch, L., Wilford, C., Boubert, L. (2011). An investigation into personality, stress and sleep with reports of hallucinations in a normal population. *Psychology*, 2, 4, 371–375.

Barrett, T. R. and Etheridge, J. B. (1992). Verbal hallucinations in normal: I. People who hear 'voices.' *Applied Cognitive Psychology*, 6, 379–387.

Barrett, T. R. and Etheridge, J. B. (1993). Verbal hallucinations in normal: II. Self-reported imagery vividness. *Personality and Individual Differences*, 15, 61–67.

Barrett, T. R. and Etheridge, J. B. (1994). Verbal hallucinations in normal: III. Dysfunctional personality correlates. *Personality and Individual Differences*, 16, 57–62.

Bass, H. (1983). The development of an adult's imaginary companion. *Psychoanalytic Review*, 70, 519–533.

Battro, A. M. (2001). *Half a Brain is Enough: The Story of Nico.* Cambridge: Cambridge University Press.

Beach, F. A. and Jaynes, J. (1954). Effects of early experience upon the behavior of animals. *Psychological Bulletin*, 51, 239–263.

Beach, F. A. and Jaynes, J. (1956a). Studies of maternal retrieving in rats: I. Recognition of young. *Journal of Mammalogy*, 37, 177–180.

Beach, F. A. and Jaynes, J. (1956b). Studies of maternal retrieving in rats: II. Effects of practice and previous parturitions. *American Naturalist*, 90, 103–109.

Beach, F. A. and Jaynes, J. (1956c). Studies of maternal retrieving in rats: III. Sensory cues involved in the lactating female's response to her young. *Behavior*, 10, 104–125.

Beach, F. A. and Jaynes, J. (1960). *Effects of Early Experience upon the Behavior of Animals.* Indianapolis, IN: Bobbs-Merrill Reprints.

Beach, F. A., Zitrin, A., and Jaynes, J. (1955). Neural mediation of mating in male cats: II. Contributions of the frontal cortex. *Journal of Experimental Zoology*, 130 (3), 381–401.

Beach, F. A., Zitrin, A., and Jaynes, J. (1956a). Neural mediation of mating in male cats: I. Effects of unilateral and bilateral removal of the neocortex. *Journal of Comparative Physiological Psychology*, 49, 4, 321–327.

Beach, F. A., Jaynes, J., and Zitrin, A. (1956b). Neural mediation of mating in male cats: III. Contributions of occipital, parietal and temporal cortex. *Journal of Comparative Neurology*, 105, 1, 111–125.

Beavan, V. (2011). Towards a definition of 'hearing voices': A phenomenological approach. *Psychosis: Psychological, Social and Integrative Approaches*, 3, 63–73.

Beavan, V., Read, J., and Cartwright, C. (2011). The prevalence of voice-hearers in the general population: A literature review. *Journal of Mental Health*, 20, 3, 281–292.

Bentaleb, L. A., Beauregard, M., Liddle, P., and Stip, E. (2002). Cerebral activity associated with auditory verbal hallucinations. *Journal of Psychiatry & Neuroscience*, 27 (2), 110.

Bentall, R. P. (1990). The illusion of reality: A review and integration of psychological research on hallucinations. *Psychological Bulletin*, 107, 82–95.

Bentall, R. P. and Slade, P. D. (1985). Reality testing and auditory hallucinations: A signal detection analysis. *British Journal of Clinical Psychology*, 24, 159-169.

Bentall, R. P., Haddock, G., and Slade, P. D. (1994). Cognitive behaviour therapy for persistent auditory hallucinations—from theory to therapy. *Behaviour Therapy*, 25 (1), 51-66.

Binder, J. R., Frost, J. A., Hammeke, T. A., Cox, R. W., Rao, S. M., and Prieto, T. (1997). Human brain language areas identified by functional magnetic resonance imaging. *The Journal of Neuroscience*, 17, 1, 353-362.

Blumenthal, A. L. (1975). A reappraisal of Wilhelm Wundt. *American Psychologist*, Nov., pp. 1081-1088.

Bottéro, J. (2001). *Religion in Ancient Mesopotamia* (trans. Teresa Lavender Fagan). Chicago, IL: University of Chicago Press.

Brett, G. S. (1912-21). *A History of Psychology*, 3 Volumes. London: Unwin and Allen.

Buchsbaum, M. S., et al. (1982). Cerebral glucography with positron tomography: Use in normal subjects and in patients with schizophrenia. *Archives of General Psychiatry*, 39, 251-259.

Cahan, E. D. and White, S. H. (1992). Proposals for a second psychology. Beyond the laboratory: Issues of application and practice. *American Psychologist*, 47 (2), 224-235.

Cangas, A. J., Langer, A. I., and Moriana, J. A. (2011). Hallucinations and related perceptual disturbance in a non-clinical Spanish population. *International Journal of Social Psychiatry*, 57, 2, 120-131.

Carr, M. (1983). Sidelights on Xin 'Heart; Mind' in the Shijing. *Proceedings of the 31st International Congress of Human Sciences in Asia and North Africa*, Aug. 31-Sept. 7, 824-825.

Carr, M. (1985a). Personation of the dead in ancient China. *Computational Analyses of Asian and African Languages*, 24, 1-107.

Carr, M. (1985b). Big Heads in Old Chinese. Paper presented at the *18th International Conference on Sino-Tibetan Languages and Linguistics*, August 27-29.

Carr, M. (1989). The *K'ôg "To dead father" hypothesis. *Review of Liberal Arts (Jinbun Kenkyū)*, 77, 51-117.

Carr, M. (1996). Ritual fasts and spirit visions in the Liji. *Review of Liberal Arts (Jinbun Kenkyū)*, 91, 99-126.

Carr, M. (2006). The shi 'corpse/personator' ceremony in early China. In Marcel Kuijsten, ed., *Reflections on the Dawn of Consciousness: Julian Jaynes Bicameral Mind Theory Revisited*. Henderson, NV: Julian Jaynes Society, pp. 343-416.

Caspi, A., Moffit, T., Cannon, M., McClay, J., Murray, R., Harrington, H., et al. (2005). Moderation of the effect of adolescent-onset cannabis use on adult psychosis by a functional polymorphism in the catechol-o-methyltransferase gene: Longitudinal evidence of a gene x environment interaction. *Biological Psychiatry*, 57, 1117–1127.

Cavanna, E. A., Trimble, M., Cinti, F., and Monaco, F. (2007). The "Bicameral Mind" 30 Years on: A Critical Reappraisal of Julian Jaynes's Hypothesis. *Functional Neurology*, 22 (1), 11–15.

Chin, J., Hayward, M., and Drinna, A. (2008). 'Relating' to voices: Exploring the relevance of this concept to people who hear voices. *Psychology and Psychotherapy: Theory, Research and Practice*, 82, 1–17.

Clark, A. and Chalmers, D. J. (1998). The extended mind. *Analysis*, 58: 7–19.

Clark, A. (2008). *Supersizing the Mind: Embodiment, Action, and Cognitive Extension*. Oxford and New York: Oxford University Press.

Cole, M. (1996). *Cultural Psychology: A Once and Future Discipline*. Cambridge, MA: Belknap Press.

Connolly, J. F. (1991). Adults who had imaginary playmates as children. In R. G. Kunzendorf, ed., *Mental Imagery*. New York, NY: Plenum Press, pp. 113–120.

Corstens, D., Longden, E., and May, R. (2012). Talking with voices: Exploring what is expressed by the voices people hear. *Psychosis*, 4, 2, 95–104.

Costall, A. (2006). 'Introspectionism' and the mythical origins of scientific psychology. *Consciousness and Cognition*, 15, 634–654.

Ćurčić-Blake, B., Liemburg, E., Vercammen, A., Swart, M., Knegtering, H., Bruggeman, R., and Aleman, A. (2012). When Broca goes uninformed: Reduced information flow to Broca's area in schizophrenia patients with auditory hallucinations. *Schizophrenia Bulletin*, 39 (5), 1087–1095.

Daalman, K., Boks, M. P .M., Diederen, K. M. J., de Weijer, A. D., Blom, J. D., Kahn, R. S., et al. (2011). Same or different? Auditory hallucinations in healthy and psychotic individuals. *The Journal of Clinical Psychiatry*, 72, 3, 320–325.

Danziger, K. (1980). The history of introspection reconsidered. *Journal of the History of the Behavioral Sciences*, 16, 241–262.

Danziger, K. (1983). Origins and basic principles of Wundt's Völkerpsychologie. *British Journal of Social Psychology*, 22, 303–313.

Danziger, K. (1997). *Naming the Mind: How Psychology Found Its Language*. London: Sage.

Darwin, C. (1958) [1859]). *On the Origin of Species by Means of Natural Selection, or the Preservation of Favored Races in the Struggle for Life*. New York, NY: Mentor Books.

Davies, M. F., Griffin, M., and Vice, S. (2001). Affective reactions to auditory hallucinations in psychotic, evangelical and control groups. *British Journal of Clinical Psychology*, 40, 361-370.

de Weijer, A. D., Neggers, S. F. W., Diederen, K. M., Mandl, R. C., Kahn, R. S., Hulshoff Pol, H. E., and Sommer I. E. (2011). Aberrations in the arcuate fasciculus are associated with auditory verbal hallucinations in psychotic and in non-psychotic individuals. *Human Brain Mapping*, 130, 68-77.

Delespaul, P., deVries, M., and Van Os, J. (2002). Determinants of occurrence and recovery from hallucinations in daily life. *Social Psychiatry and Psychiatric Epidemiology*, 37, 97-104.

Desmond, J. E. and Glover, G. H. (2002). Estimating sample size in functional MRI (fMRI) neuroimaging studies: Statistical power analyses. *Journal of Neuroscience Methods*, 118, 115-128.

Dewhurst, K. and Beard, A. W. (1970). Sudden religious conversions in temporal lobe epilepsy. *British Journal of Psychiatry*, 117, 497-507.

Dhossche, D., Ferdinand, R., van der Ende, J., Hofstra, M., and Verhulst, F. (2002). Diagnostic outcome of self-reported hallucinations in a community sample of adolescents. *Psychological Medicine*, 32, 619-627.

Dickson, P. (2006). *Dictionary of Middle Egyptian: In Gardiner Classification Order*. https://archive.org/details/DictionaryOfMiddleEgyptian.

Diederen, K. M. J., van Lutterveld, R., and Sommer, I. E. C. (2012). Neuroimaging of voice hearing in non-psychotic individuals: a mini-review. *Frontiers in human Neuroscience*, 6, 111, 1-5.

Diederen, K. M., Daalman, K., de Weijer, A. D., Neggers, S. F., van Gastel, W., Blom, J. D., Khan, R. S., and Sommer, I. E. C. (2011). Auditory hallucinations elicit similar brain activation in psychotic and nonpsychotic individuals. *Schizophrenia Bulletin*, 38 (5), 1074-1082.

Diederen, K. M., de Weijer, A. D., Daalman, K., Blom, J. D., Neggers, S. F., Khan, R. S., and Sommer, I. E. C. (2010). Decreased language lateralization is characteristic of psychosis, not auditory hallucinations. *Brain*, 133, 3734-3744.

Dierks, T., Linden, D. E. L, Jandi, M., Formisano, E., Goebel, R., Lanfermann, H., and Singer, W. (1999). Activation of Heschl's gyrus during auditory hallucinations. *Neuron*, 22, 615-621.

Diriwächter, R. (2004). Völkerpsychologie: The synthesis that never was. *Culture & Psychology*, 10 (1), 85-109.

Electronic Pennsylvania Sumerian Dictionary (ePSD) (n.d.). http://psd.museum.upenn.edu/epsd1/index.html.

Electronic Text Corpus of Sumerian Literature (ETCLS) (n.d.). http://etcsl.orinst.ox.ac.uk/.

Ellenberger, H. (1970). *The Discovery of the Unconscious*. New York, NY: Basic Books.

Engels, F. (1954 [1884]). *Origin of the Family, Private Property, and the State* (trans. Ernest Untermann). Moscow: Foreign Languages Publishing House.

Escher, S., Romme, M., and Buiks, A. (1998). Small talk: voice hearing in children. *Open Mind*, 92, 12–14.

Esquirol, J. E. D. (1832). Sur les illusions des sens chez les alienes. *Archives Generales de Medicine*, 2, 5–23.

Feelgood, S. R. and Rantzen, A. J. (1994). Auditory and visual hallucinations in university students. *Personality and Individual Differences*, 17, 2, 293–296.

Ferrari, M., Robinson, D. K., and Yasnitsky, A. (2010). Wundt, Vygotsky and Bandura: A cultural-historical science of consciousness in three acts. *History of the Human Sciences*, 23 (3), 95–118.

Fingarette, H. (1972). *Confucius: The Secular As Sacred*. New York, NY: Harper and Row.

Ford, S. C. and Beach, F. A. (1951). *Patterns of Sexual Behavior*. New York, NY: Harper and Brothers.

Forster, E. M. (1963 [1927]). *Aspects of the Novel*. Harmondsworth: Penguin.

Galton, F. (1883). *Inquiries into Human Faculty and Its Development*. London: Macmillan.

Gardner, H. (1985). *The Mind's New Science: A History of Cognitive Revolution*. New York, NY: Basic Books.

Gavalas, M. (2014). *Mycenaean (Linear b)–English Glossary*. http://www.projethomere.com/ressources/linearb.pdf.

Gazzaniga, M. S. (1970). *The Bisected Brain*. New York, NY: Appleton-Century-Crofts.

Gazzaniga, M. S. (2005a). Forty-five years of split-brain research and still going strong. *Nature Reviews: Neuroscience*, 6, 653–659.

Gazzaniga, M. S. (2005b). Cerebral specialization and interhemispheric communication: Does the corpus callosum enable the human condition? *Brain*, 123, 1293–1326.

Gliedman, J. (1982). Julian Jaynes and the ancient mindgods. *Science Digest*, 90, 84–87.

Graumann, C. F. (1980). Experiment, statistics, history: Wundt's first program of psychology. In W. G. Bringmann, R. D. Tweney, and E. R. Hilgar, eds., *Wundt Studies, a Centennial Collection*. Toronto: C. J. Hogrefe, pp. 33–41.

Greenwood, J. D. (1999). From Völkerpsychologie to cultural psychology: The once and future discipline? *Philosophical Psychology*, 12 (4), 503–514.
Greenwood, J. D. (2003). Wundt, Völkerpsychologie, and experimental social psychology. *History of Psychology*, 6 (1), 70–88.
Greer, S. (2006). A knowing noos and a slippery psyche: Jaynes's recipe for an unnatural theory of consciousness. In Marcel Kuijsten, ed., *Reflections on the Dawn of Consciousness: Julian Jaynes's Bicameral Mind Theory Revisited*. Henderson, NV: Julian Jaynes Society, pp. 233–263.
Grimby, A. (1993). Bereavement among elderly people: Grief reactions, post-bereavement hallucinations and quality of life. *Acta Psychiatrica Scandinavica*, 87, 72–80.
Guyot, Y. (1895). *La propriété: origine et évolution*. Paris: Libraire Delgrave.
Halpern, M. E., Güntürkün, O., Hopkins, W. D., and Rogers, L. J. (2005). Lateralization of the vertebrate brain: Taking the side of model systems. *The Journal of Neuroscience*, 25, 4, 10351–10357.
Halvor, E., ed. (2004). *The semantics of Qing in pre-Buddhist Chinese. Love and emotions in traditional Chinese literature*. Sinica Leidensia Series, 63. Amsterdam: Brill.
Hamilton, J. (2006). Auditory hallucinations in nonverbal quadriplegics. In Marcel Kuijsten, ed., *Reflections on the Dawn of Consciousness: Julian Jaynes's Bicameral Mind Theory Revisited*. Henderson, NV: Julian Jaynes Society, pp. 141–166.
Hartmann, von E. (1884). *Philosophy of the Unconscious*. London: Trübner and Co.
Hatfield, G. (2002). Psychology, philosophy, and cognitive science: Reflections on the history and philosophy of experimental psychology. *Mind and Language*, 17 (3), 207–232.
Hayward, M., Oveton, J., Dorey, T., and Denney, J. (2008). Relating therapy for people who hear voices: A case series. *Clinical Psychology and Psychotherapy*, 16, 216–227.
Hill, K. and Linden, D. E. J. (2013). Hallucinatory experiences in non-clinical populations. In R. Jardri et al., eds., *The Neuroscience of Hallucinations*. New York, NY: Springer, pp. 21–41.
Hill, K., Jackson, M. C., and Linden, D. E. J. (in preparation a). An interpersonal phenomenological analysis of clinical and non-clinical voice-hearers' beliefs and experiences.
Hill, K., Jackson, M. C., and Linden, D. E. J. (in preparation b). Early adversity, beliefs about voices and distress: A comparison of clinical and non-clinical voice-hearers.
Hilts, P. (1981). Odd man out. *Omni*, January, 68–88.

Hittite Lexicon (n.d.). http://www.assyrianlanguages.org/hittite/en_lexique_hittite.htm.

Hittite Online – Master Glossary (n.d.). http://www.utexas.edu/cola/centers/lrc/eieol/hitol-0-X.html.

Holloran, J. A. (1999). *Sumerian Lexicon. Version 3.0.* http://www.sumerian.org.

Honig, A., Romme, M. A., Ensink, B. J., Escher, S. D., Pennings, M. H., and Devries, M. W. (1998). Auditory hallucinations: A comparison between patients and non-patients. *The Journal of Nervous and Mental Disease*, 186, 646–651.

Howes, O. D., Montgomery, A. J., Asselin, M. C., Murray, R. M., Grasby, P. M., and McGuire, P. K. (2007). Molecular imaging studies of the striatal dopaminergic system in psychosis and predictions for the prodromal phase of psychosis. *British Journal of Psychiatry*, 191, s13–s18.

Howes, O. D., Shotbolt, P., Bloomfield, M., Daalman, K., Demjaha, A., Diederen, K. M. J., Ibrahim, K., Kim, E., McGuire, P., Kahn, R. S., and Sommer, I. E. (2013). Dopaminergic function in the psychosis spectrum: An [18F]-DOPA Imaging Study in Healthy Individuals with Auditory Hallucinations. *Schizophrenia Bulletin*, 39, 4, 807–814.

Izquierdo, A. M. (2000). A study of manifestations of hallucinations in a non-psychiatric population of Caribbean descent. *Dissertation Abstracts International: Section B: The Sciences & Engineering 2000*, 61 (5-B), 2764.

Jakes, S. and Hemsley, D. R. (1987). Personality and reports of hallucination and imagery in a normal population. *Perceptual and Motor Skills*, 64, 765–766.

Jardri, R., Cachia, A., Thomas, P., and Pins, D., eds. (2012). *The Neuroscience of Hallucinations.* New York, NY: Springer.

Jardri, R., Pins, D., Delmaire, C., Goeb, J. L., and Thomas, P. (2007). Activation of bilateral auditory cortex during verbal hallucinations in a child with schizophrenia. *Molecular Psychiatry*, 12, 319.

Jaynes, J. (1956). Imprinting: The interaction of learned and innate behavior: I. development and generalization. *Journal of Comparative and Physiological Psychology*, 49, 201–206.

Jaynes, J. (1957). Imprinting: The interaction of learned and innate behavior: II. The critical period. *Journal of Comparative and Physiological Psychology*, 50, 6–10.

Jaynes, J. (1958a). Imprinting: The interaction of learned and innate behavior: III. Practice effects on performance, retention, and fear. *Journal of Comparative and Physiological Psychology*, 51, 234–37.

Jaynes, J. (1958b). Imprinting: The interaction of learned and innate behavior: IV. Generalization and emergent discrimination. *Journal of Comparative and Physiological Psychology*, 51, 238–242.

Jaynes, J. (1966). The roots of science. *American Scientist*, 94–102.

Jaynes, J. (1969a). Edwin Garrigues Boring, 1886–1968. *Journal of the History of the Behavioral Sciences*, 5, 99–112.

Jaynes, J. (1969b). A new theory of consciousness. *Invited address at the American Psychological Association.* Unpublished.

Jaynes, J. (1969c). The historical origins of "ethology" and "comparative psychology." *Animal Behavior*, 17, 99–112.

Jaynes, J. (1976). *The Origin of Consciousness in the Breakdown of the Bicameral Mind.* Boston, MA: Houghton Mifflin. Reprinted in 1982 with a new Preface and in 1990 with a new Afterward.

Jaynes, J. (1977). Imprinting: The interaction of learned and innate behavior: V. On the essential nature of the stimulus project. Unpublished.

Jaynes, J. (1979a). Paleolithic cave paintings as eidetic images. *Behavioral and Brain Sciences*, 2, 4, 605–607.

Jaynes, J. (1979b). The meaning of King Tut: A review of the Tutankhamun Exhibition from the perspective of bicameral theory. *Princeton Alumni Weekly*, June 25. Reprinted in *University Magazine*, 1979, No. 80, 12–13.

Jaynes, J. (1981a). Ghost of a flea: Visions of William Blake. *Art/World*, 5 (1), 1–6.

Jaynes, J. (1981b). Art and the right hemisphere. *Art/World*, 5 (10), 3–6.

Jaynes, J. (1982). A two-tiered theory of emotions. *Behavioral and Brain Sciences*, 5, 3, 434–435.

Jaynes, J. (2006). Dragons of the Shang Dynasty: The hidden faces. In Marcel Kuijsten, ed., *Reflections on the Dawn of Consciousness: Julian Jaynes's Bicameral Mind Theory Revisited.* Henderson, NV: Julian Jaynes Society, pp. 337–342.

Jaynes, J. (2012). The Dream of Agamemnon. In Marcel Kuijsten, ed., *The Julian Jaynes Collection.* Henderson, NV: Julian Jaynes Society, pp. 196–206.

Jaynes, J. C. (1922). *Magic Wells.* Boston, MA: Geos H. Ellis.

Jocano, F. (1971). Varieties of supernatural experiences among Filipino peasants: Hallucinations or idiom of cultural cognition? *Transcultural Psychiatry Research Review*, 8, 43–45.

Johns, L. C. and Van Os, J. (2001). The continuity of psychotic experiences in the general population. *Clinical Psychology Review*, 21, 1125–1141.

Johns, L. C., Nazroo, J. Y., Bebbington, P., and Kuipers, E. (1998). Occurrence of hallucinations in a community sample. *Schizophrenia Research*, 29, 23.

Johns, L. C., Nazroo, J. Y., Bebbington, P., and Kuipers, E. (2002). Occurrence of hallucinatory experiences in a community sample and ethnic variations. *The British Journal of Psychiatry*, 180, 174–178.

Johns, L., Hemsley, D., and Kuipers, E. (2002). A comparison of auditory hallucinations in a psychiatric and non-psychiatric group. *British Journal of Clinical Psychology*, 41, 81–86.

Jones, M. and Coffey, M. (2012). Voice hearing: A secondary analysis of talk by people who hear voices. *International Journal of Mental Health Nursing*, 21, 50–59.

Jones, S. R. (2010). Do we need multiple models of auditory verbal hallucinations? Examining the phenomenological fit of cognitive and neurological models. *Schizophrenia Bulletin*, 36, 3, 566–575.

Jones, S., Guy, A., and Ormond, J. A. (2003). A Q-methodological study of hearing voices: A preliminary exploration of voice-hearers' understanding of their experiences. *Psychology and Psychotherapy: Theory Research and Practice*, 76, 189–209.

Kaplan, H. I. and Sadock, B. J. (1991). *Synopsis of Psychiatry: Behavioral Sciences and Clinical Psychiatry* (6th edition). Baltimore, MD: Williams and Wilkins.

Keen, S. (1977). Julian Jaynes: Portrait of the psychologist as a maverick theorizer. *Psychology Today*, 11, 66–77.

Keightley, D. (1978). *The Sources of Shang History*. Berkeley, CA: University of California Press.

Kendell, R. E. (1985). Schizophrenia: Clinical features. In R. Michaels and J. O. Cavenar, eds., *Psychiatry*, Vol. 1. London: Basic Books.

Kimura, Y., Yoshino, A., and Takahashi, Y., and Nomura, S. (2004). Interhemispheric difference in emotional response without awareness. *Physiology and Behavior*, 82 (4), 727–731.

Klausen, E., and Passman, R. H. (2006). Pretend companions (imaginary playmates): The emergence of a field. *The Journal of Genetic Psychology: Research and Theory on Human Development*, 167, 4, 349–364.

Kokoszka, A. (1992). Occurrence of altered states of consciousness: An overview. *Imagination, Cognition and Personality*, 12, 1, 89–96.

Kövecses, Z. (2000). *Metaphor and Emotion: Language, Culture, and Body in Human Feeling*. Cambridge and New York: Cambridge University Press.

Kövecses, Z. (2002). *Metaphor: A Practical Introduction*. Oxford: Oxford University Press.

Kövecses, Z. (2003). Language, figurative thought, and cross-cultural comparison. In F. Boers, ed., *Special Issue on Cross-Cultural Differences in Conceptual Metaphor: Applied Linguistics Perspective. Metaphor and Symbol*, 18, 311–320.

Kövecses, Z. (2004). Introduction: Cultural variation in metaphor. In Z. Kövecses, ed., special issue on "Cultural Variation in Metaphor," *European Journal of English Studies*, 8, 263–274.

Kövecses, Z. (2005). *Metaphor in Culture: Universality and Variation*. Cambridge: Cambridge University Press.

Kroger, R. O. and Scheibe, K. E. (1990). A reappraisal of Wundt's influence on social psychology. *Canadian Psychology/Psychologie Canadienne*, 31 (3), 220–228.

Krüger, J. G. (1756). *Versuch einer Experimentalseelenlehre*. Halle und Helmstädt: C. H. Hemmerde.

Kuijsten, M., ed. (2006a). *Reflections on the Dawn of Consciousness: Julian Jaynes's Bicameral Mind Theory Revisited*. Henderson, NV: Julian Jaynes Society.

Kuijsten, M. (2006b). Consciousness, hallucinations, and the bicameral mind: Three decades of new research. In Marcel Kuijsten, ed., *Reflections on the Dawn of Consciousness: Julian Jaynes's Bicameral Mind Theory Revisited*. Henderson, NV: Julian Jaynes Society, pp. 95–140.

Kuijsten, M., ed. (2009). New evidence for Jaynes's neurological model: A research update. *The Jaynesian: Newsletter of the Julian Jaynes Society*, 3 (1), 1–5.

Kuijsten, M., ed. (2012). *The Julian Jaynes Collection: Biography, Articles, Lectures, Interviews, Discussion*. Henderson, NV: Julian Jaynes Society.

Kuijsten, M., ed. (2016). *Gods, Voices, and the Bicameral Mind*. Henderson, NV: Julian Jaynes Society.

Kumari, V., Fannon, D., Ffytche, D. H., Raveendran, V., Antonova, E. , Premkumar, P., Cooke, M. A. , Anilkumar, P. P., Williams, S. C. R., Andrew, C., Johns, L. C., Fu, H. Y., McGuire, P. K., and Kuipers, E. (2008). Functional MRI of verbal self-monitoring in schizophrenia. *Schizophrenia Bulletin*, 36, 740–755.

LaFargue, P. (1885). *Propriété: Origine et évolution: These communiste*. Paris: Delagrave.

LaFargue, P. (1975 [1890]). *The Evolution of Property from Savagery to Civilization*. London: New Park Publications.

Lamiell, J. T. (2013). On psychology's struggle for existence: Some reflections on Wundt's 1913 essay a century on. *Journal of Theoretical and Philosophical Psychology*, 33 (4), 1–11.

Lampl, Y., Lorberboym, M., Gilad, R., Boaz, M., and Sadeh, M. (2005). Auditory hallucinations in acute stroke. *Behavioural Neurology*, 16 (4), 211–216.

Laroi, F., Sommer, I. E., Blom, J. D., Fernyhough, C., Ffytche, D., and Hugdahl, K. (2012). The characteristic features of auditory verbal hallucinations in clinical and nonclinical groups: State-of-the-art overview and future directions. *Schizophrenia Bulletin*, 38, 4, 724–733.

Laroi, F., van der Linden, M., and Marczewski, P. (2004). The effects of emotional salience, cognitive effort and meta-cognitive beliefs on a reality monitoring task in hallucination-prone subjects. *British Journal of Clinical Psychology*, 43, 221–233.

Laroi, F., Luhrmann, T. M., Bell, V., Christian Jr, W. A., Deshpande, S., Fernyhough, C., Jenkins, J., and Woods, A. (2014). Culture and hallucinations: Overview and future directions. *Schizophrenia Bulletin*, 40 (4), 213–214.

Launay, G. and Slade, P. (1981). The measurement of hallucinatory predisposition in male and female prisoners. *Personality and Individual Differences*, 2, 221–234.

Leahey, T. H. (1979). Something old, something new: Attention in Wundt and modern cognitive psychology. *Journal of the History of the Behavioral Sciences*, 15, 242–241.

Lennox, B. R., Bert S., Park, G., Jones, P. B., and Morris, P. G. (1999). Spatial and temporal mapping of neural activity associated with auditory hallucinations. *Lancet*, 353, 644.

Leontiev, A. N. (1978). *Activity, Consciousness, Personality* (trans. M. J. Hall). Englewood Cliffs, NJ: Prentice Hall.

Leontiev, A. N. (2005 [1940]). The genesis of activity. *Journal of Russian and East European Psychology*, 43, 58–71.

LeTourneau, C. (1892). *Property: Its Origin and Development*. London: Walter Scott.

Leudar, I., Thomas, P., McNally, D., and Glinski, A. (1997). What voices can do with words: Pragmatics of verbal hallucinations. *Psychological Medicine*, 27, 885–898.

Levy, J. (1977). The mammalian brain and the adaptive advantage of cerebral asymmetry. *Annals of New York Academy of Science*, 299, 264–272.

Lewinski, I. (1913). *The Origin of Property and the Formation of the Village Community*. London: Constable.

Lewis-Hanna, L. L., Hunter, M. D., Farrow, T. F., Wilkinson, I. D., and Woodruff, P. W. (2011). Enhanced cortical effects of auditory stimulation and auditory attention in healthy individuals prone to auditory hallucinations during partial wakefulness. *Neuroimage*, 57, 1154–1161.

Li, S.-C. (2003). Biocultural orchestration of development plasticity across levels: The interplay of biology and culture in shaping the mind and behavior across the life span. *Psychological Bulletin*, 129 (3), 171–194.

Lilienfeld, S. O. (2010). Can psychology become a science? *Personality and Individual Differences*, 49, 281–288.

Limber, J. (2006). Language and consciousness. In Marcel Kuijsten, ed., *Reflections on the Dawn of Consciousness: Julian Jaynes's Bicameral Mind Theory Revisited*. Henderson, NV: Julian Jaynes Society, pp. 169–202.

Linden, D. E. J., Thornton, K., Kuswanto, C. N., Johnston, S. J., and Jackson, M. C. (2011). The brain's voices: Comparing nonclinical auditory hallucinations and imagery. *Cerebral Cortex*, 21, 330–337.

López-Rodrigo, A. M., Paíno Piñeiro, M. M., Martínez Suárez, P. C. Caro, M. I., and Lemos Giráldez, S. (1997). Hallucinations in a normal population: Imagery and personality influences. *Psychology in Spain*, 1, 1, 10–16.

Lowie, R. (1927). *The Origin of the State*. New York, NY: Harcourt and Brace.

Lubbock, J. (1870). *The Origin of Civilization and the Primitive Condition of Man: Mental and Social Condition of Savage*. New York, NY: D. Appleton.

Luhrmann, T. M. (2011). Hallucinations and sensory overrides. *Annual Review of Anthropology*, 40, 71–85.

Luhrmann, T. M., Padmavati, R., Tharoor, H., and Osei, A. (2014). Differences in voice-hearing experiences of people with psychosis in the USA, India and Ghana: Interview-based study. *The British Journal of Psychiatry*, 205, 1–4.

Luria, A. R. (1976). *The Cognitive Development: Its Cultural and Social Foundations*. Cambridge, MA: Harvard University Press.

Lutz, C. A. (1988). *Unnatural Emotions: Everyday Sentiments on a Micronesian Atoll and Their Challenge to Western Theory*. Chicago, IL: University of Chicago Press.

Maalej, Z. A. and Yu, N., eds. (2011). *Embodiment via Body Parts: Studies from Various Languages and Cultures* (Human Cognitive Processing, Vol. 31). Amsterdam and Philadelphia, PA: John Benjamins.

Marks, D. F. (1999). Consciousness, mental imagery and action. *British Journal of Psychology*, 90, 567–585.

McCarthy-Jones, S., Trauer, T., Mackinnon, A., Sims, E., Thomas, N., and Copolov, D. (2012). A new phenomenological survey of auditory hallucinations: Evidence for subtypes and implications for theory and practice. *Schizophrenia Bulletin*, 40, 1, 231–235.

McLennan, J. F. (1865). *Primitive Marriage: An Inquiry into the Origin of the Form of Capture in Marriage Ceremonies*. Edinburgh: Adam and Charles Black.

McVeigh, B. J. (1996). Standing stomachs, clamoring chests and cooling livers: Metaphors in the psychological lexicon of Japanese. *Journal of Pragmatics*, 26, 25–50.

McVeigh, B. J. (2005). Explaining hypnosis, possession, and volition: A Jaynesian Approach to the varieties of consciousness. *2005 Julian Jaynes Memorial Symposium on Consciousness: "Hearing Voices Called Gods."* Psychology Department, University of Prince Edward Island Charlottetown, Prince Edward Island, Canada. September 23.

McVeigh, B. J. (2006a). The Self as interiorized social relations: Applying a Jaynesian approach to problems of agency and volition. In Marcel Kuijsten, ed., *Reflections on the Dawn of Consciousness: Julian Jaynes's Bicameral Mind Theory Revisited*. Henderson, NV: Julian Jaynes Society, pp. 203–232.

McVeigh, B. J. (2006b). Overcoming intellectual barriers to understanding Jaynes' theory. *The First Annual Julian Jaynes Conference on Consciousness*. University of Prince Edward Island, Canada (August 3–5).

McVeigh, B. J. (2007a). Elephants in the psychology department: Barriers to understanding Julian Jaynes's theories. Paper presented at *Consciousness Discussion Forum, Center for Consciousness Studies*, University of Arizona. September 12. Available at http://julianjaynes.org/julian-jaynes-society-publications.php.

McVeigh, B. J. (2007b). Ignoring the elephants: Overcoming intellectual barriers to understanding Julian Jaynes. *American Anthropological Association Conference*, Washington, DC, November 28–December 3. Paper kindly read by Dana Raphael in my absence.

McVeigh, B. J. (2008). Hallucinations as adaptive behavior: Divine voices and visions as neuropsychological vestiges. *The Second Annual Julian Jaynes Conference on Consciousness*. University of Prince Edward Island, Canada. August 7–9.

McVeigh, B. J. (2010a). Why did the unconsciousness appear in history when it did? A Jaynesian explanation. *Toward a Science of Consciousness Conference*. Center for Consciousness Studies, Tucson Convention Center, Tucson, AZ, April 8–12.

McVeigh, B. J. (2010b). Why did the unconsciousness appear in history when it did? A Jaynesian explanation. *The Jaynesian: Newsletter of the Julian Jaynes Society*. Winter, 4 (3), 2010.

McVeigh, B. J. (2012a). Hallucinations as adaptation: Divine voices, visions, and autoscopy as neuropsychological vestiges. *Toward a*

Science of Consciousness Conference. Center for Consciousness Studies, Loews Ventana Canyon Resort Hotel, Tucson, AZ, April 9–12.

McVeigh, B. J. (2012b). Mental imagery and hallucinations as adaptive behavior: Divine voices and visions as neuropsychological vestiges. Organizing Committee for the *Third International Conference of the Image*. Higher School of the Humanities and Journalism. Poznan, Poland, September 14–16 (virtual presentation).

McVeigh, B. J. (2013). Mental imagery and hallucinations as adaptive behavior: Divine voices and visions as neuropsychological vestiges. *The International Journal of the Image*, 3 (1), 25–36.

McVeigh, B. J. (2015). *The Propertied Self: The Psychology of Economic History*. Hauppauage, NY: Nova Science Publishers.

McVeigh, B. J. (2016a). *How Religion Evolved: Explaining the Living Dead, Talking Idols, and Mesmerizing Monuments*. Edison, NJ: Transaction Publishers.

McVeigh, B. J. (2016b). *A Psychohistory of Metaphors: Envisioning Time, Space, and Self through the Centuries*. Boulder, CO: Lexington Books.

McVeigh, B. J. (2016c). *Discussions with Julian Jaynes: The Nature of Consciousness and the Vagaries of Psychology*. Hauppauage, NY: Nova Science Publishers.

McVeigh, B. J. (2016d). *The History of Japanese Psychology: Global Perspectives, 1875–1950*. London: Bloomsbury.

Menary, R., ed. (2010). *The Extended Mind*. Cambridge, MA: MIT Press/Bradford.

Meshcheriakov, B. G. (2000). Vygotsky's conception: A logico-semantic analysis. *Journal of Russian and East European Psychology*, 38, 34–55.

Mill, J. S. (1843 [1974]). *A System of Logic Ratiocinative and Inductive: Being a Connected View of the Principles of Evidence and the Methods of Scientific Investigation*. Toronto, ON: University of Toronto Press.

Millham, A. and Easton, S. (1998). Prevalence of auditory hallucinations in nurses in mental health. *Journal of Psychiatric and Mental Health Nursing*, 5, 95–99.

Morrison, A. P., Haddock, G. (1997). Self-focused attention in schizophrenic patients with and without auditory hallucinations and normal subjects: A comparative study. *Personality and Individual Differences*, 23, 937–941.

Moskowitz, A. and Corstens, D. (2008). Auditory hallucinations: Psychotic symptom or dissociative experience? *The Journal of Psychological Trauma*, 6 (2–3), 35–63.

Mueller, C. G. (1979). Some origins of psychology as science. *Annual Review of Psychology*, 30, 9–29.

Münsterberg, H. (1915). *Psychology: General and Applied*. New York, NY: Appleton.

Nasrallah, H. A. (1985). The unintegrated right hemispheric consciousness as alien intruder. *Comparative Psychiatry*, 26, 273–282.

Nettle, D. (2006). Schizotypy and mental health amongst poets, visual artists, and mathematicians. *Journal of Research in Personality*, 40, 876–890.

Nørretranders, T. (1998). *The User Illusion: Cutting Consciousness Down to Size*. New York: Penguin Books.

Ocklenburg, S., Westerhausen, R., Hirnstein, M., and Hugdahl, K. (2013). Auditory hallucinations and reduced language lateralization in schizophrenia: A Meta-analysis of dichotic listening studies. *Journal of the International Neuropsychological Society*, 19, 410–418.

Ohayon, M. M. (2000). Prevalence of hallucinations and their pathological associations in the general population. *Psychiatry Research*, 97, 153–164.

Ohayon, M. M. and Schatzberg, A. F. (2002). Prevalence of depressive episodes with psychotic features in the general population. *American Journal of Psychiatry*, 159, 11, 1855–1861.

Olin, R. (1999). Auditory hallucinations and the bicameral mind. *Lancet*, 354, 166.

Pearson, D. (1998). *The Social Acceptability of Children Hearing Voices*. Doctor of clinical psychology thesis, University of Leicester.

Pearson, D. B., Burrow, A., FitzGerald, A., Green, K., Lee, G., and Wise, N. (2001). Auditory hallucinations in normal child populations. *Personality and Individual Differences*, 31, 3, 401–407.

Pearson, D., Rouse, H., Doswell, S., Ainsworth, C., Dawson, O., Simms, K., Edwards, L., and Faulconbridge, J. (2001). The prevalence of imaginary companions in a normal child population. *Child: Care, Health and Development*, 27, 1, 13–22.

Pearson, D., Smalley, M., Ainsworth, C., Cook, M., Boyle, J., and Flury, S. (2008). Auditory hallucinations in adolescent and adult students: Implications for continuums and adult pathology following child abuse. *The Journal of Nervous and Mental Disease*, 196, 8, 634–638.

Pérez-Álvarez, M., Garcia-Montes, J., Perona-Garcelán, S., and Vallina-Fernández, O. (2008). Changing relationships with voices: New therapeutic perspectives for treating hallucinations. *Clinical Psychology and Psychotherapy*, 15, 75–85.

Petrucci, R. (1905). *Les origines naturelles de la propriété: Essai de sociologie compareé*. Paris: Giard & Briere.

Polanyi, K. (1944). *The Great Transformation: The Political and Economic Origins of Our Time*. Boston, MA: Beacon Press.

Posey, T. B. and Losch, M. E. (1983). Auditory hallucinations of hearing voices in 375 normal subjects. *Imagination, Cognition and Personality*, 3, 99–113.

Potter, J. (2000). Post-cognitive psychology. *Theory & Psychology*, 10 (1), 31–37.

Puccetti, R. (1993). Mind with a double brain. *The British Journal for the Philosophy of Science*, 44, 4, 675–691.

Rees, W. (1971). The hallucinations of widowhood. *British Medical Journal*, 210, 37–41.

Romme, E. and Escher, S. (2000). *Making Sense of Voices: A Guide for Mental Health Professionals Working with Voice-Hearers*. London: Mind Publications.

Romme, M. A. and Escher, S. (1989). Hearing voices. *Schizophrenia Bulletin*, 15, 209–216.

Romme, M. A. and Escher, S. (1996). Empowering people who hear voices. In G. Haddock, G. and Slade, P. D., eds., *Cognitive-Behavioural Interventions with Psychotic Disorders*. London: Routledge, pp. 137–150.

Romme, M. A., Honig, A., Noorthhoorn, E. O., and Escher, A. D. (1992). Coping with hearing voices: an emancipatory approach. *British Journal of Psychiatry*, 16, 99–103.

Ross, C. A., Joshi, S., and Currie, R. (1990). Dissociative experiences in the general population: A factor analysis. *American Journal of Psychiatry*, 147, 1547–1552.

Rowe, B. (2012). Retrospective: Julian Jaynes and The Origin of Consciousness in the Breakdown of the Bicameral Mind. *American Journal of Psychology*, 125 (1), 95–112.

Sato, W. and Aoki, S. (2006). Right hemispheric dominance in processing of unconscious negative emotion. *Brain and Cognition*, 62 (3), 261–266.

Schmidt, C. C. E. (1996). *Empirische Psychologie* (2nd edition). Jena, Germany: Croker.

Sharifian, F., Dirven, R., Yu, N., and Niemeier, S., eds. (2008). *Culture, Body, and Language: Conceptualizations of Internal Body Organs across Cultures and Languages* (Applications of Cognitive Linguistics series, Vol. 7). Berlin and New York: Mouton de Gruyter.

Sher, L. (2000). Neuroimaging, auditory hallucinations, and the bicameral mind. *Journal of Psychiatry & Neuroscience*, 25 (3), 239–240.

Shevlin, M., Dorahy, M., and Adamson, G. (2007). Childhood traumas and hallucinations: An analysis of the national comorbidity survey. *Journal of Psychiatric Research*, 41, 222–228.

Shweder, R. A. (1990). Cultural psychology: What is it? In James W. Stigler, Richard A. Shweder, and Gilbert Herdt, eds., *Cultural Psychology: Essays on Comparative Human Development*. Cambridge: Cambridge University Press, pp. 1–43.

Siddle, R., Haddock, G., Tarrier, N., and Faragher, E. B. (2002). Religious delusions in patients admitted to hospital with schizophrenia. *Social Psychiatry and Psychiatric Epidemiology*, 37 (3), 130-138.

Sidgwick, H., Johnson, A., Myers, F. W. H., Podmore, F., and Sidgwick, E. M. (1894). Report on the census of hallucination. *Proceedings of Society for Psychical Research*, 10, 25-422.

Slade, P. D. (1973). The psychological investigation and treatment of auditory hallucinations: A second case report. *British Journal of Medical Psychology*, 46, 293-296.

Slade, P. D. and Bentall, R. P. (1988). *Sensory Deception: A Scientific Analysis of Hallucination*. London, UK: Croom Helm.

Sleutels, J. (2006). Greek zombies: On the alleged absurdity of substantially unconscious Greek minds. In Marcel Kuijsten, ed., *Reflections on the Dawn of Consciousness: Julian Jaynes's Bicameral Mind Theory Revisited*. Henderson, NV: Julian Jaynes Society, pp. 303-337.

Sommer, I. E. C., Daalman, K., Rietkerk, T., Diederen, K. M., Bakker, S., Wijkstra, J., and Boks, M. P. M. (2010). Healthy individuals with auditory verbal hallucinations: Who are they? Psychiatric assessments of a selected sample of 103 subjects. *Schizophrenia Bulletin*, 36, 633-641.

Sommer, I. E. C., Kelly, M. J., Diederen, K. M. J., Blom, J. D., Willems, A., Kushan, L., Slotema, K., Boks, M. P. M., Daalman, K. M., Hoek, H. W., Neggers, S. F. W., and Kahn, R. S. (2008). Auditory verbal hallucinations predominantly activate the right inferior frontal area. *Brain*, 131, 12, 3169-3177.

Sommer, I. E., de Weijer, A. D., Daalman, K., Neggers, S. F., Somers, M., Kahn, R. S., Slotema, C. W., Blom, J. D., Hoek, H. W., and Aleman, A. (2007). Can fMRI-guidance improve the efficacy of rTMS treatment for auditory verbal hallucinations? *Schizophrenia Research*, 93, 406-408.

Sorrell, E., Hayward, M., and Meddings, S. (2010). Interpersonal process and hearing voices: A study of the association between relating to voices and distress in clinical and non-clinical hearers. *Behavioural and Cognitive Psychotherapy*, 38, 2, 127-140.

Sperry, R. W. (1974). Lateral specialization in the surgically separated hemispheres. In F. O. Schmidt and F. G. Worden, eds., *Neuroscience: Third Study Program*. Cambridge, MA: MIT Press, , pp. 3-19.

Stephens, G. L. and Graham, G. (2000). *When Self-Consciousness Breaks: Alien Voices and Inserted Thoughts*. Cambridge, MA: MIT Press.

Sterelny, K. (2004). Externalism, epistemic artifacts, and the extended mind. In Richard Schantz, ed., *The Externalist Challenge*, New York: de Gruyter, pp. 239-254.

Stevenson, I. (1983). Do we need a new word to supplement "hallucination"? *American Journal of Psychiatry*, 140, 12, 1609–1611.

Stone, H. and Stone, S. (1989). *Embracing Ourselves: The Voice Dialogue Training Manual*. New York, NY: Nataraj Publishing.

Stove, D. C. (2006). The oracles and their cessation: A tribute to Julian Jaynes. In Marcel Kuijsten, ed., *Reflections on the Dawn of Consciousness: Julian Jaynes's Bicameral Mind Theory Revisited*. Henderson, NV: Julian Jaynes Society, pp. 267–294.

Szechtman, H., Woody, E., Bowers, K., and Nahmias, C. (1998). Where the imaginal appears real: A positron emission tomography study of auditory hallucinations. *Proceedings of the National Academy of Science*, 95, 1956–1960.

Taylor, M., Cartwright, B. S., and Carlson, S. M. (1993). A developmental investigation of children's imaginary companions. *Developmental Psychology*, 39, 737–754.

Temmingh, H., Stein, D. J., Seedat, S., and Williams, D. R. (2011). The prevalence and correlates of hallucinations in a general population sample: Findings from the South African Stress and Health Study. *African Journal of Psychiatry*, July, 211–217.

Tien, A. Y. (1991). Distribution of hallucinations in the population. *Social Psychiatry and Psychiatric Epidemiology*, 26, 287–292.

Trujillo, K., Lewis, D. O., Yeager, C. A., and Gidlow, B. (1996). Imaginary companions of school boys and boys with dissociative identity disorder/multiple personality disorder: A normal to pathologic continuum. *Child and Adolescent Psychiatric Clinics of North America*, 4, 2, 375–391.

Vallortigara, G., and Rogers, L. J. (2005). Survival with an asymmetrical brain: Advantages and disadvantages of cerebral lateralization. *Behavioral and Brain Sciences*, 28, 575–633.

Valsiner, J. (2001). The first six years: Culture's adventures in psychology. *Culture & Psychology*, 7 (1), 5–48.

van de Ven, V. G., Formisanoa, E. Röderc, C. H., Prvulovicb, D., Bittnerb, R. A., Dietzd, M. G., Huble, D., Dierkse, T., Federspiele, A., Espositof, F., Di Sallef, F., Jansmaa, B., Goebela, R., and Lindenb, D. E. J. (2005). The spatiotemporal pattern of auditory cortical responses during verbal hallucinations. *NeuroImage*, 27, 644–655.

Van Lutterveld, R., Oranje, B., Kemner, C., Abramovic, L., Willems, A. E., Boks, M. P., Glenthojo, B. Y., Kahn, R. S., and Sommer, I. E. (2010). Increased psychophysiological parameters of attention in non-psychotic individuals with auditory verbal hallucinations. *Schizophrenia Research*, 121, 153–159.

Veblen, T. (1899). *The Theory of the Leisure Class: An Economic Study in the Evolution of Institutions*. New York, NY: Macmillan.

Verdoux, H., Maurice-Tison, S., Gay, B., Van Os, J., Salamon, R., and Bourgeois, M. (1998). A survey of delusional ideation in primary-care patients. *Psychological Medicine*, 28, 27–34.
Vygotsky, L. S. (1998). *The Collected Works of L. S. Vygotsky: Vols. 1–6* (ed. Robert W. Rieber). New York, NY: Springer.
Vygotsky, L. S. and Luria, A. R. (1993 [1930]). *Studies on the History of Behavior: Ape, Primitive, and Child*. Hillsdale, NJ: Erlbaum.
Watkins, J. (1998). *Hearing Voices: A Common Human Experience*. Melbourne, Australia: Hill of Content.
Weissman, J. (1993). *Of Two Minds: Poets Who Hear Voices*. Hanover: Wesleyan University Press.
Weller, M. and Wiedemann, P. (1989). An outline of etiological and pathogenetic concepts. *International Ophthalmology*, 13, 193–199.
Werner, H. (1948). *Comparative Psychology of Mental Development*. New York, NY: Science Editions.
Wertsch, J. V. (1985). *Vygotsky and the Social Formation of Mind*. Cambridge: Cambridge University Press.
Wertsch, J. V. (1991). *Voices of the Mind*. Cambridge, MA: Harvard University Press.
West, D. J. (1948). A mass observation questionnaire on hallucinations. *Journal of the Society Psychical Research*, 34, 187–196.
Wigan, A. L. (1985 [1844]). *The Duality of the Mind*. Malibu, CA: Joseph Simon.
Wilson, R. A. (2005). Collective memory, group minds, and the extended mind thesis. *Cognitive Processing*, 6.4, 227–236.
Wong, W.-C. (2009). Retracing the footsteps of Wilhelm Wundt: Explorations in the disciplinary frontiers of psychology and in Völkerpsychologie. *History of Psychology*, 12 (4), 229–265.
Woodward, W. and Tower, J. (2007). Julian Jaynes: Introducing his life and thought. In Marcel Kuijsten, ed., *Reflections on the Dawn of Consciousness: Julian Jaynes's Bicameral Mind Theory Revisited*. Henderson, NV: Julian Jaynes Society, pp. 13–74.
Woodward, W. R. (1982). Wundt's program for the new psychology: Vicissitudes of experiment, theory, and system. In W. R. Woodward and M. G. Ash, eds., *The Problematic Science: Psychology in Nineteenth-Century Thought*. New York, NY: Praeger, pp. 67–97.
Wu, J., ed. (1979). *The Pinyin Chinese-English Dictionary*. Beijing: Commercial Press.
Wundt, W. (1900–1920). *Völkerpsychologie: Eine Untersuchung der Entwicklungsgestze von Sprache, Mythus, und Sitte*. 10 Vols. Leipzig: Engelmann.
Xu, Z., ed. (1981). *Jiagu2: Jiaguwenzidian [Dictionary of Bone Inscriptions]*. Chengdu, Sichuan: Cishu Chubanshe.

Young, H. F., Bentall, R. P., Slade, P. D., and Dewey, B. A. (1986). Disposition towards hallucinations, gender and EPQ scores: A brief report. *Personality and Individual Differences,* 7, 247–249.

Young, H. F., Bentall, R. P., Slade, P. D., and Dewey, B. A. (1987). The role of brief instructions and suggestibility in the elicitation of auditory and visual hallucinations in normal and psychiatric subjects. *The Journal of Nervous and Mental Disease,* 175, 41–48.

Yu, N. (1995). Metaphorical expressions of anger and happiness in English and Chinese. *Metaphor and Symbolic Activity,* 10, 59–92.

Yu, N. (1998). *The Contemporary Theory of Metaphor: A Perspective from Chinese* (Human Cognitive Processing, Vol. 1). Amsterdam and Philadelphia: John Benjamins.

Yu, N. (2002). Body and emotion: Body parts in Chinese expression of emotion. *Pragmatics and Cogniton,* 10, 341–367.

Yu, N. (2003). Chinese metaphors of thinking. *Cognitive Linguistics,* 14 (2/3), 141–165.

Yu, N. (2007). Heart and cognition in ancient Chinese philosophy. *Journal of Cognition and Culture,* 7, 27–47.

Yu, N. (2009a). *From Body to Meaning in Culture: Papers on Cognitive Semantic Studies in Chinese.* Amsterdam and Philadelphia: John Benjamins.

Yu, N. (2009b). *The Chinese HEART in a Cognitive Perspective: Culture, Body, and Language* (Applications of Cognitive Linguistics, Vol. 12). Berlin and New York: Mouton de Gruyter.

Zhao, C. (1988). *Jiaguwen Jianming Cidian [Concise Dictionary of Oracle-bone Inscriptions].* Beijing: Zhonghuashuju.

Index

Achilles 14
Agamemnon 14
agricultural revolution 9, 32, 35, 36
Akkadian 47, 57, 137, 161
ancestor worship vii, 33, 69, 70
  See also centrality of ancestor worship (CAW)
apophenia 129
aptic structures 97, 106, 110, 111, 113, 121
  and hallucinations 110, 111, 113
  language as 10
Archimedes 14
Aristophanes 14
Aristotle 14
"as if" mortuary practices (AIMP) vii, 34, 69
Ashurbabipal, King 14
auditory verbal hallucinations (AVH) viii, 98, 99, 100, 104, 105, 108, 113, 114, 115, 116, 117, 118, 119, 120, 121, 122, 231, 232, 234, 235
Augustine 14
authority-radiating ceremonial complexes (ARCC) vii, 34, 69
authorization 33, 36, 39, 70, 72, 130
  See also self-authorization
autoscopic extraception 129
  See also autoscopy, heautoscopy
autoscopy 11, 35, 129
  See also autoscopic extraception, heautoscopy
auxiliary divine communication (ADC) vii, 26
Avesta 16
axial age 36, 130

Baldwin, James Mark 21
Barber, Theodore X. 14

Bartlett, Frederic 18
Bascom, John 20
Bastian, Adolf 21
Beach, Frank 8, 15
bicameral breakdown 10–11, 32–33, 36, 70–71
Bicameral Civilization Inventory (BCI) vii, 33–34, 45, 67, 69
  hypothesis 33
bicameral dreams 60
bicameral mind 9, 25, 110
  bicameral breakdown 10–11, 32–33, 36, 70–71
  See also bicamerality
bicameral vestiges 3, 16, 25, 33, 41, 43, 68, 69, 76, 111, 125, 126
bicamerality 3, 9, 16, 31, 32, 33, 35, 36, 43, 45, 46, 55, 64, 70, 71, 75, 77, 101
  breakdown of 10–11, 32–33, 36, 70–71
  literate-urban 35–36, 70
  neolithic 35, 70
  vestiges of 3, 16, 25, 33, 41, 43, 68, 69, 76, 111, 125, 126
  See also bicameral mind
Binet, Alfred 14
biocultural co-contructivism 126
Blake, William 15, 17
Bleuler, Eugen 14
Boas, Franz 25
Bogen, Joseph E. 14
Book of Mormon 16
Book of Poetry (Book of Songs) 76, 77, 78, 79
Boring, Edwin G. 9, 23, 29
Brett, George S. 7

Broca's area 106, 107, 112, 116, 118, 119
  See also language regions
Bronze Age vii, 5, 32, 33, 36, 45

calendrics 130
Carr, Michael v, 28, 45, 53, 70, 77, 78, 80, 82
centrality of ancestor worship (CAW) vii, 33, 69
  See also ancestor worship
ception 129
  See also coception, extraception, introception, superception
Chalmers, D.J. 125
channeling 11, 43
Charcot, Martin Jean 14
Cheiron 9
  See also International Society for the History of the Behavioral Sciences
Chen, Yu-Hui v
China, ancient 67, 69, 70, 71, 73, 81, 83, 89
  cosmological vision of 73–75, 87, 90
Chinese 3, 42, 53, 65, 67, 68, 69, 70, 71, 72, 73, 74, 75, 77, 80, 83, 84, 88, 90, 91
  See also Mandarin
Clark, A. 125
coception 41, 129
  See also extraception, introception, superception
cognition 2, 3, 10, 19, 20, 25, 29, 32, 36, 37, 39, 40, 71, 81, 82, 110, 126, 127, 215, 212, 213
  emergency-repair 19–20
  routine-maintenance 19–20
cognitivism 19
  limitations of 27
Cohn, James v
complexity (increasing social) 10, 11, 13, 29, 35, 37, 38, 46, 67, 68
  and bicameral breakdown 10
Comte, Auguste 20
Confucianism 70, 72
conscious interiority vi, 3, 6, 8, 9, 10–11, 13, 15, 17, 19, 33, 35, 36, 37, 39, 40, 41, 43, 46, 65, 71, 121, 126, 127, 128, 130
  as cultural 10, 15, 35, 37
  cultural-historical invention of 13
  features of 20, 39–40
  metaphoric expressions 10
  not result of bioevolution 6, 13, 37, 38
  singularity of 10
consciousness vi, 2, 3, 4, 5, 8, 9, 10, 11, 12, 13, 14, 15, 19, 20, 23, 31, 36, 37, 38, 39, 40, 41, 46, 60, 72, 74, 104, 111, 122, 127, 199, 200, 212, 214, 229
  culturally-acquired 15
  features of 20, 39–40
  See also conscious interiority
consilience 39
Constantine 14
Corstens, D. 28, 122
Cretan hieroglyphs 65
cultural Psychology 2, 21, 22, 23, 25, 26, 27, 28, 30
cultural-historical psychological changes 25
cultural-historical Psychology 21, 23
  See also cultural Psychology Völkerpsychologie

dark ages 36
  See also Late Bronze Age Collapse
Darwin, Charles 11, 12, 14, 18, 25
Democritus 14
Descartes, René 14
Dewey, John 21
divination 4, 34, 36, 69, 71, 73, 141, 147
Dodds, E.R. 15
doppelgängers 35
Douglas, Mary 14
dreaming 13, 34, 60, 61, 71, 102, 18
  bicameral 60
  lucid 128
dualism 29, 43
  empirical 29
  mind–body 29, 43
Durkheim, Emile 25

Eblaite 65

Egyptian (ancient), 47, 48, 54, 58, 65, 65, 137, 138, 167
eidetic images 17, 131
Einstein, Albert 14
Elamite 65
Electronic Pennsylvania Sumerian Dictionary (ePSD) vi, 48, 50, 51, 54, 56, 61, 63, 65, 132, 134, 135, 136, 137, 138, 143, 152, 163, 160
Electronic Text Corpus of Sumerian Literature (ETCSL) vii, 48, 49, 50, 52, 54, 60, 61, 63, 65, 66, 132, 133, 14, 138, 139, 142, 161
embryonic psycholexicon (EmPL) vii, 5, 45, 46
  hypothesis 46–47
  See also undeveloped psychological lexicon
emotional valence (EV) vii, 53, 177
emotionality (negative) 45, 53, 54
  and right hemisphere 53
Engels, F. 12
epilepsy 104
ethnocultural Psychology 28
ethnopsychology 21, 28
evolution 3, 4, 5, 6, 9, 10, 12, 13, 15, 18, 25, 29, 31, 32, 33, 36, 37, 40, 41, 42, 44, 68, 109, 125, 126
  See also inter-evolution
excerption 20, 39, 40
extended mind thesis 125
  See also temporal extension thesis
extracampine experiences 129
extraception 41, 129

Fechner, Gustav 17, 22
Fichte, Johann Gottlieb 22
"flat" literary characters 65
  See also "round" characters
Forster, E.M. 65
Frankfort, Henri 15
Frazer, Sir James G. 14
Freud, Sigmund 25, 127

Galileo 14
Gazzaniga, Michael S. 14, 108, 109, 110
Geisteswissenschaften (mental/ human science) 13, 14, 17
Gibson, Todd v
Gilgamesh, Epic of 36, 47

glossolalia ("speaking in tongues") 3, 11, 16, 35, 43
god(s) 3, 10, 19, 20, 31, 32, 33, 34, 35, 36, 38, 39, 46, 47, 48, 60, 61, 62, 66, 69, 70, 71, 74, 77, 78, 81, 82, 88, 92, 93, 139, 144, 145, 147, 151, 161, 162, 163, 165, 166, 170, 176, 186, 189, 190, 199, 212, 226
  language of unhappy 81
  neurology of 97, 106–108, 112
  voices of 17
god-kings 35, 131
Goethe, Johann Wolfgang von 15, 22
Greene, Barbara v
Greer, Scott v, 8, 15

Hainly, John v
Hall, G.S. 13, 19, 23
hallucinations 2, 3, 5, 6, 9, 10, 13, 16, 28, 31, 32, 36, 38, 41, 45, 61, 95, 96, 97, 98, 99, 100, 101, 102, 103, 104, 105, 106, 108, 110, 111, 112, 113, 115, 116, 117, 119, 120, 121, 123, 129
  abnormal 229–235
  affinities with introspection 120–121
  and aptic structures 110, 111, 113
  as evolutionary adaptation 9
  among general population 99–103
  and right-side brain activity 110–118
  ubiquity of 99–103
  visual 41, 45, 61, 100, 123, 229
  See also superception, visions
Hamann, Johann Georg 22
Hamilton, J. 28
Hammurabi 14
Hartmann, Karl Robert Eduard von 127
Hearing Voice Network 4
heautoscopy 35, 129
  See also autoscopic extraception, autoscopy
Hegel, Georg Wilhelm 14, 22
Helmholtz, Hermann von 14
Heraclitus 14
Herbart, Johann Friedrich 18

Herder, Johann Gottfried 22
Herodotus 14
Hilgard, Ernest 14
Hindu tradition 75
Hittite vii, 47, 48, 50, 54, 58, 65, 132, 133, 136, 138, 161, 162, 164, 165, 167
Hobbes, Thomas 14
Homer 14
Hughlings Jackson, John 14
Hull, Clark L. 14
Humboldt, Wilhelm von 21, 22
Hunt, William Morris 17
Hurrian 65
Huxley, Thomas Henry 14
hypergraphia 43
hyper-suggestibility 35
   See also suggestibility
hypnagogic experiences 129
hypnopompic experiences 129
hypnosis 2, 3, 11, 25, 35, 43, 104

"I" 20, 38, 39, 40
   See also "me"
idiophany 99
imaginary playmates 103–104, 123
indirect divine communication (IDC) 34
individuation 40
induction methods for right-hemisphere activation (IMRHA) vii, 34
Indus script 65
inner speech 104, 105, 115, 116, 118, 119
Instructions of Shuruppak 47
inter-evolution 44, 125, 126
   and stratigraphic Psychology 125
   See also evolution
interhemispheric communication 9, 108, 110
intermediary being (IB) vii, 34, 69
internal perception (*innere Wahrnehmung*) 18, 19
International Society for the History of the Behavioral Sciences 9
   See also Cheiron
Intervoice: The International Hearing Voices Network 4

introception 39, 40, 41, 129
   See also coception, extraception, introspection, superception
introcosm 10, 38, 39, 73, 130
introspection vii, 2, 11, 17, 18, 19, 23, 24, 36, 38, 39, 40, 43, 120
   as controlled hallucinations 40
   imaginary playmates 103–104
   among university students 101–103
   See also conscious interiority, introception, superception

Jacobsen, Thorkild 15
James, William 2, 14, 17, 21
Janet, Pierre, 2, 14
Jaspers, Karl 36
Jaynes, J.C. 9, 10,
Jaynes, Julian vi, vii, 1, 2, 3, 4, 5, 6, 7, 8, 9, 10, 11, 12, 13, 14, 15, 16, 17, 18, 19, 20, 22, 25, 26, 28, 29, 31, 33, 36, 37, 38, 39, 40, 41, 42, 43, 44, 45, 46, 53, 57, 61, 67, 76, 79, 81, 83, 84, 89, 96, 97, 99, 101, 106, 110, 111, 124, 125, 126, 127, 128
   application of theories 28
   arrested 8
   and art 17
   background 7–9
   as comparative Psychologist 6
   as conscientious objector 8
   corroboration of theories 28
   as Darwin of Psychology 11
   and Edwin G. Boring 9
   as ethologist 15–16
   four-phase trajectory of mind-words 43
   hypotheses of 3
   influenced by father (J.C. Jaynes) 10
   interdisciplinary approach of 1
   legacy of 3–4, 5
   and linguistic theory 26
   obstacles to understanding 125–128
   and "other" Psychology 3–4, 5, 7, 24, 73
   as playwright and actor in England 8, 17

and "second" Psychology 20
understanding of consciousness 19–20, 37–38
Jaynesian Psychology 6, 82
primer on 31–44
Jeremiah 14
Joan of Arc 15
Josiah, King 14
Julian Jaynes Society 4
Julian, Emperor 14

Kant, Immanuel 14, 22
Krüger, Johann Gottlob 29
Kuijsten, Marcel v, 4, 28, 109

LaFargue, P. 12
Lamarck, Jean-Baptiste 14
language 1, 3, 5, 6, 9, 18, 22, 23, 24, 26, 27, 31, 32, 33, 37, 41, 42, 45, 46, 47, 48, 49, 66, 67, 68, 69, 72, 81, 83, 87, 105, 106, 107, 108, 111, 112, 117, 118, 119, 121, 123, 125, 127, 192, 235
and aptic structures 106
four-phase trajectory of mind-words 43
neurology of 97, 106–108, 112
sociohistorical scaffolding 125
See also language regions, linguistic complexity, linguistic layering
language regions 32, 105
See also Broca's area, language, Wernicke's area
Late Bronze Age Collapse 33, 36, 47
See also dark ages
lateralization 32, 109, 111, 114, 116, 117, 119, 120, 123
Lazarus, Moritz 22, 24
left hemisphere 3, 9, 32, 96, 97, 108, 109, 111, 112, 118, 123
Legalism 70, 72
Leibniz, Gottfried Wilhelm 14
Leontiev, Aleksei 21
LeTourneau, C. 12
Lévy-Bruhl, Lucien 128
Lewes, G.H. 14
Lewinski, I. 12
Limber, John v, 28
Linear Elamite 65

linguistic complexity 35, 105, 117
See also language, linguistic layering
linguistic layering 125
See also language, linguistic complexity
Linguistics Research Center—University of Texas (LRC—UTA) vii, 48, 50, 54, 133, 136, 138, 165, 167
linguo-concepts 5, 11, 36, 42, 43, 67, 77, 74, 78, 82, 83, 125
literacy 130
literature (ancient) 47
Lloyd Morgan, C. 14
Locke, John 14
Lowie, R. 12
Lubbock, J. 12
Luria Alexander 21
Luwian 65

macrocosm 39, 73, 88, 130
Malinowski, Bronislaw 25
Mandarin 5, 67, 68, 69, 76, 75, 82, 83, 84, 85, 86, 87, 89, 91, 93, 95, 176, 177, 182, 193, 194, 196, 197, 198, 199, 200, 201, 202, 203, 204, 205, 206, 208, 209, 213, 214, 215, 216, 221
See also Chinese
Mandate of Heaven 69, 70, 77
mathematics 3, 130
Marx, Karl 14
Maxims of Ptahhotep 47
Maya 65
McLennan, J.F. 12
"me" 20, 38, 40
See also "I"
Mead, G.H. 14, 21, 25
mental imagery 10, 36, 38, 40, 41, 97, 99, 104, 121, 129
affinities with hallucinations 41, 97
as controllable semi-hallucinatory experiences 41
as cultural adaptation 36–37, 38
as quasi-perceptions 97
as superception 38
See also introception, introspection

Meso-American writing 65
Mesopotamia 33, 35, 38, 47, 56, 61
metaphoricity 41, 42, 57, 69, 86, 125
   of Bronze Age psycholexemes 57–58
   of Chinese linguo-conceptualization 84
   of inner experience 125
   of mental idioms 41–42
   of mind-words 69
   See also metaphors
metaphors 3, 4, 10, 20, 26, 35, 37, 39, 41, 42, 43, 44, 47, 57, 58, 59, 67, 69, 72, 84, 85, 86, 87, 89, 91, 93, 95, 112, 124, 125, 126
   See also metaphoricity
microcosm 39, 73, 88, 130
Mill, John Stuart 14, 18
Milton, John 15
mind-as-putty metaphor 124
mind-as-vase metaphor 124
mind-space 39, 46
   See also spatialization of psyche
mind-words (MW) vii, 26, 35, 41, 42, 43, 46, 47, 53, 55, 56, 57, 67, 68, 69, 78, 79, 80, 81, 84, 88, 89, 90, 91, 92, 93, 94, 125, 137, 172, 173, 174, 215, 216, 221
   four-phase trajectory of 43
   historicity of 125–126
Mohism 70, 72
Moses 14
Münsterberg, Hugo 29
Mycenaean/Linear B 50, 65, 133, 138, 170, 171

Naturwissenschaften (natural science) 13, 14, 17
negative emotion (NE) vii, 45, 53, 54, 55, 81, 82, 117, 136, 137
Nero 15
neurocultural plasticity 7
   See also psychic plasticity
neurology of language 97, 106–108, 112
New Testament 75
Newton, Isaac 14
nomos (variant human convention) 14

nonconscious 19
   See also unconscious

objects of hallucinatory focus (OHF) vii, 24, 34, 69
Odysseus 14
Old Testament 16, 75
Olin, R. 28
Olmec 65
oracles 36, 43, 71
"other" Psychology 3–4, 5, 7, 24
   See also "second" Psychology
out-of-body extraception 129

pareidolia 129
Parkinson's disease 104, 229
Parmenides 14
Pascal, Blaise 14
Paul the Apostle 14
Penfield, Wilder 14
perceptual reactivity 19, 129
Petrucci, R. 12
phantom limb 129
physis (invariant natural laws) 14
Piaget, Jean 18
Pizarro, Pedro 15
Plato 14
Platt, Carole Brooks v
Plutarch 14
Polanyi, Karl 12, 14
political correctness 127–128
positive emotion (PE), vii, 45, 53, 54, 55, 81, 82
Post-Bicameral Civilization Inventory (PBCI) vii, 33, 45
pre-bicamerality 130
Prince, Morton 14
prophets 16, 34, 36
proto-Elamite 65
pseudo-hallucinations 97, 98, 129
psychic diversity 13
psychic plasticity 14, 125, 127
   See also neurocultural plasticity
psycholexicon (PL) vii, 5, 45, 46
psychological processes 16, 22, 24, 26, 28, 33, 42, 57, 84, 85, 124, 126
Psychology vi, 1, 2, 4, 6, 7, 8, 9, 10, 11, 12, 13, 14, 16, 17, 18, 19, 20, 21, 22, 23, 24, 25, 26, 27, 28, 29, 30, 31, 32, 33, 43, 125–127
   and anti-reductionistic

approaches 6, 27
cultural-historical Psychology 19, 21, 23, 25, 29, 127
mainstream 8, 11, 17, 19, 23, 26, 27
non-experimental approaches 2, 6, 21, 27
"other" 3–4, 5, 7, 24, 73
psychological versus vi
search for central processing mechanism 7, 25, 126
stratigraphic 33, 124, 125, 126
psychoscape 34
Pythagoras 14

Qin Dynasty 69, 72
Qin Shi Huang (First Emperor) 69, 72
quasi-perceptions 87, 97, 121
See also introception

Reimarus, H.S. 14
religious lexicon (RL) vii, 65
Rig Veda 75
right hemisphere 1, 3, 9, 10, 17, 31, 33, 35, 53, 81, 95, 97, 108, 109, 111, 118, 119, 123
and negative emotionality 53
right-hemisphere dominance (RHD) vii, 33, 107
"round" literary characters 65
See also "flat" characters
Rousseau, Jean-Jacques 14
Rowe, William v, 28
Ryle, Gilbert 14

Saggs, H.W.F. 15
Samuel 14
Sapir, Edward 25
Sarbin, Theodore R. 14
Saul 14
schizophrenia 101, 104, 111, 112, 114, 117, 118, 120
Schopenhauer, Arthur, 22
"second" Psychology 7, 14, 20–21, 23
See also "other" Psychology
secondary burial 34
self-authorization 36, 39, 130
See also authorization
self-autonomy 39

self-narratization 39
self-observation (*Selbstbeobachtung*) 18, 19
self-reflexivity 2, 38, 40
self-talk 32, 33
sense of presence 129
Shang Dynasty 17, 42, 69, 70, 71, 73, 76, 77, 83
Shelley, Percy Bysshe 15
Sher, L. 28
Sherrington, C.S. 14
Shuowen Jiezi (Explaining and Analyzing Characters) 72, 81, 82, 83, 173
Sleutels, J. 28
Smith, Joseph 16
Snell, Bruno 15
Socrates 14
Solon 15
soul 69, 74, 75, 92, 93, 164, 166, 176, 184, 185, 189, 192, 225
multiple 34
spatialization of psyche 20, 39
See also mind-space
Spencer, Herbert 14
Sperry, R.W. 14, 108
spirit possession 3, 11, 16, 25, 35, 43, 70, 71, 11
"spokesperson" self 111
Spring and Autumn period 72
Steinthal, Hajim 22, 24
Stove, D.C. 28
stratigraphic Psychology 33, 124, 125, 126
and inter-evolution 125–126
suggestibility 230
See also hyper-suggestibility
Sumer 46, 47
Sumerian 47, 48, 57, 58, 59, 60, 63, 64, 139, 142 143, 153, 167
superception 41, 96, 97, 99, 101, 123, 129
supernatural visitations (SV) vii, 4, 36, 69
See also visual hallucinations
super-religiosity 5, 32, 45, 47, 52

Tacitus 14
Taoism 72
techno-economics 130

temporal extension thesis 125
  linguo-conceptual remnants 125
  See also extended mind thesis
temporality types 12–13
  Jaynes and mid-range 13
The Origin of Consciousness in the Breakdown of the Bicameral Mind vii, 1, 2, 3, 4, 6, 9, 11, 12, 17, 23, 25, 31, 83, 112, 126, 232
theocentric social order (TSO) vii, 33, 34, 69
Thomas, W.I. 25
Titchener, Edward 18
Tolman, Edward C. 18
Tower, June F. 7, 8, 10, 11, 15, 16, 20, 23, 29
trance 2, 13, 16, 176, 178
Tukulti-Ninurta I, King 14
Tutankhamun 17

Ugaritic 65
unconscious 23, 53, 124, 127, 170
  See also nonconscious
undeveloped psychological lexicon 34, 70, 79
  See also embryonic psycholexicon
Upanishads 75

Veblen, T. 12
vestigial bicameralism (VB) vii, 35, 75
vestigial neurostructures 11, 43, 97
Vico, Giambattista 22
Virgil 14
visions 3, 4, 5, 16, 17, 31, 32. 33, 34, 41, 45, 60, 61, 64, 72, 73, 74, 75, 121, 142, 148, 196, 201, 211
  nocturnal 60, 61, 66
  See also hallucinations

visual hallucinations 41, 45, 61, 100, 123, 229
  See also hallucinations
voice-hearers 97, 100, 122, 123
voice-volition (VV) vii, 3, 18, 20, 28, 32, 33, 38, 41, 44, 71, 98, 100, 111, 121
Völkerpsychologie 2, 21, 22, 23, 25, 26, 30, 126
  See also cultural-historical Psychology
Vygotsky, Lev 21, 29, 30

Wallace, Alfred Russell 14
Warring States period 72
Watson, John 14, 18
Weismann, Judith 28
Wernicke's area 106, 107, 112, 116, 119
  See also Broca's area, language regions
Whitehead, Alfred North 14
Whorf, Benjamin 25
Wigan, Arthur 106
wisdom literature 47
Woodward, William v, 7, 8, 10, 11, 15, 16, 20, 23, 29
Woodworth, R.S. 14
Wundt, Wilhelm 2, 6, 7, 14, 17, 18, 19, 23, 24, 25, 26, 29, 30

Yangshao culture 69

Zhou Dynasty 69, 70, 71, 72, 73 76
Zitrin, Arthur 8, 15
Zoroastrianism 16

About the Author

Brian J. McVeigh received his PhD in anthropology from Princeton University. A specialist in Japan and China, he lived in Asia for 17 years. He is currently researching the impact of the theories of Julian Jaynes and how the books of the Bible reflect a transition in mentality. He is now training in mental health counseling at the University at Albany, SUNY. His previous books include:

The History of Japanese Psychology: Global Perspectives, 1875–1950
How Religion Evolved: Explaining the Living Dead,
Talking Idols, and Mesmerizing Monuments
Discussions with Julian Jaynes: The Nature of Consciousness
and the Vagaries of Psychology
The Propertied Self: The Psychology of Economic History
A Psychohistory of Metaphors: Envisioning, Time, Space,
and Self through the Centuries
Interpreting Japan: Approaches and Applications for the Classroom
The State Bearing Gifts: Deception and Disaffection
in Japanese Higher Education
Nationalisms of Japan: Managing and Mystifying Identity
Japanese Higher Education as Myth
Wearing Ideology: State, Schooling, and Self-Presentation in Japan
The Nature of the Japanese State: Rationality and Rituality
Life in a Japanese Women's College: Learning to Be Ladylike
Spirits, Selves, and Subjectivity in a Japanese New Religion:
The Cultural Psychology of Belief in Sūkyō Mahikari

www.ingramcontent.com/pod-product-compliance
Lightning Source LLC
Chambersburg PA
CBHW021342230426
43666CB00006B/380